Culture Acquisition

Culture Acquisition

A Holistic Approach to Human Learning

Mary Anne Pitman
Rivka A. Eisikovits
Marion Lundy Dobbert

and Contributors
Kyung-soo Chun   Jan Armstrong Gamradt
Betty Cooke   Kyung-hak Kim

PRAEGER

New York
Westport, Connecticut
London

GN 510
P57
1989

Library of Congress Cataloging-in-Publication Data

Culture acquisition : a holistic approach to human learning / Mary
   Anne Pitman, Rivka A. Eisikovits, Marion Lundy Dobbert and
   contributors, Kyung-soo Chun . . . [et al.].
      p.   cm.
   Bibliography: p.
   ISBN 0–275–93031–9 (alk. paper)
   1. Socialization. 2. Learning.   I. Pitman, Mary Anne.
II. Eisikovits, Rivka A.   III. Dobbert, Marion Lundy.
GN510.C83   1989
303.3′2—dc19   88–27507

Library of Congress Catalog Card Number: 88–27507
ISBN: 0–275–93031–9

First published in 1989

Praeger Publishers, One Madison Avenue, New York, NY 10010
A division of Greenwood Press, Inc.

Printed in the United States of America

The paper used in this book complies with the
Permanent Paper Standard issued by the National
Information Standards Organization (Z39.48–1984).

10 9 8 7 6 5 4 3 2 1

To Solon T. Kimball

(1909–1982)

supporter and friend

Contents

Tables and Figures

Acknowledgments

The three authors of this book have worked together closely for more than a decade in developing, formulating, and testing the theoretical positions and field research method presented here. Collaborative work over many years ends up involving more people than the authors themselves. We wish to name and thank some of them here.

We are indebted to Solon Kimball for his support in the early stages of our work and to Joan Roberts for her continuing support. Jan Armstrong Gamradt and Kyung-soo Chun were associated with us at critical junctures in data analysis and theory development. Alan Saltzman, John Mirocha, and Ken Taylor contributed to the early development of data collection methods.

We have had the assistance of numerous excellent graduate students in collecting data. For the Israeli data in Chapter 6, we would like to thank Aliza Ben-Chorin, Joseph Berkovits, Naomi Carmeli, Edna Guttman, Nurit Mandarovski, Hana Ofek, Ela Platner, Joseph Rachman, Lea Scheikoviats, Suzette Shenitzer, and Yehudit Siegelman. For the U.S. data in that same chapter, we appreciate the contributions of Gwen Anderson, Linda Capek Armstrong, Janet Burcalow, Betty Cooke, Donna Coomer, Patricia Deacon, Rick Dillner, Danielle Frederickson, Marlene Goldsmith, Nanette Graves, Kimman Harmon, Larry Hegerle, David Jackson, Judy Jax, Steve Jongeward, Marge Kosel, Ransall Lund, Glen Martin, Steve Mather, Becky Palmer, Thomas Polhemus, Leonard Przybylski, Betty Ripke, Jane Strovas, Rita Teusch, Marcia Walsh, Paul Weiner, Elizabeth Wroblewski, and one anonymous student. For their assistance in data collection for the social worker study reported on in Chapter 10, we would like to thank Fathia Agbara, Itzak Dana, Adva Lerner, Alexander Machul, Smadar

Milman, Avi Mizrachi, Hanna Sathi, Anat Shafir, Miriam Shimron, and Edna Urieli.

Still others have read earlier drafts and provided critical comment. In this regard, we are particularly grateful to Frank Waterous for consultation on conceptual design in reporting methods of analysis. The Korean draft of Chapter 9 was translated by Insub Choi; we are grateful for his careful translation, which was particularly sensitive to the presentation of the social science issues involved.

We are grateful too for institutional support: the University of Haifa for a full academic year sabbatical leave; the University of Minnesota for research grants from the Graduate School, the College of Education, and the Departments of Social, Psychological, and Philosophical Foundations of Education and of Educational Policy and Administration; the Universities of Cincinnati and Youngstown State in Ohio for grants from the University Research Councils; and the Department of Educational Foundations in the College of Education at the University of Cincinnati for financial support in the final stages of this project.

We are especially grateful to Dan Wheeler and Rick Beck for computer consultation and to the staff and students of the Computers Unlimited Program of the Cincinnati Public Schools for assistance with computer graphics; to Celia Petty and Mary Carol Hopkins for typing and copy editing; and to Lynne Smith who served as editorial assistant and provided invaluable aid in overseeing the final stages of manuscript revision and preparation. We thank our families: Lea, Joan, Nir, Zvi, Dan, and Howard. And, finally, we acknowledge the intellectual challenge of working with one another and are appreciative of each others' curiosity and commitment, qualities that were necessary to sustain the long term effort represented here.

Culture Acquisition

Introduction: Learning Culture

Throughout our evolutionary past, human adaptation has depended upon our ability to sense, process, store, and transmit information; in other words, to learn. Homo sapiens sapiens is genetically adapted for educability, as are all primates. Monkeys, apes, and humans evolved in complex environments and developed strategies for survival that depended on an ability to learn. Learning, in other words, was "selected for" in an evolutionary sense.

Within anthropology, the idea that culture is learned is axiomatic. Yet only recently are anthropologists beginning to discuss the learning process, the cultural and biological structures that both compel and constrain learning. The purpose of this book is to conceptualize and operationalize human learning as an interactive process dependent on the human primate's ability to sense, store, and manipulate information.

In one sense, as we have stated elsewhere, the question of how people learn is a "nonissue" (Pitman et al. 1984:352–54). This is because the model that we propose rests on the assumption that all humans learn in the same manner, that is, according to a fairly standard set of biological templates. Since the processes by which humans learn are universal, the real work of the anthropologist is to focus on the context of learning, that is, on the structures and processes associated with the culture of a group. Clearly, this is where the most basic, elaborate, and differentiating patterns for survival are constructed.

Mary Anne Pitman, Rivka A. Eisikovits, and Marion Lundy Dobbert were the primary authors of this chapter.

The universality of the biological substrate, therefore, is the starting point for our research on learning culture. If we failed to explicate the corporeal nature of cultural systems, our theories and methods would most likely lead us astray. An understanding of how learning comes about via the universal biological substrata also serves as a useful guide for the collection and interpretation of cultural data. It sheds light on the cultural events we observe, forcing us to view the mundane routines of daily life with new respect, providing a window into adult-child or old hand–new hand interactions, and revealing both our limitations as collectors of data and the unique and quite extraordinary power inherent in the process of anthropological inquiry.

The work to follow defines the biological parameters of culture learning; reviews previous research on cultural transmission; and conceptualizes, operationalizes, tests, and illustrates the use of a holistic, context-specific approach to learning culture. This work arises from the meeting of three streams of anthropology. The first of these has been the holistic tradition of studying entire systems, for example, of child raising or child life. The second stream of anthropology that has influenced this work arose in the early 1970s, when anthropologists began to show a concern for conceptualizing culture as process. In the field of anthropology and education, this concern has lead to a recognition of the inadequacy of the vague, global metaphor of enculturation and has opened a search for the precise mechanisms of cultural transmission. The third influence has been that of the holocultural and microcultural researchers who attempt to find solid, measurable, replicable methods for studying culture and social structure in context. Our work has been influenced by their insistence on the use of a firm, repeatable methodology closely linked to data.

These three streams of contemporary anthropological work come together to define the general challenge facing educational anthropology: creating a holistic, process-oriented method for examining culture acquisition and cultural transmission. In order to address this challenge, the analytic separation of people-as-vessels from culture-as-liquid to be poured in is rejected in favor of an analysis which includes the learner in the patterns analyzed as if there were no separation between people and sociocultural patterns. Indeed there is not, except in the minds of analysts who usually abstract people from culture and culture from people in order to simplify their analytic tasks. Because the enculturation metaphor nominalizes people (making them into things—that is, people—which receive) and cultures (treating them as things—that is, knowledge—to be passed between persons), it subtly interferes with a researcher's ability to develop a process-based approach to culture learning. The enculturation models are predicated upon some variation of a relatively passive absorption mechanism by which the learner functions as a receiver of messages (Levine 1982:61–63). The recent formulations of learning present learners as considerably more active. In Gearing's dyadic, turn-taking process, for example, learners are seen as active agents in the construction of knowledge via filtering agendas (Gearing and Sangree 1979). In our work, we have adopted the metaphor of "culture acquisition," in which all learners are viewed as active agents selecting options within a probabilistically constructed, socioculturally, ecologically patterned process.

Conceptualizing culture learning is one challenge; operationalizing it is another. To meet this second challenge, we have attempted to develop analytic methods to support holistic, process-based data. We now seek to investigate whether these have the ability to produce not only descriptions of learners but also scientifically generalizable and testable hypotheses about the effects of specific social, ecological, and ideological patterns on learners' tendencies, abilities, and actions.

The concept of culture acquisition requires explication (cf. Wolcott 1982 and Hansen 1982 for a beginning). As we are using it here, it is a concept that is much broader than schooling, than informal teaching and learning, than child raising, or even than cultural transmission. Certainly in many societies parents and other adults do a considerable amount of directing, teaching, and shaping, all of which is designed to transform children into desirable adults. But for humans, as for other primates, instructive and formative activity constitutes a very minute part of the learning process. Instead, the major forces "shaping" children and young people in the process of culture acquisition are the same as those that shape or direct all learners, namely, the structures and processes of the entire sociocultural life going on around them. In addition, the process of culture acquisition by which children and young people learn to be fully functioning adults is a holistic one. One does not become a mature adult by sequentially learning the separate elements of adult life and then putting them together to form a whole, nor does one survive as a competent old person through that process. Rather, the junior members of a society or a social group learn whole cultural patterns within the context of everyday life and then in personal action they individualize and adapt these patterns by varying some of the elements or creating new ones.

The continuing challenge in all of this is to build an explicitly *anthropological* approach to education and learning based upon the concept of culture. How can any theoretical position provide a framework for uncovering, describing, analyzing, and understanding a subject so large as the acquisition and transmission of a whole culture and yet avoid the "mystical holism" that is rightly attacked as meaningless by some critical observers of social science? How can it simultaneously avoid the equally dangerous opposite—the trite overparticularism of repetitive ethnographic documentation? It is our conclusion that in order to study human learning anthropologically, in a way that addresses all these challenges, it is necessary to capture *process*, to formulate it theoretically, to operationalize it methodologically, to describe it holistically, and then to reformulate it until theory matches real-life options in action. This is the task we undertake in the present volume.

In the first four chapters of this book we review those areas that are critical for the definition of a solidly grounded holism and for the development of an integrated theory in the anthropology of human learning. The approach to culture learning that we propose in this volume builds a conceptual interface between the quantitative approaches to the study of human growth and development and the interpretive realm of ethnographic inquiry. Just as psychologists seem to be trying to learn to "see" cultural context (Birren and Schaie 1985; Triandis and Lonner 1980), so anthropologists appear to be increasingly interested in the psychobiological underpinnings of culture (Kimball 1982; LeVine 1982; Hansen 1979). The structure of the atom is of interest to both chemists and physicists. In much the same way, new knowledge about the structure of the human organism has implications for all of the social and behavioral sciences. In our view, an adequate approach to culture acquisition must incorporate what we know about the biological, psychological, and cultural parameters that at once compel and constrain human growth and development.

The first four chapters of this book, therefore, are intended as a kind of "primer" of the theoretical and empirical frameworks that we have found to be either useful or intellectually inescapable. Chapter 1 reviews studies of primate learning and suggests applications for an adequate theory of human learning; Chapter 2 examines neurological data and information processing in humans; Chapter 3 undertakes an assessment and review of developmental theory and research on aging as it applies to culture acquisition; and Chapter 4 identifies critical junctures in the development of the study of cultural transmission in our own field of educational anthropology.

In the remaining chapters we present a theory that highlights the importance of the learner's active role and places primary emphasis on the process of culture acquisition. The learner is not passive and learners do not acquire some set of nominalized things. This framework departs from the cognitive and intellectual traditions of Western Europe that have affected contemporary science via its deeply embedded realism. Standard European languages are inherently realistic in that the noun-being verb construction *attributes* characteristics to the nominalized object represented by the noun; for example, a rock *is* hard. The medieval philosophy of realism emphasized the attribution of essence by holding the belief that the essence of a class, such as chairness, had a real existence. Empiricalism, which insists upon the direct apprehension of reality, is a modern form of realism.

Modern taxonomy theory makes variation primary (Mayr 1982) and provides an alternative to essentialism.

Ever since Plato cast shadows on the cave wall, essentialism has dominated Western thought, encouraging us to neglect continua and to divide reality into a set of correct and unchanging categories. Essentialism establishes criteria for judgement and worth: individual objects that lie close to their essence are good; those that depart are bad, if not unreal.

Antiessentialist thinking forces us to view the world differently. We must accept shadings and continua as fundamental. (Gould 1985:161)

Taxonomic categorization escapes nominalization through acceptance of the principles of indeterminacy. The first type of indeterminacy in sociocultural data is the standard variety described by Heisenberg: Social system data, like their physical counterparts, cannot be studied without intervening in the system to obtain the data. Thus, what is seen is not the subject itself but a product of the relationship between instrument of observation and subject, a relationship about which we can obtain no information that in itself is not a relational product. Indeterminacy, then, is characteristic of the research process in any scientific endeavor.

Indeterminacy also arises from the complexity of dynamic interrelationships between the parts of the system observed as a result of which it is impossible to identify either parts or wholes except on a heuristic basis. In addition, all open or living systems are adaptive and shift operations to adjust to new inputs, produce new outputs, and generally cope with environmental conditions. Thus, the ordering of parts and their relationships is constantly shifting. Models of human sociocultural systems must, therefore, account for the dynamics of human choices, which create the relations between cultural elements. When we approach the process of theorizing about human sociocultural life from a taxonomic perspective, then, we cannot assume that our terms carry a nominalized or essential fixity.

What the principle of indeterminacy makes abundantly clear is that physical or social reality and theory, even at the most elementary levels of merely naming items, have no intrinsic connection. To produce data is to have performed a set of both observational and logical operations. Consequently, data are *already* theory and as such data have no inescapable or intrinsic connection to reality. Similarly the production of generalizations, abstractions, and higher-level theories are all *logical* operations; they do not arise from either reality or data. If we "interpret" ethnographic data in order "to stay rather closer to the ground than tends to be the case in the sciences more able to give themselves over to imaginative abstraction" (Geertz 1973:24) we are still theorizing. Ethnographic representation and emically based research strategies do not provide an escape from either indeterminacy or theory. This is because emic data does not have a privileged logical or ontological status.

This is not to say that physical or sociocultural reality and the naming, data-creating, categorizing, generalizing, theorizing, or other logical operations performed on the results of our observations of that reality do not have any relationship. They do indeed have a very clear relationship, that of one-to-one correspondence between the symbolic set of the discipline, that is, its vocabulary, which names the elements of observed systems and describes the relations between elements, and the observed and observable aspects of the system under scrutiny. It follows from the indeterminacy principle that there exist an infinite number of accurate one-to-one symbolic wrappings of any reality. A veritable polyphony of interpretations and explanations is clearly possible. But as social scientists, we do not wish to take advantage of this because we are both constrained and aided by an established tradition that has already developed a number of symbol-reality relationships that, in turn, have stood the test of interobserver reliability over time.

It is possible to build a taxonomy based on the theoretical traditions of anthropology that also takes seriously the principle of indeterminacy by turning to the notion of partitioning information. The information-partitioning process copes with indeterminacy through the use of three concepts: fuzziness, dimensionality, and organization.

The notion of *fuzziness* has been developed to deal with problems stemming from the imprecision of human language when interfaced with the absolute demands of computers for binary nonambiguity (Zadeh 1965, 1971a, 1971b). A fuzzy object or concept is imprecise or lacks exact description. When fuzzy sets are formed through the clumping of fuzzy objects or concepts, two problems arise: defining the set and determining whether a given object or concept is a member of the set.

In developing theory related to the process of culture acquisition we have handled fuzziness through the qualitative approach of defining grade of membership by employing the concept of *dimensionality*. We have named specific units along a dimension and defined areas in a multidimensional space with labels taken from fairly standard usage in anthropology. As such, our labels are fuzzy-area identifiers that signify a whole set of membership grades. We neither reify nor nominalize them.

Because we accept fuzziness, we cannot logically rely solely on theoretical endeavors based in emic, or local data, which is exact and fixed. Paradoxically, however, if we accept the notion that the aim of anthropology or social science is to create models that stand in one-to-one correspondence to observables, we cannot ignore immediate data. We deal with this paradox through the use of Buckley's organization principle, or:

... the fact of organization of components into systemic relationships. When we say that "the whole is more than the sum of its parts," the meaning becomes unambiguous and loses its mystery: the "more than" points to the fact of organization, which imparts to the aggregate characteristics that are not only different from, but often not found in the components alone; and the "sum of the parts" must be taken to mean, not their numerical addition, but their unorganized aggregation. (1967:42)

Our own approach to generalizations based on General Systems Theory attempts to occupy a middle ground between local data and scientific laws. These generalizations are based on the concepts of indeterminacy, fuzziness, and organization, which are linked by the development of taxonomies. Our holistic theory assumes that components such as biology and culture interpenetrate in a manner not yet fully understood.[1] Neither comes first; neither is more essential. But you cannot add up the properties of individuals and produce a culture from them, nor can you add up the attributes of a culture and produce an individual. The holistic perspective focuses on complete systems in which the components interact. The components themselves are not givens, are not a priori entities. Rather, the form of theory building advocated here is nonreductionistic in that the whole taxonomy is stochastically determined.

These points must be attended to seriously because failure to do so will lead to misinterpretation of the model, a model that is formally neither inductive nor deductive. It is, rather, radically contemporary in its formulation and logic, eschewing Aristotelian, Baconian, Cartesian, or Lockean forms of reasoning in favor of an intellectual process derived from twentieth century biology (via systems theory), physics, and computer science.

If, then, culture acquisition is best treated as an inseparable part of an ongoing system of environment-culture interactions, how should study of the process be approached? In Chapters 5–8, we lay out a theoretical model that attempts to provide an answer to the question of how learners create informative maps of this vast, turbulent, shifting, sociocultural milieu, maps that contain the necessary complexity of information within a holistic relational structure. We propose a systems-based theory that explains the way in which learners come to see the *whole of their culture* and the place, function, and probable outcomes of myriad alternative strategies in that whole.

Our theoretical model focuses on culture patterns that include relationships and institutions. We hypothesize that people's cognitive maps are acquired, and the process of culture acquisition is the very process by which individuals come to store the cultural pattern information in their brains. Patterns are acquired and maintained in interaction with the whole event. Sociocultural patterns are learned polyphasically through many simultaneous modalities so that learning appropriate roles, for example, may depend very little upon action or interaction and much more on lateral and peripheral vision of the total structure of setting, roles, and events.

Our theoretical model of culture acquisition is knowledge-full. We contend that it is the learners' exposure to the whole of culture that results in culture acquisition because it is only through such exposure that their knowledge will constitute a complete adaptive map. What is learned is not items of information or behavioral traits, but a set of relations. That set of relations, taken as a whole, codes information about a complex ecological-social-cultural environment. This model accounts for the developmental differences of age whether culturally or chronologically defined. It accounts for the inextricable relationship between human culture and human biology. It focuses simultaneously on individual, social, and institutional variables and on the cybernetic interchange between ecology and culture: the real event in all its complexity of place, people, atmosphere, and interactive responses.

Chapter 5 posits our formal theoretical model of culture acquisition and operationalizes it by laying out a field-based research method for gathering detailed, precise, and well-contextualized ethnographic data derived from the holistic systems approach. Chapter 6 describes a test of the method undertaken through a pilot study of culture acquisition in three societies. Chapter 7 reports on three analytic experiments exploring the potential of our systems-based model to capture the cross-cultural patterning of societywide processes in a holistic yet precise and detailed manner. Chapter 8 revises the coding system in light of the comparative pilot study, thereby reassessing both the method and its underlying theory base.

In the final two chapters we assess the extent to which the theory is applicable for individual anthropologists in their own areas of research. Chapter 9 illustrates a straightforward application of the operationalized theory in a study of culture acquisition in a Korean village. Chapter 10 applies the culture acquisition concept to a professional learning context via a study of the culture of social workers.

The book has an overall additive structure reflecting the truly collaborative nature of our work and the processual quality of our systems-based holistic theory of culture acquisition/transmission. This closely integrated volume is intended to allow interested readers to familiarize themselves with the theory as well as put it to their own use. In so doing, they join us in attempting to operationalize the holistic and ecological paradigm and to do so within the discipline of anthropology, which is eminently suited to handle complex, interactive wholes, conceptually and methodologically. What we are all aiming at, in the words of biologist Sidney Brenner, "is the fundamental problem of the theory of elaborate systems" (Judson 1979:220). This book is our contribution toward the eventual resolution of that problem as it relates to human learning.

NOTE

1. For some current and positive views of the inextricable yet nondeterministic relationship between biology and culture, see Lewontin 1984; Rose 1973; Lewontin, Rose & Kamin 1984. In addition, the cognitive sciences are addressing this and related issues, especially in the fields of philosophy of mind, artificial intelligence, and neuroscience. See Hofstadter and Dennett 1981 and Laudan 1977.

1 Research on Primate Biology and Behavior: Implications for the Study of Culture Acquisition

Humans are closely related to the wild primates, sharing millions of years of evolutionary history. In this chapter we offer an approach to human learning which is based on primate biological and behavioral research. Primatologists such as Rozin and Kalat support this approach:

Given the constraints on adaptation produced by basic properties of the nervous system, the cost of evolving specializations, and the fact that most species face a common set of problems, we doubt that a separate learning mechanism would exist for every situation, or that there would be separate laws for each species. (Rozin and Kalat, quoted in Johnston 1981: 129)

Anthropologists of education often begin their formulation of theories of learning with a study of primates. We are not the first, therefore, to suggest that anthropologists examine primate research and use it to raise issues about human learning (Burton-Jones 1972; Herzog 1974; Kimball 1982; Poirier and Hussey 1982; Reynolds 1976; Washburn 1973; Wolcott 1982). Since our aim in this book is to move toward a scientifically based theory of cultural learning, our perspective on primate research is very broad. We consider *all* the major strands

This chapter is adapted from Marion Lundy Dobbert and Betty Cooke, "The Biological Foundations of Education: A Primate-Based Approach," *Educational Foundations* Vol. 1, No. 2 (Spring 1987), pp. 67–86, and Marion Lundy Dobbert and Betty Cooke, "Primate Biology and Behavior: A Stimulus to Educational Thought and Policy," in G. Spindler (ed.), *Education and Cultural Process: Anthropological Approaches*, Second Edition, Waveland Press, 1987. Used with permission. Marion Lundy Dobbert and Betty Cooke were the primary authors of this chapter.

of research on the learning-related aspects of primate biology and social structure relevant for anthropologists of education.

This chapter examines comparative studies of primate learning and socialization as well as the literature that relates primate research to human biological, social, and educational issues.[1] In organizing our findings, we have taken the following positions that arise from the literature reviewed: 1) humans must be seen first as biological beings; 2) by the fundamental nature of their biology, humans interact socially; 3) humans therefore must learn through processes that are socially oriented; and 4) these learning processes include the process of play. We present our review of the literature following this position and then draw conclusions based on it.

BODY AND LEARNING IN PRIMATES

The primate sensory system is of critical importance in developing a solidly based theory of learning. The most important sense in all primates is vision (Forbes and King 1982). It is so important that Chalmers (1980) says it is almost a defining characteristic of the order. Stereoscopic binocular color vision is the product of a long evolution in which the eyes moved forward in the head, the snout shortened, and the size of the visual cortex increased. The visual area of the brain became increasingly complex while multiple connections developed between multiple subfields (Kaas 1978). The major brain connections that developed during primate and, later, specifically human evolution are those between manipulation, fine coordination, and vision (Walker 1983). The early stages of the maturation of this circuit are seen in infant reaching and batting behaviors. Although the obvious aspects of this behavior are submerged with growth, the behavior itself does not disappear, as Piaget has noted in his discussion of the sensorimotor and concrete operations stages in humans.

A second aspect of human biology of great importance in learning is the cyclical rhythms and hormonal outputs. Cyclical and hormonal patterns in humans can be considered the equivalents of the fixed behavioral patterns we see in other orders of animals. All these fixed patterns are ultimately based in the rhythms of the biochemical, electrophysiological, and endocrine systems (Chapple 1970). The circadian rhythms are the most basic and determine the ratio of the total amount of activity to inactivity in a daily cycle (23–25 hours in humans). Aschoff (cited in Chapple 1970) has found that animals prevented from being normally active or forced into overactivity compensate for this as soon as possible. The neurohormonal outputs of the body also shape another fundamental characteristic of the individual, namely, emotional reactivity. The hormones responsible for the basic emotions are well-known: Adrenalin produces fear; rage and anger are products of noradrenalin; and acetylcholine produces feelings of well being, love, affection. These hormone-based emotional responses are involuntary and result biologically from the trigger of some stimulus. The hormonal systems that underlie emotions most certainly serve as a major base for the social system because they form the substrate of the bonds that hold societies together.

The development of affectional systems is of central importance in understanding any kind of social primate, including humans. The existence of these rhythms and hormonal states has important learning implications as well because they determine an individual's state of attention and readiness (Chance 1978).

Aside from vision and cyclical and hormonal patterns, a third biological issue is extremely important. Humans, and to a lesser extent all primates, are genetically designed to learn, to learn easily, and to learn well. This has been documented for primates in the familiar Japanese macaque films and for humans by Bloom (1964). The ability to learn quickly and to store large amounts of information is apparently an adaptation to the complex and often surprising environments faced by primates, most of whom are seriously outclassed in size and weight by both predators and other foragers who share their environments (Poirier, Bellisari & Haines 1978:157). The senses involved are not only those that sample external information, such as sight, hearing, and smell, but also those that sample internal states related to effort, tensions, and emotions. The information sensed is apparently stored in the brain in the form of a multisensory holograph (Penfield and Perot 1963) which is first indexed by and made accessible through its affective components (Zajonc 1980), although cognitive indexes are also constructed.[2] The learning ability of primates is also propelled by their high need for arousal. Poirier, Bellisari & Haines (1978), following Campbell and White, suggest that for animals with complex brains the amount of information input is the major limitation upon learning (as opposed to capacity or ability). The drive behind the primates' well-developed curiosity, explorative behavior, and frequent play, then, does more than maintain an optimal arousal state; the drive is also adaptively functional. These activities provide a source of information on how the physical and social environments function and can be manipulated. Campbell and White (cited in Poirier, Bellisari & Haines 1978:157) term it "effectance motivation"; it is at the root of the mammalian learning strategy.

The point we wish to make here is a biological one. Juvenile primates, including humans, when left to their own devices, with just a bit of supervision to prevent harm, will learn easily and well during all their preadult years, to the point where they will be ready to step into and learn adult roles through practice when they reach the proper age. This pattern can be seen among baboons and macaques as well as among humans in foraging and hunting communities. (Turnbull 1978, for example). It can also be seen in our own society where schools, whatever it is they do, do not teach the full spectrum of adult daily living roles—parenting, being a politician, bargaining, protesting, getting along on too little income, household scheduling, etc.—so that these must be learned in a more fundamental fashion.

THE SOCIAL AND DEVELOPMENTAL NATURE
OF PRIMATES

The fact that most primates are social animals residing in highly complex, bisexual, year-round social groups of varying size and composition is crucial and has long been recognized. Group characteristics do vary (in degree of dominance, for example) but most primates spend much of their lives in close association with others in their particular group. While most primates live in multi-age, bisexual social groups, it must be cautioned that not all primates have the same degree of social life. Orangutans, for example, unlike most monkeys and apes, do not live in cohesive groups or troops. They live in relative seclusion, with the exception of mothers and their young who form independent social units, but these too are relatively solitary. Others experience life in different kinds of groups at different seasons or at different points in their life cycles (Dunbar 1979; Suzuki 1979).

The social environment, regardless of its configuration, does provide the context within which most young primates learn and mature. The importance of learning within the social context and the geography of the territory occupied is emphasized extensively throughout the literature on primate learning and socialization (Chevalier-Skolnikoff and Poirier 1977; Dohlinow 1972; Herzog 1974; Kimball 1982; Lancaster 1975; Poirier 1972; Poirier and Hussey 1982). Because of the highly social nature of primates, both groups and individuals can be viewed as the adaptive units of the species. It is within the group that both direct individual learning in interaction with the environment and the passing on of group traditions occur. The learning of traditions provided within the social group "is superior to individual learning if the new behavior is difficult to acquire individually in direct interaction with the environment" (Poirier and Hussey 1982:137). Primates thus learn to become members of their species, to become members of particular social groups, and to adapt to their environment (Poirier 1977). They learn their mode of survival by living in a group, where they benefit from the shared knowledge and experience of the species. The social context in which the infant is born and nurtured is the primary reinforcement for all normal primate learning. Even independent sensorimotor activities such as observation, physical manipulation, and exploration are either facilitated or inhibited within the group setting. Variations in social structures lead to diverse learning patterns and to individuals with differing behaviors (Poirier 1977).

The growth cycle of young primates is usually divided into four specific developmental stages (Harlow and Harlow 1966; Scott and Marston 1950; Walters 1987) during all of which social group learning is crucial. These four periods are labeled differently in various studies, but consistently include a neonate period, which is dominated by long, continuous contact with the mother or primary caregiver; a period of transition between maternal and juvenile orientations, which terminates when the young outgrow infantile behaviors and leave the regular company of their mother; a juvenile period of peer socialization, when contact with individuals other than the mother becomes dominant especially contact with siblings, older females, and age mates; and an adolescent or subadult period, which is characterized by the appearance of such adult behaviors as copulatory activities. This last stage occurs just prior to full adult primate participation in the social order. Each stage has its own learning focus.

Significance of Earliest Social Experience

The earliest and most important social relationship for the growing youngster is usually with the mother, although other individuals may substitute permanently or temporarily. "In many ways the most basic theme running through primate social relations is . . . the attachment between a mother and her offspring. This bond between mother and infant is primary in the sense that it is the first bond to be formed in the life of an individual, and also in the sense that the individual peculiarities of that bond set the tone for other bonds formed later in life" (Lancaster 1975:21). The primate infant-mother relation is the most intense known (McKenna 1982; Poirier 1972). It is a "two-way relationship" based on hormonal and affectional ties in which each member of the pair both gives and receives (Montague 1970). That this relationship is initially fragile and continues to be vulnerable on into the period of transition has been established beyond any doubt by maternal deprivation studies in nonhuman primates, such as Harlow and Harlow's (1962), and in humans with studies of institutionalized infants, of maternal absence, and of abnormal mothers (Ainsworth 1973; Bowlby 1969, 1972; Henry 1971; Spitz 1945). The learning that takes place in this period has lifelong effects that lie at the level of an individual's biological growth and structure. The nature of the fundamental learning tie established in this period has strong hormonal and affective components, and these components are critical in later learning (Mason 1965) because they "bind together various individuals within a species in coordinated and constructive social relations" (Harlow and Harlow 1965:287). Thus the earliest social experience of a young primate, that of bonding with its mother, "represents the primary adaptive strategy of higher primates" (Lancaster 1975:21). "The strength, duration, and diversity of [this] affectional system" is "one of the ways in which primates differ from other animals" (Harlow and Harlow 1965:287).

The infant-mother tie has its foundation in primate biology and depends initially upon the reflexes of clinging and sucking. Of the greatest importance here is intimate physical contact, as opposed to mere nursing, because it is the foundation of the maternal bond of trust which itself is later generalized and serves as the foundation for broader social ties (Harlow and Harlow 1965). From an educational viewpoint, we need to note that in nonhuman primates, when the social ties generalize to other individuals, the mode continues to be based on physical contact, although it may be bolstered and supported by specific vocalizations that serve to express and restate the bond (see Gautier and Gautier-Hion 1982). In consequence, *all* early learning is linked closely with physical affectional ties.

Roles of Peers and Older Playmates

The single most important developmental task of the transition, juvenile, and sub-adult stages is learning to live socially. These stages in all primates are characterized by peer play, that is, play with other immature individuals of any age or sex (Walters 1987). Peer play appears to be the most appropriate method of learning, and perhaps the *only* efficient means of learning at this stage of development. During this period wild primates eat, sleep, groom, explore, and play, with play making up 70 percent of the nonsolitary behavior of young chimpanzees, for example (Mason 1965:343).

Deprivation experiments in which young and juvenile macaques were deprived of peers (but not mothers) produced prolonged behavioral abnormalities (Alexander and Harlow as cited in Chalmers 1980:116). These abnormalities spring from the interruption of the development of the affectional systems that normally follow a pattern of widening social contact and interaction. In the transitional stage, infants begin coordinated movements away from their mothers and toward both other infants and objects via approach and withdrawal, rough-and-tumble play, or contact manipulation. This initiates the development of the peer affective system, that is further developed through constant social or interactive peer play. The heterosexual affectional system is also developed in physical play through a variety of acts, including all the basic social behaviors of self-presentation, greeting, aggressive postures and gestures, as well as reproductive behaviors (Harlow and Harlow 1965). Physical contact and social experience form the cornerstones for the development of these two affectional systems, both of which are fostered in a protected atmosphere within which adults of both sexes are usually strongly attracted to the young and consequently initiate social interaction with them and protect them.

Role of Adult Males

Another part of the social context, one that is receiving burgeoning interest (Taub and Redican 1984; Whitten 1987) is the relationship between young primates and mature males. The males' socializing role is likely to be the most variable relationship experienced by the young primate in terms of the amount and kind of contact which it has with males during its early years. According to Poirier:

The adult male's contact with the infant is minimal in some species and extensive in others; . . . The adult male's role in the socialization process is influenced by such factors as social structure, habitat, one male versus multiple male groups, and the phylogenetic position of the species. (1977:20)

The adult male's role also varies according to age, dominance, specific social group, relationship between the male and the infant's mother, and individual idiosyncracies. In a study of interactions between adult males and infants in prosimians and New World monkeys, Vogt (1984) found that the mating system, specifically monogamy, seemed to be the social factor most closely related to the prevalence of direct interactions between adult males and infants. Typically, the adult male is not thought of as an infant caregiver, as a parent playing an important role in the social and physical development of the offspring. Instead it has most often been assumed that his only role arises from a protective response toward the group as a whole. However, Kleiman and Malcolm (1981, cited in Vogt 1984) found that in the primate order, the proportion of genera in which males showed some form of direct positive interaction with infants is nearly 40 percent. They defined the following set of interactions as "male paternal care: groom/play, sleep with, retrieve, feed, babysit, protect, carry and care for." Vogt concluded that "with the primates it might be supposed that interactions between adult males and infants are not only rather prevalent but also important for the proper development of the infant" (1984:346).

Two categories of paternal primate behavior, complementary and substitutive, have been noted (Snowden and Suomi 1982). The former refers to activities that are rarely engaged in by females and are primarily male-specific, and the latter refers to activities that the female can and usually does perform. Because complementary behavior is found almost universally among primates, it has been assumed that such behavior is part of the primates' genetic heritage (Snowden and Suomi 1982). However, substitutive behavior has been noted in tamarin monkeys. Male tamarins provide a major portion of parental care directly essential to infant survival, including carrying the young and sharing morsels of food with them (Abrahamson 1985). Snowden and Suomi (1982) argue, therefore, that the experience received by an individual primate throughout its development is at least as important as genetic background in determining the learning and expression of paternal care.[3]

Structure and Function of the Larger Social Context

The young primate's learning about the social context, group limits, and existence or function of dominance relationships begins through the relationship to its mother and is influenced by her status in the group and her relationships with others, including her kin. Beyond the mother-infant bond and specific peer relationships, this larger social structure and context play a major role in the learning of a young primate. Most critical to learning, perhaps, is the stability and protection provided by the group.

The group is the environment in which a young primate does [its] learning and in which traditions of feeding, ranging and the like are perpetuated. . . . Survival requires it [the primate] to live socially and, preeminently, to learn socially and to do so not only in the long period of its dependence and growth, but also throughout its life. (Hall 1968:384)

In primate groups that do have dominance ranking, shifts in individuals occupying different dominance ranks may occur, but the overall structure of leadership and power within the group persists. While there are varying degrees of permanence and of definition to the boundaries of primate social groups, there is far more stability than novelty in primate group life (Dolhinow 1972). This group stability has important learning implications in that it underlies what Chance and Jolly (1970, cited in Lancaster 1975) called an "attention structure."

This term refers to the fact that subordinate individuals are

usually very much aware of what dominant animals are doing when the subordinates may seem to be going about their business. . . . In contrast, very dominant animals do not often pay attention to the behavior of subordinates unless it actively intrudes upon them. (Lancaster 1975:45)

Two other major attention structures in primates include the mother-infant unit and the peer play group discussed above.

Various kinds of learning processes have been observed within these social group structures. The first type is *observation and modeling* (Poirier 1973) in which the young observe others doing things and try them out. Studies of wild primates reveal that the young observe intensively and try things themselves many times. The protected, leisurely atmosphere of the stable primate group is critical to observational learning because it permits focused attention and provides the emotionally relaxed atmosphere essential to readiness and approach.

A second form of learning that is important within the social group context is based on *social experience*. Social contact and interaction per se are the major building blocks of primate social structure. Mason (1978) found that social experience is critical to the building and maintenance of complex social structures. He found that rhesus groups made up of adolescent individuals deprived of early social experience lived together peacefully and apparently normally; they played frequently and aggression rates were low. But closer examination of the social structure of deprived and nondeprived groups revealed that it was simplified, dyadic, and linear in the deprived groups (p. 10). Further, any social contact, friendly or antagonistic, builds structure by definition because it reduces the time and attention available for other contact (Vaitl 1978) and because it creates relationships that are then activated in other situations (Seyfarth, Chaney & Hinde 1978).

Much holistic learning about the total social context occurs through *social conflict learning*, which can be regarded as the third variety of learning process. Poirier, quoting Berlyne, points out that conflict

is an inescapable accompaniment of the existence of all higher animals, because of endless diversity of the stimuli that act upon them and of the responses that they have the ability to perform. . . . In primate societies there is a continual interplay of friendly, sexual, aggressive, and fearful impulses, all of which must be individually balanced. (1973:22)

What such interaction both creates and communicates about the social order is the importance of social skill and experience over physical superiority and aggression (Chalmers 1980; Van Lawick-Goodall 1971; Lancaster 1975; Symons 1978;

Voland 1977). It appears that a balance of cooperation and social conflict and competition are necessary components of group interaction for young primates and lead to their learning of the social structure and their position within it.

Play is the fourth critical form of learning protected and encouraged within the context of the primate social group. As noted above, play is estimated by many (such as Lancaster 1975; Poirier, Bellisari & Haines 1978) to be the most significant modality for learning.

Differing play orientations correlate strongly with separate maturational periods. The body-oriented locomotor play of neonates promotes motor learning by activating and strengthening limb-brain feedback pathways. Their exploratory play, often with the mother's fur, digits, limbs, or other body parts, strengthens the central mother-infant affectional bond (Harlow and Harlow 1965). The infant's playful response is probably as important an element in bond strengthening as is nursing. At the transitional stage, play tends to pull the infant away from the mother (Poirier, Bellisari & Haines 1978) and toward other young animals. It is the attractiveness of play and of young play partners that moves the infant away from the mother and focuses affections toward the larger social group (Harlow and Harlow 1965). These tentative movements develop into the full rough-and-tumble, fighting, rolling, chasing, and climbing activities typical of primates during the peer socialization of the juvenile period. Contrary to what has been believed in the past, dominance hierarchies are not the only structures developed through this play (Voland 1977:899; Gard and Meier 1977:372–73; Brueggeman 1978:205–12). Rather, what is developed are the peer and heterosexual affectional systems and the social skills that go with approach, withdrawal, and responsiveness, and later an ability to deal with aversive elements in social relations (Harlow and Harlow 1965:313–14). During the adolescent or sub-adult period, specific elements enter into the play systems, beginning with the secondary sexual behaviors and postures of threat, but soon developing into proper sexual orientations and experiments with correct postures.

Throughout all these stages, primate play facilitates learning by making use of the physical, cognitive, and behavioral elements of adult life. These are picked up and tried out over and over again, in many sequences and combinations, often in an exaggerated or magnified form, and in a context where performance failure has few negative outcomes and lacks serious consequences of any kind. Harlow's work was the first to highlight the importance for general intelligence of this seemingly trivial type of trial and error learning (see Schrier's 1984:95–97 defense of Harlow). Among primates such as Japanese macaques and chimps, studies show that juvenile play is a source of new behavioral strategies. Baldwin and Baldwin (1978) have examined this data closely and have documented the formal structural similarities between the creative process and the play process. Even for rats, play with the mother develops more flexibility in the young (Fagen 1981).

Nevertheless, we know that for wild primates play is not essential for the development of *relatively normal* behavior (Leonard 1978:15; Baldwin and Baldwin 1974, cited in Lancy 1980). But Mason's (1978) careful work in studying the ontogeny of social systems in rhesus macaques offers support for the speculation that play is essential for *optimal* development. Social experience, including play, contributes to the development of social ability. In humans we have a great deal of evidence suggesting that disabilities that lead to inability to play either through isolation, lack of physical ability, or through peer rejection produce psychological and social abnormality (Lancy 1980; Williams 1972); and lack of mother-infant play, whatever the cause (Aldis 1975:237), also seems to be conducive to abnormal development.

PRIMATE AND HUMAN LEARNING: THE STUDY OF CULTURE ACQUISITION

If we accept the basic research claim reviewed in this chapter that all primate learning is essentially a social process which takes place in a necessary social structure, then we are logically forced to move away from a theoretical stance that emphasizes cultural transmission. From a social perspective, we are compelled to see learners, especially children, as major actors in the process of cultural construction and continuity. As a consequence, our theories of cultural perpetuation must be oriented toward a focus on culture acquisition. This refocusing is mandated by the findings of primatologists, which indicate that the major forms of primate learning are observation, modeling, social experience, and play (Poirier 1972; Lancaster 1975).

We conducted a survey of major contemporary works on anthropology and education and on culture and personality to determine the standing of biological, social, and contextual learning factors in current anthropological conceptions of growth, maturation, and education. We found that these factors are underrated. Table 1.1 summarizes the findings for 14 works published since 1965.

We find that many of the fundamental primate learning factors are neglected in favor of factors related to schools and formal learning. The average proportion of chapters and pages focused on play in this sample of comprehensive volumes is 0.3 percent. Emotions, biological development, and the roles of males are equally neglected. Some attention is given to observational learning (usually under the heading of imitation). The best coverage is given to social environment and the achievement of social identity, but even these are inadequately covered when one considers that they are the major accomplishments of troop-dwelling primates. An average of only 23 percent of the pages and chapters focus on environment and identity. This relative neglect is not surprising when we consider the Western cultural biases that value work, and therefore school, and dismiss watching, emotion, and play as less appropriate for scientific study. These pervasive biases have been extensively commented upon (Berlyne 1971; Freedman and Omark 1973; Gibson 1976; Huizinga 1950; Mead 1963b; Norbeck 1974; Schwartzman 1978; Washburn 1973). These biases lead to an exaggerated em-

Table 1.1

Percentage of Chapters Focused on and Percentage of Pages Indexed for Major Primate Social Learning Factors in Texts on Psychological and Educational Anthropology

Author	Publ. Date	Age Stages, Development, Growth		Emotions & Affections		Observational, Modeling & Social Conflict Learning		Socialization, Identity & Social Environment		Children and Males		Play		Aspects of Formal Education (Anthropology & Education Texts Only)	
		# chs*	# pp**	# chs	# pp	# chs	# pp	# chs	# pp	# chs	# pp	# chs	# pp	# chs	# pp
Hsu	1972	0%	9%	0%	16%	0%	.8%	7%	15%	0%	0%	0%	0%	-	-
Levine	1982	0%	1%	0%	.5%	0%	0%[1]	12%	0%	0%	0%	0%	0%	-	-
Wallace	1970	0%	3%	0%	4%	0%	0%	17%	2%	0%	0%	0%	0%	-	-
Williams	1983	0%	.6%	0%	6%	0%	0%	30%[2]	51%	0%	0%	0%[3]	0%	-	-
Hansen	1979	0%	0%	0%	0%	5% subchs.	0%	5% subchs.	21%	0%	0%	0%	4%	45% subchs.	82%
Kimball	1974	0%	NI	0%	NI	5%	NI	26%	NI	0%	NI	0%	NI	34%	NI
Kimball & Burnett	1973	3% subchs.	NI	3% subchs.	NI	10% subchs.	NI	34% subchs.	NI	1% subchs	NI	2%	NI	27%	NI
Kneller	1965	0%	0%	0%	0%	12% subchs.	0%	29% subchs.	2%	0%	0%	0%	0%	43%	26%
Roberts & Akinisanya[4]	1976	0%	1%[5]	0%	3%[5]	0%	9%[5]	10%	7%[5]	0%	0%	2%	NI	48%	NI
Sady	1969	0%	0%	0%	2%	0%	2%	0%	21%	0%	0%	0%	0%	0%	23%
Spindler	1974	0%	2%	4%	4%	0%	0%	30%	12%	0%	0%	0%	0%	63%	52%
Wax, Diamond & Gearing	1971	0%	5%	0%	.5%	10%	2%	10%	17%	0%	0%	0%	0%	73%	53%
Median		0%	1%	0%	2-3%	0%	0%	17%	12-15%	0%	0%	0%	0%	43-45%	52%
Mean		.25%	2.2%	.1%	4%	4%	1.1%	18%	23%	.1%	1%	.3%	.4%	42%	47%

[1] Socialization chapter discusses theories, not children.
[2] Based on chapters referring to children in social context.
[3] Nor is play one of the glossary terms.
[4] Patterns and configurations volume only.
[5] No index - estimate based on counting pages.

*by title
**in index

phasis upon schooling. As seen in the last column of Table 1.1, the schooling focus is very strong in the structure of general anthropology and education texts, that is, those texts whose titles suggest a broad examination of education or socialization from an anthropological perspective. An average of 43 percent of the chapters and 44 percent of the pages comment on schooling.[4]

A closely related bias assumes that culture is systematically transmitted. While culture is most certainly systematized, the transmission or acquisition of culture may not be systematic. Primate social-learning models do not assume systematic transmission with respect to the acquisition of a complex lifeway (see Poirier 1973; Walker 1983 for discussions of the high levels of complexity involved in primate learning). Rather, they proceed on the assumption that the entire lifeway of the troop is an environment which the young or juvenile members must test and learn to live with.

Looking at studies of primate growth and learning and at the ways that primatologists and anthropologists study growing and learning in nonhuman primates, then, provides anthropologists of education with a body of data against which to measure their work. Among anthropologists of education, only Kimball, in *Culture and the Educative Process* (1974), actually states and attempts to sketch out an absolutely parallel position for the study of human learning. However, the literature reviewed here suggests a number of areas to which additional attention should now prove fruitful:

1. An anthropological learning theory that focuses on the importance of vision and observation;

2. A biologically well-grounded anthropological theory of learning that seeks to understand the roles of biological rhythms in culture and in the process of culture acquisition/ transmission;

3. Some studies of the ways various societies define and treat emotions and affections, both in a range of particular circumstances, as did Eggan (1956), and in normal settings, in which children are expected to learn mundane cultural tasks and, in particular, in the earliest stages, where critical emotional attitudes and social strategies are learned;

4. An anthropology of education that addresses maturation from a stance emphasizing active acquisition rather than transmission, viewing human learners, like all primates, as natural learners who are propelled by their high need for arousal, their curiosity, and their attraction to the novel in their environments, all of which are supported by their complex brain and polyphasic learning mechanisms;

5. The role of biological maturation vis-à-vis the development and adaptation of lifelong learning capacities, including an increased emphasis on the study of the earliest stages, where critical emotional attitudes and social strategies are learned, and an extension of our concepts of social learning to cover the entire human lifespan;

6. Broadened conceptions of the critical social milieu and the way children learn entire lifeways;

7. An anthropology of education that emphasizes the role of peers and of peer relations, as suggested by primate studies that focus on the presence of and interaction with peers as major social learning factors;

8. The role of adult male group members, an area being addressed in primate research and in cross-cultural research on the status of women, but not in our own field;

9. An anthropological learning theory that views play as a serious form of learning essential in developing optimal adult function and flexibility and in promoting novelty, the latter probably more central in the overall human adaptive strategy than it is in the strategies of other primates.

Certainly no individual educational anthropologist can incorporate all of these factors into his or her work, but that is not what we mean to suggest. Rather, our purpose in reviewing this literature is to suggest a redefinition of the parameters of the field, of the conceptual space in which we set our individual work. What we are suggesting here is that the field utilize a broad, multifaceted approach to culture acquisition, one modeled on a holistically constructed primate base. This will temper our Western cultural biases and encourage a fully process-oriented approach to culture acquisition and cultural transmission.

NOTES

1. Both the comparative literature and the primary sources underline the importance of recognizing that biological and behavioral details and contexts differ by species even for analogous traits. We must never make the mistake, therefore, of thinking that similar processes in nonhuman primates and in humans are identical. The biological and behavioral building blocks of human and monkey or ape daily living systems are similar, but in the different species they contribute to quite different overall systems. Some primates are troop dwelling, some solitary; with some, sex is the basis of the primary social structure; with others it is dominance relations (Baldwin and Baldwin 1979; Dolhinow 1972; Poirier 1972; Suzuki 1979). It is usually thought that the best evidence for factors that are strongly important in understanding humans will come from our phylogenetically closest relatives, but modern research has modified this dictum. There is some evidence that measured intelligence in primates correlates better with a terrestrial lifestyle than with evolutionary position (Rumbaugh 1975).

2. This interpretation is also consistent with the notion that animal call systems are fundamentally expressions of emotional states (Lancaster 1975). Taken together, these studies suggest that emotional factors are more basic in mammalian function than cognitive factors.

3. Such experience appears to be a prerequisite for displaying adequate infant caregiving behavior for adult female primates as well.

4. A chapter or portion of a chapter was considered as focusing on schooling if a section was headed with a schooling title or if word usage in a page indicated a solid schooling focus.

2 Developmental, Neurological, and Information-processing Research: Applications to Culture Acquisition

Jan Armstrong Gamradt

This chapter looks at humans as processors of information. It examines some of the neurological and psychological processes involved when humans acquire information about the world around them. It also focuses on some of the psychological and presumably neurological mechanisms that compel, constrain, and channel human learning.[1] Like Chapter 1 of this volume, this chapter views learning as a biological adaptation to social life and discusses the implications of several fundamental research findings for constructing an adequate theoretical and empirical approach to the study of culture acquisition.

BEYOND THE CARTESIAN IMPASSE: THE HUMAN BRAIN

As a part of the central nervous system, the brain is part of an ever-vigilant sensing system that extends throughout the body. An organism's nervous system permits it to sense and react to the external world and to coordinate those physiological systems that make it possible for the animal to eat, drink, breathe, move, mate, and so on. While each of these latter functions is controlled by a seemingly separate neurological subsystem, it is important to remember that the nervous system is characterized by a remarkable degree of integration. Anatomically, every part of the human brain appears to be connected to every other part of the brain, and the brain itself is anatomically and functionally connected to every part of the body. The implications of this essential integration for social and psychological theory are important, and too often ignored.

Although it is the convention to say that information is stored in the brain, it might make more sense to say that the *body* is the repository of stored information about the world. Our inclination to conceive of and observe "mental" and "physical" systems separately has led us into a nearly inescapable intellectual dilemma—"the Cartesian impasse" (Vessey 1965; Sarles 1977). As Sarles explains, "By constructing the problem of human knowledge within a framework of dualist thought, in which one must impale himself on one horn or the other or try precariously to ride both, the issues have been obscured" (1977:231). As a result, we often tend to overestimate the importance of cognitive processes and to underestimate, even ignore, "the empty half of the mind-body antagonism" (1977:231).

There is probably no better illustration of this misguided Cartesian thinking than contemporary attempts to associate human intelligence with computer technology. The brain does not process information in the same way as a computer (Dreyfus and Dreyfus 1986; Searle 1984; Calvin 1983; Dreyfus 1979; Hubel 1979). A computer cannot integrate the abstract with the corporeal (see, for example, Jacobson 1982); a computer does not need to interpret contemporaneous sensory inputs within the context of its own past experiences and future expectations; a computer cannot encode kinesthetic, auditory, visual, tactile, and other sensory information simultaneously when it stores information in its memory; and the more information a computer contains, the slower it tends to operate, whereas the more information a human brain contains, the more efficiently it seems to work.

Unlike the computer, the brain of the human neonate contains the seeds of its own lifelong transformation. At birth, the human brain contains as many neurons as it ever will: about 30 billion cells (Changeux 1985:51).[2] Neurological development involves the addition and subtraction of connections between neurons, not the growth of new cells (Bloom, Lazerson & Hofstadter 1985; Wittrock et al. 1977). Early in development, there is "excessive sprouting of nerve cells . . . followed by massive neuronal depth" (Gardner 1986:270). As development progresses, a kind of neuronal pruning seems to occur. Eventually, only a small percentage of the original number of intercellular connections remains. The reasons for this sprouting and pruning process are not well understood.

Neurological change both facilitates and constrains human development. In much the same way, the individual's experiences can either foster or inhibit neurological development. There is widespread agreement that early environmental factors can affect the density and distribution of intercellular connections (Martinez and Kesner 1986; Wittrock 1980; Oakley 1983; Black and Greenough 1986). In general, when it comes to early environmental experiences, the old adage "use it or lose it" seems to pertain. Thus, it is far easier to become bilingual while one's brain is developing rapidly during infancy than it is in adulthood. Feral children, never exposed to human language early in life, seem unable ever to catch up linguistically (Curtiss 1977).

Although experience is an essential precondition for human development, recent empirical studies of infant development shed new light on the structure and function of the human nervous system itself. As the next section will show, one of the consequences of these studies is that many social scientists may need to update their notions about the initial condition of the human being.

RESEARCH ON THE SOCIAL NATURE OF HUMAN INFANCY

Until recently, the newborn infant was believed to be a neurological and, by implication, psychological primitive. All classical theories of development assume that the newborn infant is a relatively unstructured organism (Meltzoff 1985). The traditional view is that the infant's limited sensory and motor capacities comprise the building blocks of cognitive and social development. Implicit in this perspective is the assumption that the infant enters the world possessing only a few primitive reflexes (sucking, grasping, crying, etc.) and an ability to read sensory input. Then, through its largely reflexive interactions with the material and social world, the infant will gradually become a social organism. For example, contemporary behaviorists hold that the infant becomes social because it is uniquely sensitive to contingency relationships (Watson 1979, 1985). Thus, an infant prefers to interact with other humans (rather than with inanimate objects) simply because humans are more likely to respond contingently to its behaviors.

Arguing within a very different theoretical framework, Piaget (1952) postulates that the infant's ability to grasp and manipulate objects permits it to discover object constancy. This, in turn, is required for the development of concept formation, which makes possible the discrimination of self from other, which in turn will allow the infant finally to participate in truly social interactions.

Bowlby's (1969) approach to development represents yet another distinct paradigmatic tradition, one grounded in psychoanalytic and ethological theory and research. It, too, emphasizes the importance of the infant's reflexes, which ensure proximity to a caretaker, and thereby allow the infant to *become* a social organism. Thus, all of the classical standard models of development portray the newborn infant as an asocial organism that gradually, by acting upon a differentially responsive environment, acquires the cognitive and affective structures that will eventually make social development possible.

Recently, a new view of infant development has emerged within the psychological literature, representing a substantial departure from traditional assumptions about human nature. It assumes that the human infant, even at birth, is "preadapted for social engagement" (Murray and Trevarthen 1985:212). Those who work within this paradigm believe that even newborn humans are socially attuned organisms. For example, infants learn to identify their caretaker's unique qualities very rapidly. At birth, infants prefer human speech sounds to sounds made by inanimate objects, and prefer female to male voices (Eisenberg 1975). Even before birth, the fetus responds to its mother's voice (Spence and DeCasper 1982). Shortly after birth, the infant can discriminate its mother's voice from other voices (DeCasper and Fifer 1980), can recognize its mother's face (Field and Fox 1985), and will show a preference for its mother's scent over that of another mother (McFarlane 1975).

Other studies of infant development strongly suggest that young humans learn through multiple sensory modalities and seem to possess an inherent ability to integrate multimodal sensory information. These capacities allow even very young humans to imitate the facial expressions and hand gestures of those around them, translating visual information into a motoric representation (Meltzoff and Moore 1977, 1983; Meltzoff 1985). By the time an infant is two months old, it can engage in and partially regulate interpersonal interaction. As Murray and Trevarthen describe it, "The 2-month-old uses expressions of feeling in direct face to face encounters to assist the mother in establishing a balance of mutual awareness that supports expressive motives in the infant and allows 'turn taking' in proto-conversations" (1985:194; see also Condon and Sander 1974; Lewis and Rosenblum 1974; and Kozak and Tronick 1985).

Taken as a whole, the recent literature on infancy suggests that human beings do not become social, but are social from the start. They possess a nervous system that is sensitive to multimodal information, that is geared toward processing social stimuli, and that enables them to participate in reciprocal relationships at a very young age. Far from the primitive bundle of reflexes it was once thought to be, the infant is a highly competent, sophisticated, structured, social organism. Only within the last decade or so have researchers come to fully appreciate the extent to which all of our cognitive capacities are social (that is, multimodal and context bound). Human memory is a case in point.

THE PARADOXICAL NATURE OF HUMAN MEMORY

Psychologists refer to the conversion of particular experiences into long-term memory as "consolidation." The term suggests that some sort of tangible solidification occurs when memories are formed. But at the neurological level, the empirical reality is that memory is an ephemeral, paradoxical phenomenon (Mayes 1983). Recent research suggests that the points at which neurons are linked (the "synapses") are of central importance in the learning process (Woody 1986; McGaugh 1983; Dunn 1980). Whether a piece of information exists for only a few seconds or for a lifetime is thought to be determined by the nature of the links that are formed between neurons (Kupferman 1985a).[3] But even though synaptic changes are an observable consequence of learning, neuroscientists have for the most part given up the notion that memories are stored in specific sites within the brain (see, for example, Woody 1986; Pietsch 1981; and John and Schwartz 1978).

Some years ago, Karl Lashley dedicated himself to tracking down what he called the "engram," the site of memory. As a part of his research, he removed various parts of the brains of laboratory animals and then tested their ability to carry out tasks they had learned prior to surgery. He was never able to find any specific place that held learned material. He found, rather, that the amount of memory loss was directly related to the amount of brain that he had removed. The particular location from which he had removed brain tissue did not seem to matter (Lashley 1950).

Summarizing the anatomical evidence, Changeux (1985) has concluded that an important consequence of the way that neurons are linked together in the cortex is that "neurons interact in a cooperative manner, as in a crystal, but are dispersed like vapors throughout multiple parts of the cortex, with no simple geometric relationship" (Changeux 1985:141). The "vaporlike" nature of neuronal activity lies at the heart of what many writers refer to as the paradoxical nature of memory research (Woody 1986:434–35; Pietsch 1981). Thus, John and Schwartz have argued that "reductionist attempts to localize function . . . failed to confront the fact that complex perceptual and cognitive processes involve dynamic integration of vast regions of the brain" (1978:7). In a similar vein, Woody has noted that "experimental studies over the past 50 years have provided ample evidence that memory and learning are represented over many neurons, and the latter [are] distributed over broad portions of the nervous system" (1986:434). To restate this somewhat, the formation of long-term memories appears to involve many parts of the brain—the hippocampus, amygdala, cerebellum, and neocortex—all of which are characterized by extensive connections to the entire organism's affective and sensory/motor systems. Thus, the process whereby long-term memories are formed appears to be a whole-brain (which is to say a whole-body) process.

Just as humans learn through many sensory modalities, they also encode and recall information transmodally. Memory is almost always characterized by multiple associations (Norman 1982). A particular memory can be triggered or retrieved through any one of several sensory or cognitive channels. In other words, humans often seem to store information in a physiological context. Memory retrieval can even be state dependent, as when an alcoholic is unable to remember the location of a hidden bottle until he or she becomes inebriated again (Overton 1985; Eich 1980).

In general, the way humans encode information is overwhelmingly affected by contextual variables—a fact that psychologists have only recently acknowledged. As Jenkins (a reformed associationist-reductionist) put it:

What is remembered in a given situation depends on the physical and psychological context in which the event was experienced, the knowledge and skills that the subject brings to the context, the situation in which we ask for evidence for remembering, and the relation of what the subject remembers to what the experimenter demands. (1974:793)

Ten years later Horton and Mills concluded: "If there is a single principle that best describes the current status of the cognitive psychology of human memory, it is that the contextualist thesis is alive and well at both the empirical and theoretical levels" (1984:362). People are able to recall learned information better when they are asked to retrieve that information in the same setting in which they originally learned it. But how well do humans learn about and remember context itself? Is the human nervous system a kind of omnicorder that continuously encodes and permanently stores a multimodal record of all of the individual's experiences? The issue is an important one for anthropologists, particularly for those of us interested in how cultural information is acquired by each new generation.

THE OMNICORDER VIEW OF HUMAN MEMORY

Some authorities maintain that all of our experiences are somehow recorded and permanently stored in the brain. Like Freud (1967), who proposed an inaccessible human unconscious, they argue that our inability to recall past events is due to problems with retrieval rather than storage. For example, Wilder Penfield's studies of cerebral localization led him to conclude that the human brain contains "a permanent record of the stream of consciousness." He found that memories elicited via electrical stimulation of the cortex during surgery on epileptic patients were "more complete and detailed than memories that can be voluntarily recalled" (Penfield and Rasmussen 1957:214–15). The content of these recollections usually involved social experiences. Patients most often remembered "times of watching or hearing the action and speech of others and times of hearing music." Interestingly, none of Penfield's patients ever recalled eating, drinking, executing skilled motor acts, experiencing sexual arousal, performing mathematical calculations, speaking, or decisionmaking (Penfield and Perot 1963:687).[4]

Penfield believed the hippocampus to be a "repository of ganglionic patterns" that preserves a complete record of conscious human awareness (that is, the stream of consciousness).[5] The hippocampus, located in the temporal lobe, brings together signals from a number of sources. It receives information from all of the main extroreceptive senses (information from the outside world) and is also connected to the parts of the brain that signal reward (the medial forebrain bundle) (Kupferman 1985b). The hippocampus is widely believed to play an important role in the learning process and appears to be very important as a kind of "cognitive map" (O'Keefe and Nadel 1978). But is it the site at which all of our past experiences are recorded? Is it a kind of gateway through which one's entire personal history might be reached? Probably not. There are two lines of research that argue against Penfield's hypothesis. First, laboratory animals that have had their hippocampi removed are still able to remember how to perform previously learned tasks. And second, there is the famous case of HM.

HM, an epileptic patient whose hippocampus was surgically removed, was able to remember previous experiences (dating back from approximately three years before the surgery), but he was never again able to form any new long-term memories. He could remember old friends, but was never able to remember the names or faces of the people he met for the first time after the surgery. And although he was able to acquire new motor skills, when asked, he was unaware of having acquired them and would be surprised at his apparently new ability (Milner 1972, cited in Bloom, Lazerson & Hofstadter 1985). HM's deficits suggest that the hippocampus probably plays an important part in long-term memory consolidation, and it may hold, or rather, process memories for three years or so, but it is not the repository that Penfield and others once thought it to be. One of the striking aspects of HM's case is his ability not only to acquire but to retain new skills. Some theorists have interpreted these findings to mean that humans have more than one way of learning and remembering, that is, memory involves more than one neurological system (Squire 1986; Kesner 1986; Tulving 1985).

MULTIPLE MEMORY SYSTEMS

In 1975, Weinberg referred to two types of memory: procedural and declarative. Cohen and Squire (1980) refer to these two memory systems as "knowing how" and "knowing that." The evidence suggests that procedural memory, knowing how to do things, and declarative memory, knowing that something has happened, involve different kinds of processing. Procedural memory may involve biophysical changes only in the neural circuits directly involved in the learned procedure. Habituation (becoming insensitive to a persistent stimulus), sensitization (becoming hypersensitive to a particular stimulus), and classical conditioning are forms of procedural learning.

In contrast, declarative knowledge is believed to involve a kind of remodeling of neurological patterns. Squire (1986) argues that declarative knowledge involves an "explicit, accessible record" of an individual's previous experiences, and a sense of familiarity about those experiences. He believes that declarative memory is processed in the temporal region and thalamus, and he hypothesizes that the temporal region creates linkages with memory storage sites in the cortex and other regions of the brain. Neurological communication between these regions eventually leads to a reorganization of memory that is brought about by physical changes in the neurons involved. Squire believes that this process may take up to several years and that when the process is complete, the temporal region is no longer required because the information is distributed across many regions of the brain. For this reason, HM and other patients like him are able to acquire new skills (knowing how), but have no memory of having acquired this new knowledge (that is, they have no ability to store declarative information because the temporal region is no longer intact).

The lengthy processing time apparently required for long-term storage is surprising. Many authorities hold that perceived events must be rehearsed before they can make the transition from short-term to long-term storage, and most readily admit that this storage process is affected by a wide range of contextual and organismic factors: level of arousal, novelty, previous experience, age, cognitive style, etc. We are all subjectively aware that our ability to learn/remember material is affected by such factors, but we have no subjective sense of the very long time it apparently takes for our neural circuits to become altered permanently. Yet, in light of the findings described above, it seems unlikely that any single event or set of events automatically becomes a permanent part of our consciousness. (Regarding "consciousness," see "automatic encoding," below.) In fact, taken as a whole, recent investigations of how the brain functions have generated a compelling case against the Watsonian ideology of unlimited plasticity (Gazzaniga 1985). The research reviewed here suggests that a permanent alteration of the human brain may require a good deal of environmental/experiential redundancy. This intriguing possibility suggests some implications for anthropologists, to be discussed later in the chapter.

In reference to the omnicorder theory of human memory, then, there is little empirical support for the notion that humans remember all of their experiences (see Loftus 1980 and Loftus and Loftus 1980 for useful reviews of the evidence on both sides of this argument). There is, however, a body of new and rather impressive evidence that humans do record certain kinds of information automatically. Moreover, the learning processes involved and the screening and filtering processes that direct this learning are beyond the individual's subjective awareness.

NONCONSCIOUS INFORMATION ACQUISITION

Zajonc has argued that human preference (that is, attraction to stimuli) increases as a function of "mere exposure" (1968; see also Harrison 1977). In other words, we tend to grow to like the things in our surroundings more with the passage of time, with repeated exposures. In recent years Zajonc has also demonstrated that the neurological circuitry that assesses familiarity requires no cognitive mediation (1980, 1984).[6] Thus, according to Zajonc, preference (which is a consequence of familiarity) acts as a kind of internal filter that influences subsequent cognitive processing. This in turn leads to the striking conclusion that we may know whether we like something before we know what (or who) it is.

The primacy of affect thesis has important implications for social theory, some of which were noted in Chapter 1. It might help to account for the conservative nature of cultural systems, for ingroup/outgroup consciousness, and for the persistence of affective attachments between individuals throughout the life course.[7] The model suggests that early experience may have consequences that extend far beyond those predicted by models that assume fewer global learning mechanisms. It also illuminates the potential significance of the ecological context (what we have referred to as the setting—group composition, atmosphere, and larger cultural patterns; see Chapter 5) in which children live out their early years. Zajonc's work suggests that our attraction to stimuli is guided by an unconscious, automatic process. Recently, information-processing theorists have begun to document other kinds of automatic learning processes.

THE AUTOMATIC PROCESSING OF FUNDAMENTAL INFORMATION

Until recently, most cognitive psychologists believed that the acquisition of factual knowledge requires conscious involvement on the part of the learner. In recent years, however, a number of studies have demonstrated that nonconscious learning is not only possible, but absolutely unavoidable. Hasher and Zacks have labeled this form of knowledge acquisition "automatic encoding." They argue that there is an "inevitable encoding into memory of certain fundamental aspects of experience" (1984:1372). According to Hasher and Zacks (1979, 1984), humans automatically absorb temporal, spatial, and frequency-of-occurrence information. Automatic encoding does not require consciousness or intentionality on the part of the learner. An individual's ability to encode these kinds of information cannot be improved by training or explicit feedback. And even more remarkably, the process is not affected by the age, motivation, education, or ability of the learner.

Automatic encoding has an impact on a wide range of cognitive and social processes. For example, we have knowledge structures (schemata) that guide our expectations about what is likely to occur in a particular situation (for example, going to a movie, attending a lecture). We also have schemata that help us to categorize classes of people (high-strung, easy-going) and places (an office, kitchen, etc.). It seems likely that the formation of these classification structures is at least in part a consequence of frequency-of-occurrence information (Hasher and Zacks 1984:1382). Thus, not only does frequency-of-occurrence have an important impact on affective preferences (via the exposure effect discussed above), but "frequency information may play a central role in a number of the cognitive and social accomplishments of childhood, including the acquisition of knowledge about categories, the development of ability to make accurate probability judgments, and even sex roles" (Hasher and Zacks 1984:1384). In support of their claim, they cite evidence that children do not imitate all of the same-sex role models that they encounter. Rather, they seem to require information about whether a potential role model is typical of their own gender group, and then only imitate individuals who appear to be representative of their gender (Perry and Bussey 1979, cited in Hasher and Zacks 1984:1384; Nihlen and Bailey 1988).

Thus, even the behavior of young children appears to be guided by a complex set of information-processing heuristics. These powerful and apparently ubiquitous cognitive processes exist independently of the language system; they are nonconscious. The extent to which implicit cognitive rules are biologically programmed remains problematic. It seems overwhelmingly clear, however, that just as the tabula rasa model of the infant has been challenged, the "black box" view of the human mind is being displaced by a structured organism perspective. This shift in zeitgeist is further illustrated by Lewicki's work on nonconscious social information processing.

NONCONSCIOUS SOCIAL INFORMATION PROCESSING

Lewicki has argued that human information processing is guided by a variety of nonconscious cognitive algorithms.[8] He claims that these algorithms are "never learned at the level of consciousness," "operate totally beyond one's conscious control," and "are available to a person who follows these algorithms in no other way than by an 'outsider's viewpoint' observation of how they operate" (1986:1, 2, 3, 11). Further, Lewicki claims that "these cognitive algorithms . . . seem to be ubiquitous and directly responsible for outcomes of various 'high level' processes traditionally attributed to a conscious level of processing, like judgments, inferences, or evaluations" (p. 11). For this reason, nonconscious learning may regulate a number of important social phenomena: personality dispositions, social behaviors, emotional reactions, mood, preferences, attitudes, and so on (1986:11–12).

Lewicki presents experimental evidence that demonstrates that the formation of an internal processing algorithm (IPA) requires "surprisingly little consistent evidence" (1986:220). His research also indicates that IPAs are self-perpetuating and quite resistant to change. As he puts it, "If there is a lack of salient contradictory evidence (i.e., evidence contradictory with an IPA), then, once initiated, the IPA may develop (become stronger) even in the absence of any supporting evidence" (p. 220). One of Lewicki's conclusions seems especially relevant to the culture acquisition process:

The results demonstrate the *enormous sensitivity of the human cognitive system*. Even nonsalient stimuli—which due to a limited, controlled processing capability cannot be processed in a consciously controlled manner—are still nonconsciously registered and stored in a form capable of influencing subsequent, relevant cognitive processes (p. 220; emphasis added).

While psychologists are only beginning to appreciate the significance and scope of nonconscious information acquistion, anthropologists have always known that many kinds of cultural knowledge are transmitted from one generation to the next without conscious intent.

IMPLICATIONS FOR THE STUDY OF
CULTURAL TRANSMISSION

Studies of infant development make it clear that humans enter the world with a sophisticated, neurologically based capacity to interact as social beings. Our nervous systems continue to be biased toward the social throughout the life course. Because even very young infants are social organisms, anthropologists who study culture acquisition need to be particularly sensitive to bidirectional and multidirectional effects. In other words, empirical work on culture acquisition needs to focus not only on the ways in which a society's old hands train its new hands, but also on the ways in which new society members compel and constrain their seniors.

Studies of people with lesions in the temporal lobe (like HM) suggest that it takes a surprisingly long time for a particular memory to become "permanent." Although the human brain is biologically designed for plasticity, it may be that neurological stability can only be achieved through environmental redundancy. This suggests that the ordinary, everyday, repetitive background stimuli (what is labeled "setting" in Chapter 5) may be just as significant as the more salient but less frequent rites and rituals upon which we tend to focus our attention. In regard to culture acquisition, as educational anthropologists we may need to rethink some of our assumptions about the relative importance of the entire context in which we find our learners.

This is not to say that seasonal rituals, patriotic displays, rites of passage, and so on, are not important. Clearly, the neurological evidence suggests that all regularly occurring events—particularly those with a powerful affective load— are likely to be important. In fact, the neurological evidence gives us a hint as to why human groups tend to engage in repetitive rituals, surround themselves with symbolic messages, and recount the same fables again and again. It was just such environmentally redundant cultural patterns that Mead and Benedict were exploring in their search for cultural configurations.

The existence of multiple memory systems also has important implications for the study of culture acquisition. While formal educational institutions are geared toward declarative knowledge acquisition, the multiple memory research suggests that humans possess more than one memory system, and that some of these systems are not accessible to either subjective awareness or linguistic expression. These findings suggest that those who study culture acquisition may need to take nonformal learning environments more seriously. For example, many of the effects of the "hidden curriculum"—body postures, facial expressions, emotional display patterns, dominance/submission, and so on—are manifestations of procedural learning. Those of us who are serious about finding the most meaningful loci of cultural differences need to remind ourselves—often— that human social life may rest as heavily upon implicit learning mechanisms as on explicit (salient) ones. Clearly, conventional information-gathering tools (for example, questionnaires, interviews, tests) are nct likely to be effective as sources of information about the contents of procedural memory. This means that holistically oriented ethnographers may be among the few social scientists able to explore the real-world manifestations of both procedural and declarative memory systems.

Finally, empirical work on automatic and nonconscious cognitive processes demonstrates that there may, indeed, be an information-processing equivalent to Freud's Unconscious. Our personal preferences, the heuristics we employ when making social judgments, and the knowledge base upon which such judgments rest are all, at least to some degree, a consequence of automatic learning processes. Once again, the importance of context as a social dimension becomes evident. The social and material settings in which people live are often described as a kind of backdrop for the really meaningful data. For many social scientists, the task of social description focuses primarily on the nature of the transactions that take place between participants and the way in which these participants construct social meaning. There is no question that these are important social phenomena, but the automaticity research strongly suggests that humans do not have linguistic access to many important aspects of their psychological and social lives. While the locus of this information is within them, its exact nature is best understood contextually.

All of the models described above support our contention that human learning is a multimodal, constant, and inherently social process; that humans are extraordinarily sensitive to contextual (that is, cultural) information; and that the mechanisms by which humans acquire and transmit knowledge are very, very complex. The models also suggest that anthropologists, by virtue of their shared commitment to methodological and theoretical holism, may be among those best suited to construct social theories that integrate the corporeal with the macro-cultural, theories that will take us beyond the Cartesian impasse.

NOTES

1. A word of warning is necessary before proceeding with this review. There is no single literature on human learning. There are a multitude of literatures, each of which could fill many volumes. The information presented in this chapter focuses on selected recent theories and empirical findings that appear to shed new light on the question of how culture (in the broadest sense) is acquired by one generation interacting with a previous one. Excellent reviews of the "classical" theories of learning and development that informed earlier anthropological investigations are available elsewhere. LeVine (1982) has provided an overview of several of the classical approaches to research on socialization and personality development. In addition, Crain (1985) has written a straightforward synopsis of all of the major theories of development beginning with Rousseau's. Overviews of recent empirical work in the areas of developmental psychology, child psychology, learning, and memory appear in the *Annual Review of Psychology* (for example, Cairns and Valsiner 1984; Horton and Mills 1984; Masters 1981). *The Handbook of Child Psychology* (Mussen 1983) is yet another source of information on these and other relevant topics, as is *Developmental Psychology: An Advanced Textbook* (Bornstein and Lamb 1984). Useful reviews of cross-cultural research on perception, cognition, and motivation, and on the development of memory, language, and cognitive skills appear in *The Handbook of Cross-Cultural Psychology* (Triandis and Lonner 1980), and in *Cultural Perspectives on Child Development* (Wagner and Stevenson 1982).

2. Larry Squire, on the other hand, claims that the brain has "ten trillion or more neurons" (1986:171). Cherniak (1987) has found tremendous variation in such "basic

facts'' about the brain's anatomy. He has also discovered that neuroscientists have no sense that a considerable degree of ''quantitative incoherence'' exists within their field. He attributes this to ''a kind of idealism [that] pervades all levels of cognitive science.'' Cherniak argues that many scientists have adopted a model of humans derived from economic theory (that is, the ''rational man'' model). As a result, they tend to overestimate the complexity of neuronal structures, the cellular density of these structures, and the degree to which humans are neurologically equipped for ''true'' rationality (See Cherniak 1986). The Cartesian impasse manifests itself once again. True Believers in the veracity of biological ''facts'' may want to take note.

3. Information is carried across the synapses with the aid of chemical substances called neurotransmitters, which are secreted from the sending cells (Stevens 1979). The organism's level of arousal, emotional state, and previous experience all have an effect on its nervous system's chemical environment. This, in turn, affects both the overall pattern of synaptic intercommunication (the firing pattern) and the nature of the connections between particular neurons (McGaugh 1983).

4. Penfield and Perot speculated that the reason for the absence of these kinds of memories might be due to the fact that ''these times do not call for interpretation, and the activity is not really within the focus of attention in quite the same way as things that are heard and seen'' (1963:688). But they go on to speculate that ''these things that are absent from our experiential recall may all be recorded somewhere and may be made available by other means'' (p. 689).

5. By 1963, Penfield no longer believed that the entire stream of consciousness was contained within the hippocampus: ''Our evidence indicates that this neuronal record is not in the temporal cortex itself. It lies in other neurone circuits at a distance'' (Penfield and Perot 1963:689–90).

6. Lazarus (1982) has criticized Zajonc's model. According to Lazarus, Zajonc mistakenly equates cognition with rationality, emphasizes a nonexistent distinction between cognition and affect, and employs an inappropriately linear information-processing model of cognition. Nonetheless, he agrees that affective responses can be triggered without lengthy processing and believes that humans are neurologically ''wired'' to assess the meaning of stimuli very quickly. In other words, Lazarus agrees that Zajonc ''is right, but for the wrong reasons'' (p. 1020).

7. In evolutionary terms, it seems clear that an affective-cognitive bias toward the familiar might well have had survival value. But it is equally clear that humans—particularly young humans—are also compelled to explore the unfamiliar. The ''optimal drive'' theories of White, Berlyne, Solomon, and others (see Chapter 1) attempt to account for the human primate's apparent need for novelty. These theories suggest that all animals try to maintain an optimal level of stimulation (arousal, complexity, etc.). In human communities, each culture responds to the child's need for familiarity and for novelty in a distinct manner. Clearly, these two basic impulses are involved in a number of important psychosocial phenomena: the attachment process (Bowlby 1969), cognitive development (Piaget 1952), curiosity behavior, play, fantasy, creative activities, and so on. Rheingold (1985) has reviewed much of the literature on the roles played by familiarity and novelty as aspects of human development. She suggest that novelty and familiarity should perhaps not be thought of as opposites on a continuum because they may actually be independent dimensions.

8. Lewicki uses the term internal processing algorithm (IPA) to describe ''the result or cognitive consequences of a nonconscious acquisition of information about covariation''

(1986:29). Covariation is a fundamental information-processing category, "a basic aspect of any cognition" (p. 28). For example, in order to recognize an object, we must find interrelationships (covariation) between some of its features. An IPA contains information about the covariation of at least two features or events and this information, in turn, influences the way individuals interpret and react to their experiences. For example, the IPA that makes it possible for us to judge a person's age from the appearance of his/her face also affects the way in which we interpret the person's actions. Our interpretation of these actions may, in turn, be affected by our expectations about how people of a given age are *likely* to act (that is, the covariation of age and behavior patterns).

3 Culture Acquisition as a Lifelong Process: Perspectives from the Social and Behavioral Sciences

The conceptualization of human learning we propose is not only founded on primate and biological research but is concerned with that uniquely human adaptation, culture. Culture consists of patterns of relating, knowing and believing, and surviving that each particular human community has constructed via the process of choosing from and reconfiguring available options. When educational anthropologists have turned their attention to the patterns of culture, they have concentrated much of their research and theorizing regarding the process of pattern formation on the earliest experiences of humans. Henry (1960), Hilger (1960), Mead (1928), and Whiting (1963) focused on children's behavior, child life, and child development. Children have been viewed as the primary (and sometimes sole) learners in a culture.

This focus on children has seemed logically correct and scientifically warranted. Studies of primates, as reported in Chapter 1, clearly establish the significance of early learning experiences for nonhuman primates. As reported in Chapter 2, recent studies have found neonates to be highly involved in structuring the relationships in their lifespace. As adults ourselves, it is simply evident to us that children must and do learn a great many things. As self-conscious observers of human communities, groups, and behaviors it is equally obvious to us that learning does and must occur at least in childhood.

But the seemingly obvious, here, as in all study of human behavior in context, can obscure our view of embedded patterns, of underlying structure and process,

Mary Anne Pitman was the primary author of this chapter.

of what is *really* going on. For that reason, it is necessary to look beyond childhood in order to hypothesize successfully about how cultural patterns are acquired, transmitted, maintained, and adapted. It is necessary that we view cultural knowledge and learners and the structure of socioecological systems as interactive components in a fluid process, a cybernetic process in which cultural patterns are simultaneously acquired, maintained, and adapted via the actions (choices) of the culture members. Though some of these will be children, the above perspective directs attention to persons of varying levels of cultural competence and indicates that children will not be the only or even the primary learners in a community.

RESEARCH ON ADULTS

Studies of adult learners and of aging per se are a recent development in U.S. social and behavioral sciences. Adult development became an identifiable field in psychology only recently,[1] precipitated in part because longitudinal studies in the field of child development needed to move forward in the lifespan in terms of both data and theory as their subjects reached adulthood in the 1960s and 1970s (Elder 1974; Kagan and Moss 1962). Some of the researchers (Bagley 1963; Kagan 1977) then suggested that the lifespan become the framework for all studies of human development, including child development, and that adulthood be viewed as a significant developmental period in its own right, not just as an epilogue to youth or an antecedent to aging. Gerontologists, too, needed to look backward in the lifespan, placing aging in the context of lifelong processes (Birren and Schaie 1977; Binstock and Shanas 1976).

Studies of adult processes, therefore, have increasingly become a focus of research. This chapter describes the two important perspectives which that research contributes to our conceptualization of culture acquisition. The first perspective identifies basic components thought to be inevitable, ongoing, and automatic in the developmental process. The second identifies structures thought to be constructed, deliberate, made, put together via a network of available choices. These two perspectives are considered in association with adult development theory and age stratification theory, respectively. They will be examined here for clues to analytical categories that address culture acquisition as a lifelong process.

Research on adults has often been framed within competing or incompatible theoretical positions. It is the conclusion of this chapter that an emerging consensus is being introduced, via the anthropological literature on age, that promises to move us beyond yet another Cartesian impasse (see Chapter 2), that of innateness versus acquiredness or nature versus culture. This consensus has informed and influenced our analytical categories as we have attempted to move toward a scientifically based theory of cultural learning.

THE PSYCHOLOGY OF LIFESPAN DEVELOPMENT

The psychological study of age has experienced a redefinition in recent years that is contributing to our anthropological formulations of learning. Some psychologists suggest that this redefinition signals the advent of "a kind of paradigm shift . . . in the way developmental psychology is conceptualized" (Baltes, Reese & Lipsitt 1980:67). Others note the fruitfulness of this endeavor as evidenced by the publication of over a thousand scientific articles per year on the topic between 1983 and 1985 (Birren and Cunningham 1985:3). This shift or redefinition is from the identification of already laid down schemata—biologically based behavioral schemata—to a description of the ongoing pattern of development during which behaviors become organized, change, differentiate, and eventually become disorganized (Birren and Cunningham 1985:4). This attention to lifelong processes is called "life-span developmental psychology." Its adherents include both those who view developmental stages as biologically structured, intraorganismic, unidirectional, and universal and those who view developmental patterns as culturally mediated. Both views have important implications for the development of a scientific, holistic model of culture acquisition.

Those who posit that developmental stages are biologically structured provide support for our contention that all humans learn in the same way, within a similar set of biologically defined parameters. These developmental studies follow the tradition established by Freud, Piaget, and Erikson, all of whom posited an inherent structure to human development, one that is cumulative and irreversible and determined by prior structures. The entire tradition finds chronological age, which is to say biological age,[2] to be the most powerful organizer of and influence on adult development.

Research being conducted by Daniel Levinson and his colleagues on adults in the United States adheres to this model and illustrates its use (Levinson et al. 1978; Levinson 1986). Levinson contends that the life cycle evolves through a series of stages that are partially overlapping, with the overlap constituting a complex process of disequilibrium and crisis (thus, the popularized "midlife crisis"). Consistent with Erikson's life-cycle theory, Levinson's subjects had to complete one developmental task or phase before launching out on subsequent periods of stability. Levinson hypothesizes "that there is an *underlying* order in the human life course" in that the sequencing of stages, "the basic nature and timing" of the structure of growth and change, "holds for men and women of different cultures, classes and historical epochs" (1986:8, 11).

Wider or carte blanche applications of particular formulations of the basic model, such as Levinson's, to whole communities or cultures, however, have been viewed by some scholars as highly problematic. Gilligan (1979), for example, attempted to generalize a similarly invariant but particular formulation to a population made up entirely of (U.S.) women. A life-span developmental psychologist interested in moral development, Gilligan found the paradigmatic formulation of moral development (Kohlberg 1958) inapplicable to women. The reason that that particular formulation of invariant structure was not generalizable to her population, according to Gilligan, lay in its conceptualization of what constitutes the developmental task, namely, establishing ego strength. Ego strength is seen as the ability to separate, to individuate, to form strong ego boundaries. Gilligan found this conceptualization of the task of human development to be central to the three theories that form the basis of life-span psychology. For Freud and Piaget, a developing sense of personal boundaries was the essence of growth, and Erikson's eight stages of psychosocial development likewise focus, with two exceptions—stages one and six—on issues of autonomy and individuation. Levinson's most recent formulation reiterates this basic developmental tenet by defining the "macrostructure of the life cycle" as a series of steps "in a continuing process of individuation" (1986:5).

Gilligan (1977) devised an alternative structure of moral development based on the morality of mutual responsibilities. The work of sociologist Nancy Chodorow (1974, 1978) provided Gilligan with the basis for her claim that interaction rather than individuation formed the structure of women's developmental patterns. Chodorow traced the differences between masculine and feminine personalities to the entire context of their formation, primarily to the fact that women are the universal child rearers of both boys and girls, at least during the earliest and most formative period of a child's life. This led her to suggest that the development of a girl's sense of identity proceeds by means of interactive modeling, while for a boy, it proceeds essentially by denying the model that is present and identifying with the male position rather than with the male person, who is absent and unavailable. Gilligan applied Chodorow's work to her study of women in the United States by emphasizing the contextual, relational process over the abstract, individual one. She claimed that interactive responsibilities were primary in the structuring of women's moral development, rather than the competing individual rights that may be primary for men. In other words, positing universal differences between masculine and feminine personalities, Gilligan denied that any developmental sequence (in particular Kohlberg's) is transferable across gender lines. Nevertheless, she assumed that the developmental constructs she had defined were universal when applied to women. Thus, she agrees with the basic premise of life-span psychology, namely, that development proceeds in a unidirectional, sequential, cumulative fashion; early structures determine subsequent development; chronology is the dominant organizer.

What is valuable in the above studies for educational anthropologists who wish to formulate holistic theories of cultural learning is the recurrence of an assumed inherent and therefore biological structure in all of these formulations. The future of particular formulations, such as Levinson's, Kohlberg's, or Gilligan's, does not affect the logical status of the whole position. Their work certainly creates a dissonance that reveals the challenges scientists face in attempting to filter out the biases inherent in their own cultural definitions of variables. There is disagreement on the units of the formula. Still, they and others consistently validate the structure of the formula itself, and with it the logic of defining biology as some component of the paradigm of human development.

What is missing, in turn, is an explanation that accounts for differences, a description and explanation of variation in the structure of adult lifeways. By relying on social scientific constructs (via Chodorow) and focusing her analysis on gender, Gilligan introduced mediating factors into the conceptualization of human development. Research such as hers opens the door to a consideration of the social, cultural, and environmental contexts of human development, and identifies the need for "new paradigms to help [us] ease out of the rigid molds of characterizing phenomena as either biological or social" (Birren and Cunningham 1985:31). However, such holistic paradigms are as little evident as yet in developmental psychology as they have been in educational anthropology (see Chapter 4). Personal life events, historical events, social roles, and social norms receive little serious analysis by life-span developmental psychologists (see Gutmann 1977 for an exception); their primary interest continues to be the identification of those developmental processes that can be defined as innate. In the words of Daniel Levinson, "the basic nature and timing of life structure development are given in the life cycle at this time in human evolution" (Levinson 1986:11), and it is the work of developmental psychologists to design constructs to explicate that patterning.

AGE STRATIFICATION AND THE LIFE COURSE

An alternative model of human development has focused on social processes as the determinants of developmental change. Contemporary advocates of this position are more likely to refer to "life course" than "life-span." Though some authors use these terms interchangeably, "life-span" more typically refers to those individual, intrapsychic shifts that are studied by developmental psychologists. "Life course," as used by sociologists and social psychologists, refers to "age-related transitions that are *socially created, socially recognized*, and *shared*" by a group or cohort (Hagestad and Neugarten 1979:35). The cohort is a demographic concept introduced by Ryder (1965) and refers to those persons who are age-mates and who, as a generation, experience similar social events. In this context, the life course is the path that an individual as a member of a cohort fashions for her or himself through the various role changes occurring in a lifetime. In life course analysis, the construct of cohort (year of birth in 20-year intervals) is seen as interacting with those of age and period (Maddox and Campbell 1985). Thus, one studies a group or cohort of people born about the same time who age together under the similar but changing conditions of a single historical period. This perspective eschews individual, psychological, and biological mechanisms in favor of the study of structural changes in social processes. As such, it contributes another important dimension—the social and cultural conditions missing from life-span analysis—to a holistic conception of human learning and development.[3]

An example of what this perspective can contribute to a holistic, systemic conception of human learning is found in the work of social psychologist Bernice Neugarten who, along with her colleagues at the University of Chicago, has been a leader in developing a social age norms theory of adult development in Western (predominantly U.S.) societies (Neugarten 1968). According to their view, a psychology of the life cycle is a psychology of social timing or of normative, historically inescapable influences and of nonnormative life events. Developmental change is thus precipitated both by the age norms prevalent in a person's culture and society and by life events that occur in the contexts of health, such as medical trauma and accidents; of work, such as career changes or unemployment; and of family, such as divorce or death. Due both to the exigencies of life and to the changing macro-structure of social norms, the life course of cohorts will differ noticeably from one generation to the next. The pattern of that course will be structured not by biology but by social context, and it is the introduction of social context that is important to us here.

In sociological research on aging, each cohort is viewed as a stratum in a social structure. Its behaviors and their effect on adjoining strata is the focus of research in most age stratification models (Riley and Foner 1968; Riley, Johnson & Foner 1972). The repertoire of beliefs and behaviors available to any given cohort at any given time will be circumscribed by the social environmental realities and by history. Likewise, similar changes in the collective biographies of a cohort can affect the social environment in such a way as to produce social change. "Cohort analysis opens the door to deeper understanding of the systematic interdependence between changes in the lives of individuals and changes in society, both past and future" (Riley 1979:112).

San Giovanni's (1978) age-stratification study of 20 ex-nuns who had left a Roman Catholic convent community and joined the secular society attempted to exemplify how the social context of aging can supersede the developmental imperatives of chronological age. These women created their own roles and shaped their own transition processes by combining some of the behaviors typical of younger cohorts, such as buying a car, having a first date, and getting a paycheck, with their own established skills, such as job competency and independent thinking. San Giovanni suggests that as a result the ex-nuns became role models for their own cohort by demonstrating the possibility of a changing definition of U.S. women's family and career roles, moving toward competency and independence. For San Giovanni, this confirms the age stratification hypothesis that causal links exist between individual biography and social change, or rather that developmental changes are social phenomena that respond to social structural (not biological) events.

Both life-span developmental psychologists and age stratification sociologists have been criticized for identifying changes that may, in fact, be only historical as being biological and social. Rossi (1980), for example, has argued that the role changes and accompanying stressful transitions reported in the experiences of both men (Levinson et al. 1978; Vaillant 1977) and women (Friedan 1963; Rubin 1979) were precipitated by the special economic conditions of the 30 years between 1930 and 1960. She notes that the Levinson's timetable for male development may "be a reflection of the bureaucratic organization of work in an industrial economy. The right sequencing of male schooling and career progression may reflect the phasing of modern business and professional life" (Rossi 1980:16). Thus, chronological age becomes the assumed organizer for what may, in fact, be a career ladder defined by the economic exigencies of the time. Rossi further notes that Neugarten's model of social age norms was developed during the 1950s and the early 1960s, a period when life-styles were relatively stable and appeared more predictable than they had been in the post-Depression era and than they would become in the 1970s. Perun (1981) agreed, noting that the facts of history "may account for more of the patterns of behavior observed than the *developmental change* presumably being studied" (Perun 1981:245). In this context history may be synonymous with existing cultural patterns and hence Perun suggests that those patterns should be accounted for if we mean to understand human development and change.

We can expect to see researchers emphasizing longitudinal data as they continue to formulate and test their hypotheses about human development. Nevertheless, the evidence in support of both life-span developmental psychology and age stratification sociology is already impressive. More important here, however, is that each contributes significant and necessary dimensions to a multidimensional, consensual, holistic paradigm of human development.

ANTHROPOLOGY OF AGE AND AGING

In their introduction to the second edition of the *Handbook of Aging and the Social Sciences*, Maddox and Campbell (1985:19) conclude that "better theories of adult development will necessarily be multidisciplinary and comparative." The discipline of anthropology entered the discussion of age and aging in the 1980s and is bringing to it characteristic anthropological perspectives that are emic, comparative in the cross-cultural sense, and holistic in their simultaneous attention to biology, social structure, and culture. Anthropologists who have begun to study age have relied on both age stratification and lifespan development theories. Their resulting propositions lay the groundwork for the design of a holistic formulation of culture acquisition/transmission as a biologically based, ecological, interactive, socially constructed, lifelong process.

Traditionally, sociocultural anthropologists addressed those aspects of social organization assumed to be malleable, defined by human processes rather than prescribed by human biology. These include, for example, linguistics, economics, and politics. Age, "perhaps because of its continuous and dynamic biological base" (Keith and Kertzer 1984:20) and sex were assumed to belong to the natural order and were therefore not proper subjects for social scientific investigation

(Fry 1985:218). However, since the late 1970s, numerous studies have demonstrated the great cultural variety that exists in regard to cultural definitions of sex and gender (Collier and Rosaldo 1981; Ortner and Whitehead 1981; Pitman and Eisenhart 1988; Rosaldo and Lamphere 1974; Sacks 1979; Sanday 1981), and current studies of age are demonstrating that it, too, is a cultural phenomenon exhibiting considerable variation.

These anthropological studies of age (Amoss and Harrell 1981; Bernardi 1985; Brown and Kerns, 1985; Fry 1979, 1981, 1985; Fry and Keith 1982; Keith 1980, 1985; Keith and Kertzer 1984) address such issues as cultural definitions of the life course, cultural varieties in the use of age as an organizing principle, and studies of the aged (Fry 1985; Keith 1985) from the several perspectives of the subfields in anthropology. In so doing they have begun a rapprochement between advocates of nature versus culture. "The intricacy and subtlety of the biological/ cultural interweave that makes age a difficult subject also offers a fitting topic for anthropological analysis," according to Keith and Kertzer (1984:21) and, one might add, a necessary one for anthropological explanations of the processes involved in culture acquisition/transmission. The metaphor itself, weaving, suggests that no one variable—learning/teaching, children/adults, biology/culture— nor any linear or oppositional relationship between them is sufficient to capture either the structure or process of lifelong learning and adaptation in human communities. "Since all of human culture rests on a biological foundation, each community's definition of the nature/culture boundary is part of a cultural map, and a promising topic for anthropological investigation" (Keith and Kertzer 1984:21). Thus, the synthesis of physical and sociocultural anthropology will allow us to account for human learning and development beyond maturity as both biologically constrained and culturally variable.

Anthropological research has begun to demonstrate that the life course itself is culturally or emically defined, that different cultures vary in their definitions, degrees of perception, and evaluations of the process (Fry 1985; Keith 1985; Keith and Kertzer 1984). For some cultural groups, life is perceived as following a linear course. Thus life course is an emically correct description. For others, life cycle is more accurate because of beliefs about reincarnation or because the functions of the very old are similar or identical to the functions of the young, as among the Akwe-Shevante of Brazil (Maybury-Lewis 1984, cited in Keith 1985). Within any one cultural group, definitions of the life course can also vary on the bases of sex, public versus private domains, career and family cycle, and/ or kinship network. What is clear is that "the biological definition of the life course as beginning at birth (or conception) and ending at death" (Keith and Kertzer, 1984:20) is itself inapplicable in some human communities, those which view life itself as something that transcends earthly and material domains. More important for a study of learning, the anthropological constructs regarding age suggest hypotheses that posit that the varieties of linear or cyclical progressions, their beginning and end points, and the biocultural events that move them are not all prefashioned with roles and statuses assumed and moved into in lockstep fashion. Rather, they are presumably learned via the neurological processes of importing information that is redundant in the environment and via the socioe-motional process of both choosing from and constructing available options. The life-course structure and process and notions of it are variable, therefore, and are based firmly in neither culture nor biology to the exclusion of the other. Nor are these processes, structures, and events reserved for only some age groups, whether age is defined chronologically, biologically, or culturally. Rather, these are lifelong processes of continual construction and adaptation.

Myerhoff's (1984) study of an aged, immigrant U.S. population cut off from its native culture by the Holocaust in Eastern Europe and from its children by assimilation and geographic isolation demonstrated how old people create norms and structure roles and rituals for their own transition. They "had to become their own witnesses to their own stories. . . . Wherever they could, and by what-ever means possible, these individuals have improvised and performed a lively, syncretic culture, made up of a common childhood past combined with their values and experiences of adulthood and old age" (Myerhoff 1984:317–18). Likewise, educational anthropologists, though not directly concerned with a theory of learning, have focused on the changing roles of individuals and groups in the course of particular time-limited social events through the lens of rites-of-passage theory (Eddy 1969; Leemon 1972; Holloman 1974; Neville 1984; Pitman 1985; Dobbert and Pitman 1986). These studies all demonstrate that rituals which dramatize and enact changes in social status are constructed from the living traditions of the current social milieu, not from historical traditions or particularistic traditions of religious or ethnic groups. Between the old status and the new is the transitional period, the period of what is now generally known as "liminality" (Turner 1969, 1974). Turner sees the liminal period as the locus of lifelong learning, a period pregnant with possibility, risk, and invention (Turner 1982). According to Myerhoff, "Moral choice, creativity and innovation are possibilities that emerge from the agony of isolation and the joy of com-munitas which may accompany the liminal stage" (1982:117).

From the perspective of learning or culture acquisition, this emergent con-struction supports a hypothesis that culture is continually being learned. It is not simply received, like a gift, and then used until no longer needed, presumably at death. Learning is more than a kind of passing of information down the chronological chain. Learning is interactive, with learners sampling the options available in a cultural system, choosing some and in the process restructuring the systemic constellation available to them and others. When age is included as a variable in research on culture acquisition, a "more subtle interpretation of the mechanisms by which norms are transmitted, enforced, and created" becomes possible, and the focus on youth which has "emphasized transmission of existing standards" becomes controverted by studies that "show the old people as creators of norms" (Keith and Kertzer 1984:39–40). Thus, the learning process, the process of constructing norms and actions in response to available options remains unchanged, but learning itself will continue throughout the span of life. Neither the content learned nor the process of acquiring it has a biological clock attached. Learning is lifelong, interactive, automatic, and continual.

CONCLUSION

The new anthropological study of age encourages us as educational anthropologists to identify a model of culture acquisition/transmission that is based on biological processes while at the same time accounting for cultural variety in the dynamic sense of culturally learned patterns as rapidly and regularly modifiable throughout the course of life. Humans as learners ''are not passive recipients of knowledge, rules and standards from enculturators who are older, bigger, stronger or more important than they are'' (Fry 1985:217). Culture shapes behavior, but does not determine it. And culture itself is shaped by individuals, who choose, act, and believe. That includes *all* individuals, not just the young, because the cultural map is drawn and redrawn in a lifelong process of social and environmental systemic interaction. Those who would develop a theory of culture acquisition must therefore model the process in such a way as to account for learning throughout the span of life. Culture is not a thing. It is patterns for survival that are constructed via the interactive choices of all the members of a cultural community, including the young, the established stakeholders, and increasingly the elderly.

NOTES

1. For a history of the field of adult development, see Baltes and Willis (1979); Baltes, Reese & Lipsitt (1980); Birren, Cunningham & Yamamoto (1983); Birren and Cunningham (1985); Rossi (1980).

2. Chronological age calculates ''time elapsed since birth'' according to a scale or index derived from some standard calendar, typically the Western calendar. See Beall (1984:83–84) for a discussion of the way physical anthropologists distinguish biological and chronological age.

3. However, life course analysis is similarly handicapped because it views these social and cultural factors not as mediating conditions in a cybernetic system, but as unicausal determinants of a group's structure and process.

4 Cultural Transmission: A Review of Existing Theory and Method

The previous chapters review some of the key constructs and major findings in primate research, in the psychology of learning and brain research, and in research on aging and development that are critical for holism in the anthropology of human learning. This chapter narrows to review those constructs as they appear in the work of educational and psychological anthropologists and of anthropological methodologists who have addressed issues of cultural transmission. We describe how their work, taken as a whole, contributes to the building of a solid theoretical and methodological base for an anthropology of culture acquisition. These works will be reviewed in light of three criteria for theory formulation: the first criterion relates to the conceptualization of culture as process; the second to holism; and the third to standards for precision in data collection and data analysis.

DEVELOPING A PROCESS-ORIENTED THEORY OF CULTURE AND SOCIAL STRUCTURE

Most of the classic definitions of culture antedate process-oriented social science and do not incorporate the dynamic elements of age, sex, class, faction, ethnic strategy, etc., that have characterized the foci of contemporary social science. Such static definitions of culture have led, in turn, to static definitions of cultural transmission. A. F. C. Wallace commented on this phenomenon:

Marion Lundy Dobbert and Mary Anne Pitman were the primary authors of this chapter.

In many investigations, the anthropologist tacitly, and sometimes even explicitly, is primarily interested in the extent to which members of a social group, by virtue of their common group identification, behave in the same way under the same circumstances. For the sake of convenience in discourse, they may even be considered to have learned the "same things" in the "same cultural environment." Under such circumstances, the society may be regarded as culturally homogeneous and the individuals will be expected to share a uniform nuclear character. If a near-perfect correspondence between culture and individual nuclear character is assumed, the structural relation between the two becomes nonproblematical, and the interest of processual research lies rather in the mechanisms of socialization by which each generation becomes, culturally and characterologically, a replica of its predecessors. (1970:22).

In contrast to models of culture and cultural transmission that emphasize "the replication of uniformity," Wallace proposed models that explain "the organization of diversity":

. . . It is sometimes more interesting to consider the actual diversity of habits, of motives, of personalities, of customs that do, in fact, coexist within the boundaries of any culturally organized society. When the fact of diversity is emphasized, the obvious question must immediately be asked: How do such various individuals organize themselves culturally into orderly, expanding, changing societies? . . . Culture, as seen from this viewpoint, becomes not so much a superorganic entity, but policy, tacitly and gradually concocted by groups of people for the furtherance of their interests, and contract, established by practice, between and among individuals to organize their strivings into mutually facilitating equivalence structures. (1970:22)

Such a process model refocuses the attention of social scientists interested in education. When culture is seen as concocted "policy" or as the organization of "strivings," the whole emphasis of socialization studies necessarily shifts from the identification of cultural schemata to be handed down to a description of how those schemata develop, become organized, and are continually adapted by individuals and small groups, each learning to fit its own desired outcomes into the social whole.

Following Wallace, Gearing and his associates[1] have attempted to develop a set of propositions for looking at information flow on an interindividual (but not cultural comparative) level. In doing so, they have focused upon the interactive event, or dyadic dance, as the locus of cultural learning via selective information exchange (or failure thereof). This work both assumes and refocuses the language and identity studies of Gumperz, Cazden, and others. It adopts and extends Goodenough's cognitive anthropology into a scrutiny of emic *behaviors* by viewing each individual's acting out of personality, status, role, and other individual characteristics as culturally conditioned, cognitively patterned organizations of information.

According to Gearing's formulation, the cultural system of any group is maintained via dyadic face-to-face encounters during which the actors take turns positioning and repositioning themselves in a transaction of equivalences of meaning. These encounters are conducted according to "agenda," which are codifications of each person's expectations of what promises or threatens to occur. Agenda can vary from "open" to "troubled". Their structures are revealed in each person's positioning of self vis-à-vis the other in terms of those expectations. Equivalences of meaning that have been transacted through recurrent encounters in a social group result in cultural transmission.

The notion of equivalence structures, drawn from Wallace (1970), and of encounter, drawn from Goffman's collective works, excludes psychological variables. It is not the knowledge or internalized motives in the psyches of individuals that are to be scrutinized. It is the behavioral patterns, including speech, displayed in face-to-face interactions that influence, manage, control, and constrain the transmission of culture. According to Gearing, then, culture *is* "the complex network of transacted equivalences and not-yet transacted equivalences" (1973:5).

Learning, or in Gearing's terms "the work of education," occurs *not* during the transaction of "open agendas," those transactions in which parties agree and share, but during "filtering agendas," those transactions in which equivalence is not immediately and equally achieved. Because open agendas involve widely known and shared information, Gearing views them as peripheral in a cultural theory of education, even though the greatest number of likely encounters involve such agendas. Agendas in which the filters are "stable" because information is limited by power, position, or ownership that is culturally understood by both parties are viewed as central to the theory because through them complex information is being communicated. "Troubled" agendas involve barriers to information based on premises that are not culturally shared. Thus, information is totally blocked.

The social structural, ecological, and ideological patterns of a group are thus transmitted in certain specified face-to-face negotiations. But it is not, in Gearing's view, necessary to study the internalized maps underlying the negotiations of reciprocal behavior, because the transactions of stable agendas regenerate the information that constitutes the epistemology of the group. Therefore, according to Gearing, by making use of the concepts of equivalence and agenda, a cultural explanation may go from face-to-face to panhuman and need not concern itself with the specific local constraints of ecology, ideology, and social organization, that is, of community. A general theory, however, would map encounters in many societies to determine each one's system of equivalences. This would be done in the manner of an ethnoscience of kinesic behavior by defining the emic categories that explain the behavioral displays of analytic pairs. Once the categories are defined, the analysis would go on to focus not on "the replication of uniformity," that is, on open agendas, but on "the organization of diversity," that is, on filtering agendas.

Thus, Gearing's non-holistic but process-oriented formulation of cultural transmission rests on Wallace's definition of culture (cited above) as policy and contract. It draws the focus of attention in educational anthropology to culture as constructed or processual. If this focus could be combined with holistic approaches characteristic of pre-process models, anthropological learning theory would be substantially advanced.

ACHIEVING HOLISM

Historically, the anthropology of education was closely associated with the standard holism of either social or cultural anthropology. The first major works on the anthropology of education exemplified the holistic tradition of studying entire systems of child raising or child life. Works such as Read's *Children of Their Fathers* (1960), Mead's *Growing Up in New Guinea* (1930), Raum's *Chagga Childhood* (1940), Hilger's *Field Guide to the Ethnological Study of Child Life* (1960) and her numerous related studies provide good examples of this tradition. However, in the early 1960s a shift occurred.

Beginning with the publication of Henry's *Culture Against Man* (1963), the field of anthropology and education in the United States turned its focus from the holism of social and cultural anthropology and narrowed to a problem-oriented school and classroom focus. The socially conscious scholars of that period wished to analyze the social problems being perpetuated and aggravated by the existing structure and content of U.S. schools, to document them, to come to understand them, and to take action to alleviate them. Most applied research in education lacked a traditional theoretical base from which to derive recommendations for action. They were derived, instead, from idiosyncratic values and from isolated or ad hoc approaches.

Not all anthropologists of education narrowed their focus to problem-oriented work. Solon Kimball, who together with his colleague Conrad Arensberg was one of the leaders in introducing anthropologists to concepts and methods for the study of modern Western societies, tried to strengthen the theoretical potential of educational anthropology by centering attention on community. In *Education and the New America* (1962) he and James McClellan described the historical community types in the United States and their associated educational forms and then attempted to define and describe the succeeding modern U.S. community and educational forms. By classifying modern U.S. structure as corporate-bureaucratic, they were able to raise questions about the form of education appropriate to that culture type. In doing so, they achieved a high level of sophisticated holism in analysis, one that cannot be approached when education is considered in terms of isolated models of schooling.

Twelve years later Kimball continued his advocacy for a holistic, community-oriented approach to education and learning:

An essential characteristic of the anthropological method is the examination of all aspects of a people's way of life. Historically, this emphasis upon the whole arose from the fact that the tribal groups studied were relatively limited in population and homogeneous in cultural attributes and possessed few and simple social arrangements. These circumstances led to consequences of immense conceptual importance. Among them was the realization that human behavior, of whatever type, could be understood only within the context of its relation to other aspects of the same society and that cultural and social behavior must be viewed as interdependent systems operating within a given set of conditions. Specifically, the number and variety of social groups, the kinds of activities characteristic of each, the nature of the values and symbols, even the manifestations of personality, were considered to be expressions of and related to the whole. . . . *The realities of the learning process, then, must be viewed in the context of the total social arrangements and cultural practices that constitute education and the environment within which it operates.* (1974:77–78; emphasis added)

In *Culture and the Educative Process* (1974), Kimball wrote extensively on the relationship between culture and learning. He looked at the "Cultural Influences Shaping the Role of the Child"; he took particular note of the all-encompassing nature of the symbol system of a society. These, together with the underlying social, conceptual, and material structures, serve to organize both adult and child actions, constraining them in ways that he felt were beginning to be ignored in educational anthropology. Kimball pointed out the impossibility of developing an anthropology of education if the field were to employ the individualistic focus that is the basis of the psychological approach and that underlies the U.S. value system (1982: Chap. 11; also 126) or if it were to focus exclusively upon schooling and school-related learning issues (see, for example, his extended comment; 1974:110).

In "Community and Hominid Emergence" (1982), one of his last published articles, Kimball chose to argue for the importance of a holistic, community-based approach to education by looking at the human evolutionary tradition. In doing so he returned to a theme that had been developed in the early 1970s (Kimball and Burnett 1973; Wax, Diamond & Gearing 1971; Herzog 1974), the theme of the human primate heritage: "The evolutionary process, operating within an environment of community, favored the appearance of species that joined organic development and cultural learning as essentials for adult maturation" (Kimball 1982:126). He went on to hammer home his point by indicating the significance of this fact for theory building.

Relatively few anthropologists have made contributions to an anthropologically oriented learning theory, even though cultural transmission is acknowledged as a major area of concern. This deficiency may be attributed to a continued domination by a tradition in anthropology that emphasizes descriptive ethnography, and to the theoretical biases of structuralism, materialism, or symbolism where cultural transmission has not been considered significantly relevant. (Kimball 1982:127–28)

John Ogbu is another educational anthropologist who argues against narrowing one's ethnographic focus. He claims that such narrowing trains one's focus on unquestioned folk theories about the nature of the relation between society, race, and education that tend to locate the problems of inequality in each child's immediate home environment (1978:2). In *The Next Generation* (1974) and in *Minority Education and Caste* (1978), Ogbu calls for a broader approach that looks at the social construction of adult work life and at the actual outcomes of the patterned relationships among varying social groups.

In *The Next Generation* he shows how both parents and the school cooperate to try to give minority children the best possible formal education, which the children may use to build an economically and socially satisfactory life-style and to extricate themselves from poverty. He employs a comparative structural approach to show how observation and the consequent knowledge of the social facts of life teach ghetto children a different lesson, a lesson about the job ceiling for blacks in the U.S. and about the hopelessness of striving to achieve a new life-style through education. In *Minority Education and Caste*, Ogbu utilizes a cross-national approach to demonstrate the way in which educational issues related to racial discrimination can be set in a comparative cultural context. Like Kimball and McClellan in *Education and the New America*, he produces new insights, his regarding castelike social processes, by utilizing the holistic approach. He calls on all social scientists to query both their findings and their questions at the highest level of social theory (1978:3–5).

Another holistically based, comparativist approach to educational issues is found in Ashley Montagu's edited volume *Learning Non-Aggression* (1978). This work is concerned with educational issues related to the problems of the origins of warfare and aggression or of peaceableness and gentleness in society. Montagu invited seven anthropologists to address the following educational questions:

The evidence suggests that as a consequence of natural selection . . . human beings can learn virtually anything. Among other things, they can learn to be virtually wholly unaggressive. . . . How [does] it come about that some societies are so little aggressive compared with others? What are the conditions that make for aggressiveness both in the individual and in the society? How do some societies manage to control the expression of aggression? (1978:6–7).

The anthropologists were to reflect on these issues and provide specific ethnographic data to illustrate the varied ways in which human beings may learn to be aggressive or nonaggressive. The importance of the book lies in the fact that it, too, raises serious educational questions and attempts to answer them using a holistic, comparative basis. Although the methodology that holds *Learning Non-Aggression* together is informal, this work, like Ogbu's, demonstrates how major sociocultural questions about culture acquisition/transmission are best approached through ethnographic study from the perspective of multiple cultures.

STANDARDS FOR PRECISION IN DATA COLLECTION AND ANALYSIS

Over the course of the history of anthropology, the methods of and standards for gathering and recording data have become increasingly codified, making recent standards both more formalized and more demanding. This trend has been particularly noticeable in educational anthropology. Margaret Mead, for example, was a leader in the movement to formalize anthropological methodology. As early as 1928, with the first publication of *Coming of Age in Samoa*, Mead included a methodological appendix in which she described her sample, explained the methods and instruments used, and provided a number of data tables. In *Growing Up in New Guinea* (1930), she continued this tradition and even provided a few samples of raw data. In the 1956 volume *New Lives for Old*, she included a 7,000 word methodological appendix with samples of notes taken in the native language. In this appendix, Mead took care to contrast the methods used in 1928 with those used in 1953, noting that the more recent methods guaranteed collection of "fine-grain material, which is so incomparably more detailed than the material of twenty-five years ago" (p. 292).

Mead's methodological concerns led to experiments with tape recordings, film, and still photography. These materials, some later published or made into educational films,[2] were not intended for use in the display of cultural findings, but were designed to be used as data "to capture her subjects and give unimpeachable documentation to her work" (Harris 1968:417). Her attention to accuracy and detail was not solely a response to the criticism of her work (see Harris 1968:416) since it antedated any such criticism. It probably arose from her training under the scientist Franz Boas, who decried sloppy work and was a stickler for detail. He "wanted a real corpus of materials to work on, large bodies of material which would make possible the cross-checking of each detail and would provide a basis for making certain kinds of negative statements" (see Mead's description 1959:9–11, 16). Harris (1968:417) ranks Mead's introduction of the use of equipment to improve the accuracy and objectivity of anthropological data-gathering as her most enduring contribution to the discipline.

The demand for higher standards of scientific accuracy and performance received further impetus from the Redfield-Lewis and Pueblo controversies. In commenting on these controversies, Pelto (1970:30–34) demonstrates how they arose out of a lax set of standards for scientific procedures. He goes on to say, *"The single most serious problem in anthropological research is the failure to pay careful attention to definition of units and variables."* He continues: "The procedures of observation related to the essential, defined elements must be described in enough detail so that another anthropologist . . . can clearly understand what steps would be necessary to replicate the observations involved . . . " (p. 35; Pelto's emphasis).

Within the field of educational anthropology, Frederick Erickson and his colleagues have displayed a similar concern for accuracy and detail. Building upon

Birdwhistell's work and the communications theory of Edward T. Hall, they have pioneered the use of modern videotape and film technology in connection with the study of education. The resulting studies have been variously termed "microethnography" (Erickson 1975), "constitutive ethnography" (Mehan 1978), "ethnographic monitoring" (Hymes 1980), "sociolinguistic microanalysis" (Gumperz 1982), and "ethnography of communication" (Jacob 1987). Within this tradition, researchers focus not on people, that is, individuals and related intrapsychic phenomenon, but on interactive processes, people "making choices and conducting social action together" (Erickson 1986:47). Because of their assumption that learning "is not optional for humans" (1986:90), these researchers focus their investigations "on particular cultural scenes within key institutional settings" (Erickson and Mohatt 1982:137), usually classrooms, in order to explain differential learning. This focus has been explained and defended by Erickson:

We can assume that all students are learning something. The basic issue is that many students . . . do not appear to be learning what the teacher and the school claim to be teaching. Both the claims regarding what is being taught and the claims regarding what is being learned need to be scrutinized, in the context of . . . the local meaning systems that are created as teachers and students influence one another. . . . The particular means they construct for collaboratively accomplishing [their] ends are expected to vary across each specific classroom, and . . . can only be discovered by studying particular instances in close detail, since the universal principles are realized in ways that are locally unique. (1986:90–91)

The methods that have been developed for studying these interactive learning instances in great detail and then comparing them to similar cases studied in a similarly detailed manner have been described by Erickson and Schultz (1981) and illustrated by Erickson and Mohatt (1982). The entire body of research within this genre represents a major contribution to the development of a standard for scientific accuracy in the recording of detail in anthropological studies in educational settings.

Problems with accuracy in research are compounded for educational anthropologists who wish to investigate culture acquisition/transmission at the macrocultural level of community. A major problem related to data gathering at a macrocultural level is that of defining and obtaining an adequate sample. Still, there is a critical need for large structural studies. They are essential to balance both the schooling bias of modern educational anthropology in the United States and the persistent cognitive psychological biases of our field and the field of child development. As both Burton (1978) and Funnel and Smith (1981) have noted, these biases typically are not conducive to the development of a theory of cultural transmission. When culture is considered as merely cognitive, important biological, ecological, and social structural constraints are reduced to the status of simple individual preferences. Modern holistic, cybernetic approaches, to use Funnel and Smith's term, include all these elements and thus may have wider explanatory power. But macroculturally defined settings cannot be studied as wholes. They must be sampled from as they cannot be recorded or filmed comprehensively as can microcultural events.

However, one cannot merely sample the cultural setting in order to define the body of cultural knowledge to be learned. As we have learned from Wallace and from other proponents of a negotiation perspective, there is no fixed body of material to be sampled. Contemporary data from research on families, for example, does not even support a hypothesis that children replicate the values and beliefs of the adults closest to them, their parents (Troll, Bengston & McFarland 1979). Child life is not a miniature version of adult life but is independent, reflexive, and complementary (Burton 1978). Similar findings are emerging from the research on life course/life cycle, showing that both the old and those in the prime of life who have social power engage in creative interplay and learning (see Chapter 3).

In order to develop theory, then, the field needs a coherent way to link the study of these processes with broad sociocultural perspectives so that children, child life, old people, adult learners, and the processes of culture acquisition/ transmission can be studied within the holistic, community context. McDermott and Roth (1978) propose a solution for anthropology in general that is applicable to educational anthropology. They suggest that the distinction between micro-studies and macrostudies should be done away with by viewing both within a single framework. Macrostructures, they claim, are regenerated and confirmed in each moment by face-to-face actors operating within a framework of constraints that originate externally but are made internal within the action, an idea borrowed from Sapir and also given expression in Gearing's hypotheses (see above). Finding a way to sample from the cultural universe in such a way that this entire framework of acts, interactions, and environments is accounted for becomes the essential research problem.

The best solution may be provided by time allocation (TA) studies that comprehensively sample an entire array of activities in a manner that eliminates age and gender biases and aids in covering all activities, including those unexpected or unpredicted (Gross 1984:521, 523). TA may be used in conjunction with continuous, fixed interval, or spot samples (1984:539–41). Continuous sampling provides data on the "texture" of lives. Fixed interval sampling with random or representative beginning times provides a way to look at a representative universe using established cycles as starting points. Spot samples are the method of choice for obtaining high levels of detail and validity. Time allocation methods, then, provide the types of samples that can embrace the broadly conceived classes of data needed to develop theory in the field of cultural transmission. This type of sample construction permits a combined focus on both the macro and micro levels. Therefore, it can meet the standards set by microsystem analysts and at the same time address our concerns for attention to complex, macrolevel, interactive wholes.

BROAD MODELS FOR THE STUDY OF CULTURAL TRANSMISSION

In educational anthropology the available models most concerned with operationalizing theoretical constructs at a broad community and national level are those of George and Louise Spindler and John and Beatrice Whiting. The Spindlers have developed the idea of instrumental linkages as the mechanism for preservation and change in community structure, and the Whitings have looked at the effects of social and ecological environment upon personality and child-raising systems. Both pairs of educational anthropologists were seriously concerned with finding a way to define and study mechanisms of ordinary life responsible for the transmission and acquisition of culture.

Spindler expressed his impatience with static, omnibus socialization and enculturation models, which arise from the assumptions behind replication-based theories of cultural reproduction, saying that the models can do no more than "orient," are quite incapable of defining, and do not help "explain what we find" (Spindler 1974b:2). The Spindlers' conception of instrumental linkages (Spindler and Spindler 1965; Spindler 1974a) is a model for defining how information is processed by individuals who share an environment and a social system. They have postulated that cultures are integrated through sanctioned and unsanctioned instrumental linkages organizing values, desired ends, and specific actions into units characteristic of a given culture. When taken as a totality, these linkages provide the skeleton for a unified socioconceptual structure (1965). According to this model, an instrumental linkage is the relationship between a goal and the behavior used to achieve it. Culture becomes learnable because children can see these linkages in action, hear comment upon the use of them by other members of the society, and find their elders recommending certain linkages and rejecting others. When the linkages, what they are and how they function, are taught to or learned by children, cultural transmission is achieved. The transmission process is studied by examining "alternative linkages." The focus is on individuals within a cultural system as they proceed to challenge established instrumental linkages and perceive, select, and order alternative linkages.

Linkages may be studied by means of an instrument developed by the Spindlers, the Instrumental Activities Inventory (IAI), which is "a series of line drawings of real cultural alternatives . . . that elicit the cultural knowledge" of the subject (Spindler and Spindler 1981:301). The IAI builds upon procedures and concepts used in both culture and personality and cognitive anthropology research, but does not introduce researcher opinions as the personality assessment does (see LeVine 1973 regarding comment on personality testing). Following the procedure of cognitive anthropology, the instrumental model employs emic categories, but it also expands on ethnosemantics by introducing visual emic stimuli (the options of the instrument) to elicit emic data. Further, both the stimuli and the data are multimodal, though not necessarily simultaneously so. The results obtained from administering the IAI may be used to define both group norms and individual variations (by sex, age, role, experience, etc.) in those norms (Spindler 1987).

Thus, the instrumental linkage model adapts most of the approaches to cultural transmission that preceded it. The notion of an instrumental model of a cultural system "draws from functional, systems, and cognitive theory" (Spindler and Spindler 1965:248) and is holistic because it unifies cognitive, communicative, and social structural elements. Because the Spindlers are "concerned with the nexus between individual psychology, social action and cultural organization"(1981:302) and with intracultural variation (as for example in *Dreamers without Power* 1971), their model is also fully compatible with a multisided, dynamic, process-oriented view of culture:

. . . [We] early developed a multiple acculturative adaptation model. It was apparent to us that our communities were not homologous and consisted of people with varying degrees of groupness whose strategies of adaptation . . . were different from each other. . . . (Spindler 1974a:3)

Further, the model is, as Spindler notes (1974b:249), open and is capable of handling change.

During rapid culture change or urbanization, established instrumental linkages are challenged by new information, behavior modes and belief systems. . . . In using this model, one may be concerned with either the culture system processes that result in new instrumental linkages or with the perception, selection and cognitive ordering of alternative linkages by individuals. (1974a:4)

John and Beatrice Whiting and their colleagues have also made a major contribution to the explanation of child life in terms of the social and ecological conditions underlying cultural patterns. John Whiting originally explored Kwoma teaching techniques via psychoanalytic theory (1941), but went on to seek a more general theory of behavior (Whiting and Child 1953:13) and of personality in the context of culture. In *Child Training and Personality* the focus was on culture-personality connections; the approach taken to testing for the existence of such connections was, of necessity, cross-cultural. The methodology chosen was the statistical testing of carefully stated hypotheses, using data derived from 75 cultures. In later work, John Whiting adopted an even more holistic stance, seeking to further relate his findings to broader cultural or ecological features via correlational testing procedures.

The work represented in Beatrice and John Whiting's *Children of Six Cultures* is also the result of this deliberate broadening of focus. Because they realized that the existing ethnographic literature contained "restricted and parochial" descriptions (1975:vii), a gigantic effort was launched to gather systematic data on children and their communities in six cultures. The final comparative analysis of the data for all six cultures focuses on the influence of culture on child behavior, for example, on the kinds of social features that lead to mature, responsible behavior in children versus those that lead to competitive, achievement-oriented behavior or on the social/behavioral patterns that result when children or their mothers work. Although the data base is small, the results suggest that the use of a method that defines, describes and tests precise, carefully limited pattern statements about children is a fruitful source of scientific hypotheses.

Some anthropologists may not feel comfortable with many of the Whitings' techniques and with the other statistical techniques applied by cross-cultural (holocultural) anthropologists. These methods usually utilize various rating or ranking techniques or rely on factor analysis, and most rest upon the assumptions of frequency probability theory, which are inappropriate for cultural work because data are analyzed as if each instance, act, or item were independent. Nevertheless, the Whitings' approach is exemplary because it is based on explicitly stated theory that is formally tested against data about children and their milieus.

Harris defends this type of generalization against the ethnographic, Boasian critique that it lacks the necessary anthropological holism because it breaks data into small pieces and is riddled with errors. In so doing, he cites Campbell's historically based explanation of the way sciences grow.

The healthy infancy of the successful sciences seems to have been predicated upon the stimulating nourishment of crude but effective ceteris paribus laws. . . . The abstractive-generalizing social scientist knows that in dealing with natural groups ceteris are not in fact paribus, and he [sic] therefore expects exceptions which represent the operation of many other laws which he as yet knows nothing of. (Campbell 1961:347, cited in Harris 1968:453)

Because the methods of the holoculturalists are so limited, they militate against the production of fully holistic studies. However, their work is influential and provides a model for other social scientists because of its general intent to find and establish scientific verification for the sociocultural laws that link apparently disparate aspects of human endeavor, such as food surpluses and shortages with child-training behaviors (Barry, Child & Bacon 1959). It is, then, not the holo-culturalists' techniques, but their insistence on the use of a firm, repeatable methodology and their adventurous testing of novel data-based hypotheses that provide direction for the development of theory in educational anthropology.

CONCLUSION

While it is generally true that "anthropologists have shown more interest in reporting what transmitters try to transmit than what learners are actually learning" (Wolcott 1982:2), it is clear from this review that that situation has been changing. Following Wallace, anthropologists of education have become more concerned with the interactive and processual. We have begun to recognize the constancy of learning as lifelong and not limited to childhood. Learning in naturally occurring social environments constitutes the focus of the Spindlers' IAI and the Whitings' cross-cultural research, providing some balance to the institutional focus of much contemporary microcultural research. The latter, however, has provided us with a methodology that captures detail in a systematic and replicable way that is now applicable to larger social environments. Kimball's call for a holistic, sociocultural approach to the study of education within the discipline of anthropology is once again persuasive to educational anthropologists concerned, as Kimball was, with the possibilities of building theory. Subsequent research can now proceed on a solid and broadly conceived base, moving theory-building work toward the understanding of the macrocultural level while attempting to meet the requirements for a solid scientific procedure.

NOTES

1. See Gearing (1973, 1979); Gearing et al. (1975, 1979). Gearing et al. (1979) and Gearing (1979) are introductory and concluding chapters of a book edited by Gearing and Sangree (1979) for the purpose of presenting his theory to a community of peers. Those peers—over 20 of them—offer comments on the theory in the middle section of the book and, in so doing, reveal the then chilly climate of receptivity to a process-oriented theory of culture acquisition/transmission within the educational anthropology community.

2. For example, *Growth and Culture: A Photographic Study of Balinese Childhood* with F. C. MacGregor, and *Balinese Character: A photographic Analysis*, and the films *Karba's First Years* and *Bathing Babies in Three Cultures*, all produced with Bateson between 1942 and 1953.

5   Culture Acquisition: Operationalizing a Holistic Approach

The first four chapters of this book reviewed the dimensions, theoretical constructs, and methods that appear essential for a holistic understanding of human learning. Taken as a whole, this body of primatological, neurological, developmental, and educational research suggests designs for the anthropological study of learning that are broadly encompassing and at the same time carefully specified. The criteria for studies of learning in social contexts that emerge from this work justify and perhaps demand research strategies that are holistic, but these strategies must also be carefully detailed in the micro sense. Therefore, designing comprehensive strategies for the study of cultural learning is a demanding task.

The general process orientation of contemporary anthropology encourages us to begin by defining learners interactionally, in terms of their interaction both with living people and with fluid, social, and ecological structures. Adults and children can be pictured as instrumentally active social agents constructing concepts, aims, and accomplishments of their own within a given milieu. This view calls for an orientation within educational anthropology toward an interactive notion of learning. If we define learning, as Mead (1970) did, as all nonmaturational change, as all change that is not bio-genetically preprogrammed, then it follows that the interaction that leads to the acquisition of culture is a holistic

This chapter is adapted from Marion Lundy Dobbert, Rivka Eisikovits, Mary Anne Pitman, Jan Armstrong Gamradt, and Kyung-soo Chun, "Cultural Transmission in Three Societies: Testing a Systems-Based Field Guide." Reproduced with permission of the American Anthropological Association from *Anthropology & Education Quarterly* 15:4, 1984. Not for further reproduction. Marion Lundy Dobbert, Rivka A. Eisikovits, and Mary Anne Pitman were the primary authors of this chapter.

and—at all times and in all places—ongoing process. It is the purpose of this chapter to present a theoretical approach and a research method that captures this polyphasic, process-oriented nature of learning in cultural context.

THE GENERAL SYSTEMS THEORY BASE

We begin with a learner in the context of everyday life. From there we build a formal theory of culture acquisition/transmission. Figure 5.1 pictures this at a general level. On the left hand, in the subsystem box labeled 1.0, we have represented a learner with specific characteristics of age and sex, with abilities and skills learned previously or, if physical, inherited, and with a configuration of cultural knowledge about what to do and how to do it. The learner also possesses a capacity to act both in response to the cultural environment, box labeled 2.0, and upon the environment. This is shown by the "choose" and "range of possibilities" arrows between the learner and culture patterns boxes.

The second element of our formal theory is the culture or way of life that the learner is to encounter. This is represented incompletely in Figures 5.1 by the previously mentioned subsystem box, on the right, labeled 2.0. But we need a way of picturing culture that is more complete, complex, and interactive, because culture or the lifeway of a community cannot be treated as a thing. Rather, it is generated via a living, changing web of meanings, meetings, and actions with a particularly dense network of constant interaction as its core.

We can specify this more accurately and transform it into formal theory through use of the information concept from general systems theory (von Bertalanffy 1968). In systems theory, the concept of information refers to a set of probabilities (Ashby 1968). This means that in defining relations between parts of a system, one defines the set of possibilities that exists between them. When one part of a system encounters another part or when a system encounters its environment, it samples the state of the observed system and takes note of that system's probabilities, that is, it obtains information. The information is stored informally as a map that symbolically represents the probable states of exterior systems. We can say that in this way learning occurs. Further, as a system maps those states and matches them symbolically to its own states, meaning is obtained. In information theory, then, any kind of activity or cognitive construction implies symbolic correspondence and adjustment of structure. It does not imply replication. An analog of this learning process may be seen in the relationship between genetic systems and environments. Genetic systems correspond with and take into account the major factors in an environment in order to survive, but the structures of the nucleic acid chains do not resemble, in any way, the structures of the natural environments being mapped. The concept of information also explains the way in which organization in a system is maintained through the process of importing new resources. For example, in the physical system of an animal, the method of maintaining organization (that is, life) is evident—food, which is energy, is imported and incorporated. The situation in a cultural system

Figure 5.1
General Cultural Analog

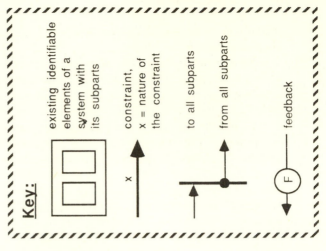

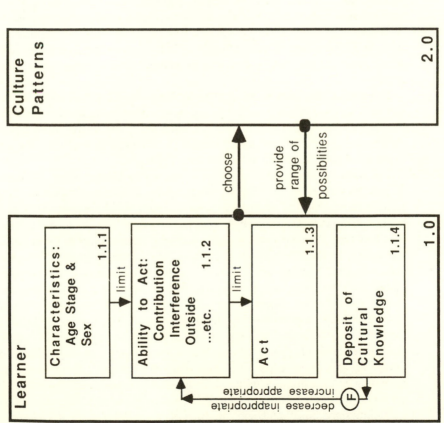

is analogous: The cultural system imports and incorporates information and thus maintains structure.

Using the notions of information and correspondence, we can formulate a definition of culture that accounts for its interactive complexity. Each aspect of a culture may be thought of as a subsystem that samples the states of other subsystemic parts of that culture, maps them, and adjusts accordingly. Learners may be thought of in the same way—as subsystems that map possibilities and match states. The following definition of culture is based on this process of correspondence and the importing of information as an organizer:

Culture is a system that maps information from an environment and configures it as a structure of conceptual patterns, patterns for social interaction and patterns for getting a living.

Figure 5.2 elaborates upon this definition of culture. The box on the right, labeled 2.0, indicates (at this point noninteractively) the essential elements that a learner will encounter in any single interaction. These are: settings, groups, activities, atmospheres, and objects. In order to avoid the danger of reification, the model must consist of two parts on two separate levels. The first part represents humans, who store information in their nervous systems, and the second represents culture, which stores information in structures or patterns corresponding to the environment.

To complete the formal theory, it is necessary to show how information that is stored in the structures, actions, and beliefs that make up the cultural map interacts and moves around the system, and how it may be transmitted between groups and generations in a society. Figure 5.3 models the essential interactions in such a theory of culture acquisition/transmission.

The model operationalizes the general theory by depicting the relationships of specific learners to the specifics of their own cultural environments. In order to read the model and simulate the types of situations it explicates, one must begin with an individual person (1.0) called learner (1.1). The learner is a person of a given age and specific sex, who possesses certain abilities for action (subsystem box 1.1). Both the age and sex of the learner may limit the person to certain cultural settings and activities (2.0). In some cultures, for example, an infant would be limited to a household setting, or a boy to specific grazing locales (boxes 1.1.1 to 2.0). Regardless of a learner's age, sex, or status, the settings (2.0) themselves define and limit the possible activities that take place within them, so that the actions a learner may encounter are organized differently by setting. A household ritual, for example, would be different from a ritual in the village square. These options and limitations are indicated by the three arrows extending from cultural settings (2.0) to learner's behavior (1.1.3), to other person's values (1.2.2), and to social interaction patterns (3.1).

Within a setting, the learner will encounter a culturally organized social interaction pattern (3.1) that may be formally organized and institutionalized

Figure 5.2
Expanded Cultural Analog

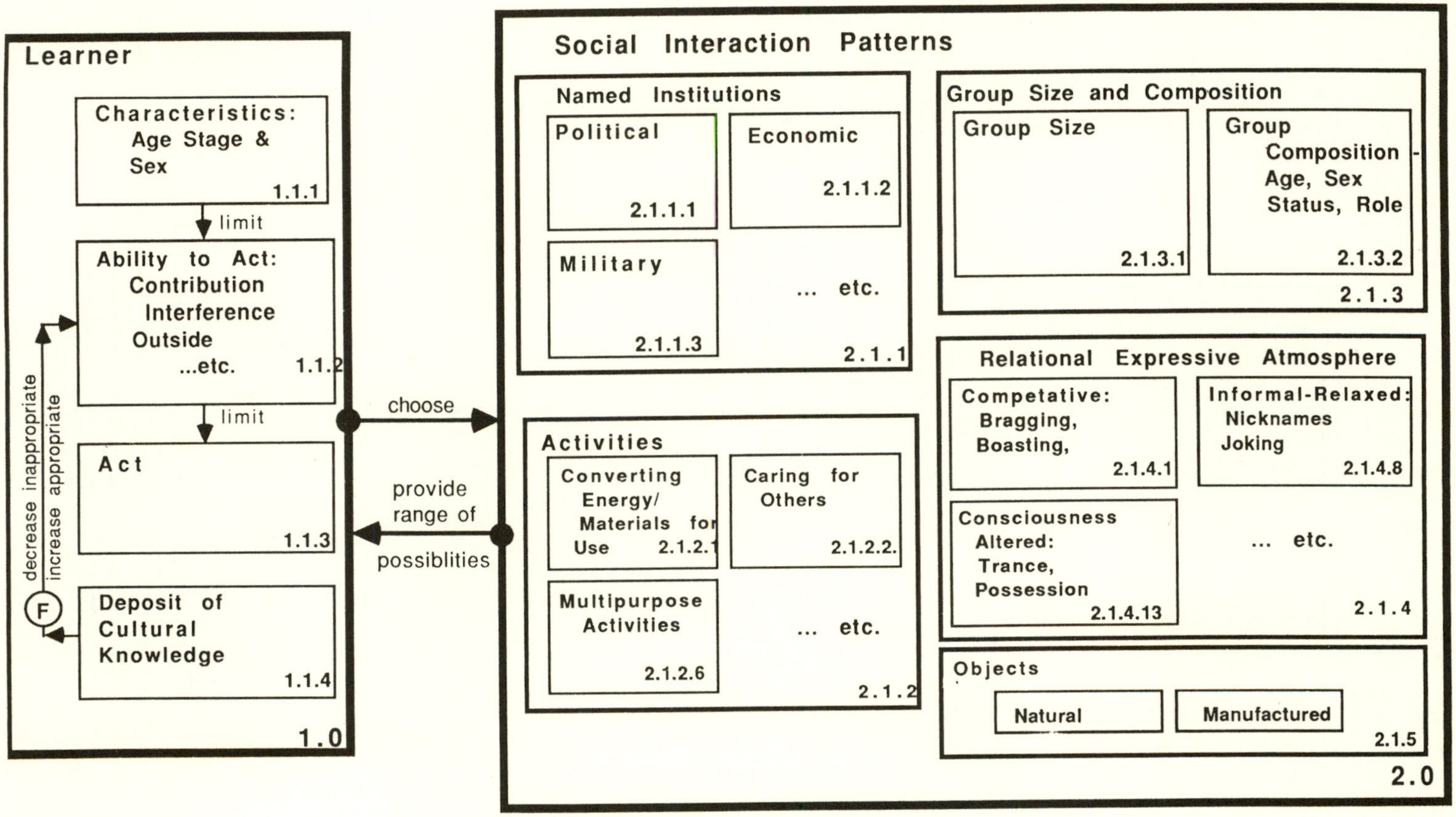

Figure 5.3
Model of Systemic Interactions in Culture Acquisition/Transmission

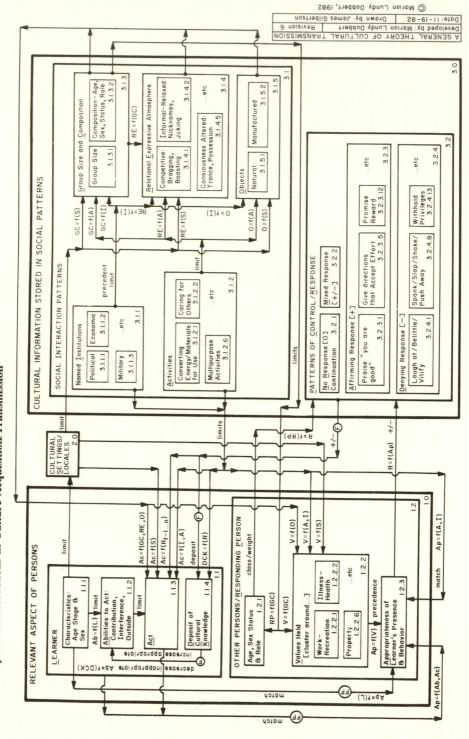

(3.1.1) or that may be a more informal activity pattern (3.1.2). In either case, each institution or activity will have characteristic aspects the learner will automatically receive information about and learn about in the process of achieving symbolic correspondence between personal cultural knowledge and current parameters of the sociocultural pattern. These parameters include the size and composition of the groups that engage in such activities (3.1.3), the characteristics of the emotional atmospheres and relational modes encountered (3.1.4), and the objects either used or present when such activities are occurring (3.1.5). For example, in an informal household setting for making beer among the Ngoni, a girl would also learn about beer pots, grain, and fire; would learn that this is a small-group activity; and would learn that this is a time for happy joking (Read 1960).

The nature of the institution and activity (3.1.1 and 3.1.2) also limit the kind of people who might interact with the learner (1.2.1), as well as the range of values and ideals associated with activity within that institution (1.2.2). All of the factors related to the nature of the institution or activity in turn limit the types of acts a learner may choose (1.1.3). This limitation process is indicated by the arrows flowing from the institution (3.1.1) and activities (3.1.2) subsystems, through group size and composition (3.1.3), atmospheres (3.1.4), and objects (3.1.5), on to responding persons (1.2.1), and out through appropriateness of learner's act (1.2.3) to response (3.2) and to learner action (1.1.3). In the Ngoni beer-making situation, for example, the learner stores information indicating that the personnel are grown women, never men; that values about social interaction and pride in work apply, but not values about warfare; and that an ideal of peaceable cooperation governs the interaction. Then let us assume that a young boy and a young girl both try to join the activity and stir the beer. The women present will react to the children on the basis of the appropriateness of the act for the child. Both gender appropriateness and relevant values will be considered. Let us say that the grandmother reacts to the small boy on the basis of gender-appropriate behavior values (1.2.1 and 1.2.3 to 3.2). Grandmothers have great importance in Ngoni life and so do gender-related values. Thus, the negative reaction (3.2.4) will be very strong and will decrease strongly the boy's likelihood of choosing that action in that setting again (3.2 to 1.1.3 and 1.1.4). The little girl, however, was noticed by a young woman of the household, a person of lower status, and was praised for being willing to work, a value of less importance than the gender-appropriateness value. The low-level positive response (3.2.3) may slightly increase the girl's likelihood of choosing that action or setting again.

Through this looped process, the cultural pattern consisting of a place (2.0), an activity (3.1.2), objects (3.1.5), appropriate group composition (3.1.3), specific relational expressive content (3.1.4), a set of persons (1.2), and relevant values and ideals (1.2.2 and 1.2.3) becomes part of the learner's knowledge (1.1.4). The model weights the strength of the knowledge through the loop which begins in 1.2.2 and 1.2.3 to inform the response selected in 3.2, which then becomes part of the learner's map in 1.1.2.

FACILITATING DETAILED HOLISTIC STUDIES

Studying culture acquisition/transmission from the kind of holistic perspective we have operationalized here requires attention to a seemingly endless depth of detail. A field guide, which may be defined as an instrument for aiding systematic data collection on any chosen topic, is particularly useful for the study of complex situations and processes. It serves as a basic checklist, assisting the fieldworker in paying attention to as many details as humanly possible. Here we present a field guide derived from all the elements of our operationalized model. The field guide consists of two primary parts. Part I is a set of forms that guide the fieldworker in recording essential data and provide a format for achieving a holistic picture of the learning process in a variety of settings. Part II is a set of ethnographically derived categories that will assist researchers in coding data. Taken as a whole, the field guide creates a structure for gathering and comparing ethnographically dense data across cultures, age levels, or settings.

It must be noted that the optimal time to begin systematic data gathering with this guide is after the fieldworker has become familiar with the setting and has spent a period of time collecting a broad base of ethnographic data. When able to map out and describe the setting with its subsystems in considerable detail and to understand key terms in the local language or the technical jargon of institutional settings, the researcher is ready to construct a sampling plan and to commence the field-guide–aided stage of data collection.

Field Guide: Part I—Forms

To aid the researcher in obtaining all the necessary data, we have designed three forms: a learner cover sheet, a series cover sheet, and a data gathering sheet. These forms are all-purpose, generalized guides to the types of data needed in studies of learners. For individual studies, the forms must be modified to fit the context or the constraints created by specific research questions, issues, and settings.

Cover Sheets

The two cover sheets provide base data derived from participant observation and informant interviews and aid in interpreting the actual culture acquisition/ transmission incidents by setting them within their cultural and social contexts. These data are essential for explanation and comparison both intraculturally and cross-culturally.

The learner cover sheet (Figure 5.4) provides space for recording data on the individual learner's background and on the cultural context of the observations. The background material includes the learner's name, both the one regularly

Figure 5.4
Learner Cover Sheet

Name (s) of
Learner: _____   **Age:** _____   **Sex:** ____

PARENTS, GUARDIANS, MENTORS, SPONSORS

    1. First name: _____ Age: _____ Sex: _____

Occupation: _____

Level of schooling, training, or knowledge: _____

    2. First name: _____ Age: _____ Sex: _____

Occupation: _____

Level of schooling, training, or knowledge: _____

GEOGRAPHIC LOCATION

CULTURAL REGION (general and specific)

SUBCULTURAL SPECIFICATIONS
Relevant ethnic, subcultural, kin, or network factors important to learner in
setting:

Figure 5.4 Continued

Observer assessment of ethnic, subcultural, kin and network factors:

Social class factors important to learner and others in setting:

Observer assessment of social class factors:

DESCRIPTION OF MAJOR LEARNING SETTINGS OBSERVED

Number of occupants, ages, sexes, and relation to each other and learner:

Describe the interpersonal relations in the major settings:

Figure 5.4 Continued

What is the general social and public reputation of this setting/group?

DESCRIPTION OF LEARNER

What is this learner's general social and public reputation?

Among peers:

Among elders:

Observer's perspective on learner's personality and individual characteristics:

Figure 5.5
Series Cover Sheet

LEARNERS	
SETTING	

DATE | | TIME beginning/ end | |

CYCLE DATA

Day of week or of Market Cycle, etc.:

Season in Agricultural,Economic,Business Cycle:

Ritual or Festival Day or Period?:

Today's weather:

WHAT CHARACTERISTICS of the settings, activities and persons,etc.included in this series are critical to understanding this series of observations correctly?

Figure 5.5 Continued

```
┌─────────────────────────────────────────────────────────────────────┐
│                                                                       │
│  SOCIAL  CLASS  FACTORS important to learner and others in setting:   │
│                                                                       │
│                                                                       │
│                                                                       │
│                                                                       │
│                                                                       │
│  OBSRVER ASSESSMENT of social class factors:                          │
│                                                                       │
│                                                                       │
│                                                                       │
│                                                                       │
└─────────────────────────────────────────────────────────────────────┘
┌─────────────────────────────────────────────────────────────────────┐
│  DESCRIPTION OF MAJOR LEARNING SETTINGS OBSERVED                       │
│  Number of occupants, ages, sexes, and relation to each other and     │
│  learner:                                                             │
│                                                                       │
│                                                                       │
│                                                                       │
│  Describe the interpersonal relations in the major settings:          │
│                                                                       │
│                                                                       │
│                                                                       │
│                                                                       │
└─────────────────────────────────────────────────────────────────────┘
```

used and alternate forms; information about the persons primarily responsible for the learner; geographic and cultural information; subcultural specifications, such as ethnic identity or social-class data relevant to the study; descriptions of key settings and the ongoing human relations in them; and information about how people think about and react to the learner.

The series cover sheet (Figure 5.5) is used to record data essential for interpreting learning incidents in a cultural context by making explicit the cultural knowledge that may be taken for granted by the fieldworker. If, for example, a child is participating in a religious ritual, the cover sheet will provide a general description of it, of its usual complete form, process, role occupants, and its value and meaning for its participants. Unusual details about the specific case from which the observations are taken are also noted. The series cover sheet facilitates understanding of the incident records following it (that is, the data

Figure 5.6
Data Gathering Sheet

Date: Time: Obs. Series: Codes

Learner

Lrn

Surrounding Persons

Grp. Size

Grp. Comp

Setting

Set

Institution

Inst

Activities

Activ

Figure 5.6 Continued

Action/Interaction/Response

Act

Abil

Resp

Resp Pers

Atmosphere (describe
observable markers)

Atmos

Objects

Obj

Values (and explanatory
statements expressed or
clearly implied)

Exp

Imp

Comments (which clarify
the incident)

---

gathering sheets described below). Consequently, one cover sheet is filled out for every sequence of observations in a single setting.

Data Gathering Sheet

Since no observer can watch a learner and see everything that is happening, we have developed a data gathering sheet (Figure 5.6), which is used to record a series of incidents or slice of life. The types of educational, culture acquisition acts to be observed and recorded on the data gathering sheets are not defined differently or separated from other kinds of daily acts. Following the systems-based theory, it is assumed that children as well as adults learn from all their encounters. We thus define a learning incident or episode as any bounded mini-event involving a learner. An incident might be defined as a ''natural'' bounded unit or a sequence of behavior. The definition of what constitutes a natural boundary will most likely be derived from the ethnographer's knowledge of the field setting. In addition, Hill-Burnett (1973) has suggested some ways to define incidents through delineation of bounding events—by change of setting, personnel, objects, and activities. We would add change in emotional atmosphere, change in salient values, change in learner act in relation to activity in a single setting, change of response to all the learners as a group or to the observed learner specifically in the setting, and change in orientation toward the setting. Taken together, these limiting components tend to define an incident as a single complete exchange. A conversation, one child's turn in a game, an order issued by a parent, a small child's attempt to sweep—all these may be called learning incidents or episodes.

The Data Gathering Sheet (Figure 5.6) is designed to guide the collection of data in all areas covered by the theoretical model. The sheet is sequenced to facilitate on-the-spot data gathering. It begins with data on the main individuals involved—the learner and the surrounding persons. Next, there are spaces for descriptions of the setting, the institutional context, and the major activities that characterize the setting as a whole, including topics of discussion not addressed to the learner but which the learner might overhear. The learner's acts and abilities and the interactions with and responses to the learner are then recorded as a single interactive event. The researcher then records atmospheres, objects, and relevant values. Space is also provided at the bottom for observer comment. The right-hand edge provides spaces for coding data. Observers using the sheets on different projects may wish to resequence the recording spaces to fit their own observational styles or to add additional foci, but any revision should address the data recording fields included here. This is because in order to conduct a holistic analysis, it is essential to consistently collect data in each major area described in the theory. The following section, therefore, explains the logic behind the inclusion of each category on the data gathering sheet.

The form begins, like any data recording sheet, with space for noting the date and time of observation along with some notation about the specific observation series to which the sheet belongs. The form is then used to record a specific learning incident in detail.

Learner and Learner Characteristics. Although the major description of the learner is found on the cover sheet, name, age, and sex are noted here for easy reference. Observable characteristics, such as clothes, grooming, initial emotional state, posture, or gestures, are noted in detail as are other factors that might mediate learning in the specific instance, such as linguistic ability, first time in situation versus frequent attendance, previous lessons in or about the activity, previous statements about the activity or setting, and so on.

Surrounding Persons. Here the observer describes the persons visible or audible within the setting, specifying their involvement with the various activities and noting their sex, age, and relationship to the learner. Other distinguishing characteristics are also noted, but more precise detail is included for those persons who strongly affect the central activity. Other persons are characterized in groups but with accuracy.

Setting. This space is used to describe the cultural setting both as a space and as a culturally organized and meaningful locale. The distance between this setting and the geographical and psychological center of the learner's intimate life is central to the study. For this reason, the researcher should take care to describe the relationship between the setting and the learner's usual lifespaces.

Institution or Ritual. Institutions and rituals may be either secular, sacred, or semisacred. If the learner is in a place that can be defined as a named, established institution, such as a market, a court, a school, or a church, or is part of a ritualized setting, this is the fact that should be identified on the data gathering form since these formalized settings have pre-established behavioral rules governing activities within them that any learner must eventually become familiar with. If, however, the learner is in an informal, noninstitutionalized setting, that too would be noted in this space.

In order to create comparability and consistency within and between studies, it is necessary to define "institution." A formal institution may be defined by four characteristics: (1) it is named; (2) it occurs in places predictable by members or students of the culture; (3) it has a formal set of roles and/or a formal program or a defined order; (4) it is scheduled or tripped by a preceding event. By way of example, we examine two ambiguous cases. The first is a Western middle-class family meal in a dining room. The meal begins with a prayer, proceeds through the main course, and is followed by a dessert, after which the children go off to play or do homework while the adults have coffee and chat. This event is not an institution or ritual, although there is some formalized activity, such as praying. The term "family meal" does not necessarily imply the events or sequences seen here. No individual or role or sequence of events need necessarily be present. The second case is a child's birthday party in the United States. A birthday party is more formalized than the meal just described. The term "birthday party" brings to mind decorations, birthday cakes, party games, and presents.

These are generally provided whether the party is held at home or at a restaurant. Three formal roles are essential—a birthday child; guests, who are usually the child's peers; and an adult party manager (traditionally a parent), who paces, sequences, and produces necessary items. For various parties, an element may be missing but native informants can distinguish between a ''real party'' and a family birthday dinner. The party, then, has the required characteristics necessary to be considered an institution or ritual, while the family meal does not.

Activities. This category refers to the activities happening in the learner's immediate environment, within seeing and hearing distance. It does not refer to what the learner is doing. Rather it tells us what *everybody else* is doing and, therefore, what the learner will be gaining information from and about. The focus is on the activities of the accomplished members of the society, those senior to or of higher status than the learner, and secondarily on the learner's peers or subgroup.

Returning to the beer-brewing activity of the Ngoni (Read 1960), referred to earlier in this chapter, let us suppose that the focal learner for the incident to be recorded is a little boy sitting on the ground about 15 feet from the women, playing cattle herding with his friend and using pebbles as cattle. In this case, the main activity recorded is still beer brewing. The little boy's game will be recorded in the space for ''Learner's Act/Interaction.'' If at the same time, another group of six little boys were playing court nearby (with the learner in the same location), then the activities space would record activity at two levels: (1) the adult level and (2) the peer-group level. Thus, the information will capture the relationship between the entire sociocultural context and a focal learner. Because the learner has the opportunity to learn from all surrounding activities, the description will necessarily be detailed, not merely noting that ''mother is working over the fire (or in the kitchen)'' but ''mother is stirring the corn meal into the water (or cutting the carrots).'' Similarly, the location of the learner's primary caregiver, trainer, or supervisor is also noted if the learner knows it. For example, a little girl playing school in the basement recreation room with three friends may know or guess that father is preparing supper in the kitchen. While she is not learning the details of the father's activity, she is learning about the dimensions of his role. Topics of discussion is an important subcategory of activities. In many situations the topic of discussion that accompanies an activity is not related to the activity. Persons washing clothes at a well in India or at a laundromat in the United States do not necessarily discuss water getting or clothes washing. To the contrary, they will be exchanging the latest news, discussing plans for someone's wedding, talking about how someone's spouse or kin has lost a job. Or perhaps the TV or radio will be on, conveying information about the outcome of an election, showing an exercise program, or advertising soap. Since the polyphasic learner has the potential for absorbing the information from these, an observer would note discussion topics and verbal information that form part of the total learning environment.

Learner's Act/Interaction and Others' Responses. This space is used to record the selected incident. Some researchers may prefer to use it as a single area in which to record the interactions in a paragraph form of the sort one might find in a very detailed page of narrative field notes. Other researchers may prefer to divide the space into columns and record each individual's acts and responses in parallel sequence. Characteristics such as age, sex, status, and role of persons to whom the learner relates either directly—by talking to them, by joining their activity, or through a response such as watching—or indirectly—by playing or working within their sight or hearing—are recorded here as each of these may influence the seriousness with which the learner and the community take the responses. Additional details about the responders that aid in understanding the situation are also noted here. The interactions with or responses to a learner that are recorded need not have been directly or overtly expressed. A very important way of dealing with a learner's acts is to give no response. "No response" then is actually a kind of response and care should be taken to record it and to distinguish it from deliberate disregard.

Atmosphere. A complete description of an atmosphere includes general noise level, human participants' noise level, types of noise (such as yelling, loud laughing, chuckling), degree of physical activity, facial expressions, muscular tension and tone, voice tones, gestures, and concrete clues regarding the emotional atmosphere. Data in this space do not describe the emotional state of the learner but the emotional atmosphere of the setting. The emotions of the learner and the immediate peers or authority figures may be quite different from those prevalent in the setting itself. The former are noted in the description of the characteristics of the learner or responder or as part of their interactions.

Objects. We learn a great deal from objects, their form, and placement, although often the learning is not consciously recognized. Specialized tools, for example, inherently contain skills-teaching programs, since if they are not used correctly they will not perform correctly. A hand saw is a good example: It will work only if pulled up and down lightly and smoothly over its entire length. The arrangement of physical objects often teaches social facts. A classroom with a large front desk facing rows of many small desks demonstrates that the teacher is a central focus and has a different status than the children. A classroom with a round table and eight matched chairs indicates multiple foci and a different distinction between teacher and students. Facts about social status and social processes are also conveyed through architecture, level of maintenance, and type of materials used in construction. Objects in cultural settings designed for children, juniors, or specific groups of learners provide clues to cultural conceptions about them and the learning process.

Values and Explanatory Statements. A value or explanation that refers to a fundamental worldview and is stated by any person involved in the incident under observation is noted here and if possible quoted. Motivational and incentive statements are classified as values expressions. Any value or explanation that, in the judgment of the observer, is clearly implied, is also noted and the words or gestures which implied it are indicated. Thus, data in this space, as well as in the following "Comment" space, may rely less on direct observation and more on the fieldworker's knowledge about and interpretation of the culture being studied.

Comments. In this space the observer notes anything that will help interpret the incident described on the sheet. These notes may include things that have happened since the last incident recorded, the usual way this family or cultural group does the activity recorded, a history of the critical personal relationships involved, and so on.

Quality, Completeness, and Sampling with Forms

A good record will be concrete and factual and contain as much detail as can be comfortably written up as the incident occurs and within the 10–15 minutes immediately after. The record will use definitive nouns, adjectives, and adverbs that are photographically descriptive of a given object or interaction and include all its relevant aspects. Dialogue will be quoted or closely paraphrased. Only records with a high level of detail will allow for the specific analyses, re-analyses, and hypothesis testing that make up the spiral process of the natural history paradigm upon which anthropology builds its theory (Kimball 1974:59–74). Table 5.1 contrasts two data sheets, one containing and the other lacking the kinds of detail needed for quality data.[1]

In designing this guide we have emphasized the recording of entire learning contexts because we are not concerned with child life but with building models of culture learning processes. Thus, we record an entire learning context even if we must neglect the observation of additional learning incidents to do so. The systems perspective supports this decision. To record less than the entire context would omit essentials, because patterns are learned as wholes that the learner maps in totality. Consequently, our data-gathering strategies emphasize the entire material and socioemotional context. Thus, for example, if we are following a rapidly moving learner who does not stay in a setting long enough to allow us to record all the information before the learner leaves, we nevertheless complete our record of the incident by remaining as long as necessary. To further ensure completeness and accuracy, we review data sheets for omissions, vague generalities, hidden opinions, or inferences. The holistic, detailed nature of the data we record often leads to rerecording the same data in several spaces. This is to be expected, both because humans extract multiple meanings from things and events and because the form itself is redundant.

A full study of culture acquisition would consist of a large number of these incident observations organized around a general theoretical issue or a specific research question. However, since the data are gathered in context, they can be utilized for purposes not envisioned when the data were first collected. Such reusability is enhanced by the format in which the field guide insists that data be collected, namely, in complete context and in the terminology of detailed markers.

Accuracy cannot be achieved by careful note-taking alone. The proper sampling of incidents to record is also essential for theoretical utility. The theory

Table 5.1
Contrast between Vague and Well-detailed Data

DATA	Vague, Overly General	Solid, Well-Detailed
Learner	girl, 9	female, 9 years old, Caucasian, wearing pink, coordinated pants and sweater set
Persons	her parents	mother, age 30-35, middle class, wearing slacks (not jeans); father, age - + 30-35, new sweater, jeans
Setting	child's home	learner's home, a two-story, five-room apartment in the university married student housing
Activity	reading and writing	father is taking notes at the dining room table; mother reading in LR in arm chair; learner writing letter at dining table
Action/ Interaction/ Response/ Topics	learner begins to cry mother and father tell her it's not important	child stares at letter, leans head on hands and begins to cry, at first silently, but increasingly loudly (about 1 minute) Mo: What's the matter? Why are you crying? Ch: I forgot what I was going to say (crying) Mo: That's not something to cry about. You cry over nothing. Write about something else and it might come to you. Fa: Now, come on - that's not important. Why don't you get on with it? Ch: But it was meant to begin the letter (voice strained, but crying ceased) [note use of quotes]
Topics	none	no conversation, radio or TV
Institution	not relevant	not relevant
Surrounding persons	see above	see above
Atmosphere	mixed	mother and father serious, absorbed in work, child unhappy, restless
Objects	normal household objects	pencil, aerogramme
Values	cry baby	getting on with the job - work as a necessity; self-control
Comments	---	parents disapprove

and method described here are focused on the process through which whole sets of complex culture patterns are learned via the intricate, multifaceted events of everyday life. While many of the major patterns of culture in general have been described along economic, social-organizational, political, and even psychological axes, we do not know much about the structures of the specific patterns of culture acquisition. These have been approached and described only at an elementary level.[2] Our ignorance has important consequences for sampling. When we have very little idea of what we are ultimately looking for, our sampling system must guarantee complete coverage of all normal situations. Further, culture acquisition is polyphasic, and therefore we must sample information taken in by all of the sense modalities and by such means as modeling, social conflict, and habitat learning. This suggests that the only valid data-gathering methods will be based on time sampling, at least for the basic or foundational data. The authors have experimented with various sampling intervals and have concluded that incident samples collected at intervals of half an hour to an hour provide optimal coverage of a culture's range of patterns.

Two other forms of sampling are also relevant for detailed, long-term study, but only after the basic time sample has been completed and the outline of the sociocultural system has been clarified. The first of these is "event" sampling, a detailed documentation of learners in the daily, weekly, monthly, and annual routines of the people being studied, paying particular attention to the minor events and "nonevents" (or interludes) of everyday occurrence. A second form of sampling that would appear relevant is network sampling. Learners are probably treated differently and behave differently with people of distinct status and relationship to themselves. It may prove informative to sample incidents involving representatives of the entire range of the learner's network.

While the focus of a series of incidents recorded on a set of individual data sheets is always a single learner, the focus of a culture acquisition study is a coherent group of individual learners selected according to their relevant sociocultural characteristics so as to (1) provide general coverage of the variations important for the study, such as age and sex, and (2) constitute a defined and representative focal group relevant to the problem selected for study, such as children of middle-class origin or adult immigrants. An advantage of collecting data on a defined, coherent sample is that doing so also facilitates the examination of variation between families, by age, by sex, and across settings. Were we to examine randomly selected children at, say, 30-minute intervals, our data would not be representative because we would lose the structure inherent in real-life learning sequences. We might, with such a sample, capture cross-cultural variations at a general level, but we would be unable to examine the details of acquisition/transmission patterns.

Field Guide: Part II—The Coding System

The use of a systems-theory base does not narrow the data, but rather encourages a broad perspective during the recording phase and aids in the collection of detailed, holistic data that retain their emic structure and cultural context. Researchers and theorists holding varied theoretical positions could ask questions focused at social structural, conceptual, interpersonal, or behavioral levels and could analyze the data recorded on the data gathering sheets by using general ethnographic methods. A broad ethnography of child or group life could be constructed. One could use standard natural history methods common to analysis in anthropology, such as thematic, event, or network analysis as well as sociolinguistic, biographical, or culture and personality approaches. Here, however, we discuss a form of analysis that arises directly from the method of approaching learning incidents as wholes composed of multiple subsystems.

Analysis of qualitative data always begins with the process of constructing generalizations by grouping items on the basis of some theoretical or practical schema for judging similarities. For the study of culture acquisition/transmission, it is necessary that the schema for aggregating data be applicable to observations taken in any of the world's 3,000 to 5,000 different cultures; from Western and non-Western societies; from gathering-hunting, horticultural, pastoral, agricultural, or industrial societies; from bands, tribes, chiefdoms, and states. The classification schema we present below embraces as comprehensive a view of the culture acquisition process as possible. By relying upon the systems-theory depiction of the process, our schema can account for broad cultural variables. Learning is viewed from a structural and sociocultural position developed from an information-mapping perspective.[3]

The coding system (Table 5.2) was derived inductively and ethnographically for each separate subsystem of the theory. In first defining and then delineating each subsystem, we relied on numerous general and educational ethnographic studies in both the British and American traditions. We identified every word, process, behavior, grouping, and concept we could find in them relating to possible options in that particular subsystem and also used them as inspirations for brainstorming about various cultural possibilities for each. The code lists we developed eventually consisted of scores of terms. We then grouped these terms in such a way as to construct inclusive classification systems for each element or subsystem of the theoretical model (Figure 5.3) and to specify the observational foci found on the data gathering sheet (Figure 5.6). Codes are provided for learner (1.1.1), learner's ability (1.1.2), learner's act (1.1.3), responding persons (1.2.1), values and explanations (1.2.2), setting (2.0), the organization of action (3.1), including the degree of institutionalization (3.1.1), activities (3.1.2), group composition (3.1.3), atmosphere (3.1.4), objects (3.1.5), and response (3.2).

To validate the classifications, we had to test their ability to represent the full range of human cultural variation. Consequently, we reversed the process used to derive the coding system. The classifications were tested against a set of ethnographies from diverse cultures that had not been used in deriving them. The code list was tested first for its ability to embrace all the data in this latter set of ethnographies and second for its ability to classify unambiguously yet without violating the meaning and structures of the culture described while at the same time fitting the theory and its specifications. The classification systems were modified and remodified to achieve valid, workable results. Table 5.2 presents our original classification schema with its major (numbered) and minor (unnumbered) subcodes.[4] In the next chapter we will illustrate the use of this form of analysis. A revised version of the code based on later work is discussed

Table 5.2

Specification of Subsystems for a General Theory of Cultural Transmission (with labels and codes)

1. Relevant Aspects of Persons
   1.1. Learner
      1.1.1. Characteristics
         1.1.1.1. sex --   male (M) female (F)
         1.1.1.2. Age Stage -- infant (I), young child (Y), post-pubescent child (P)
      1.1.2. Ability to Act
         1.1.2.1. With Reference to Adult or General Activity -- tries it/does part/does child version (Rd), does it with skill (Rd), initiates new task/part of task (Rd),
            observes adult activity or asks about it (Ro)
         1.1.2.2. Interferes with Adult or General Activity (I) -- does it incorrectly, poorly, ineptly, gets in the way, does not do task/share/requested part, asks about unrelated issue/suggests unrelated activity, refuses instruction/ request not related to adult activity
         1.1.2.3. Acts outside of Activity (O) -- imitates activity going on in location, stops doing adult activity or leaves, obeys adult instruction/request not related to activity, plays/amuses self (models activity not present, informal play, organized sport), explores/curious, individual state
      1.1.3. Act (includes propensity to choose specific patterns); codes are identical to those in 3.12
   1.2. Other Persons/Responding Persons
      1.2.1. Age-Sex-Kin and Formal Characteristics -- same sex parent (Sp), opposite sex parent (Op), same sex sibling (Ss), opposite sex sibling (Os), same sex kin (Sk), opposite sex kin (Ok), child (C), stranger (S), other ethnic (E), same sex adult (Sa), opposite sex adult (Oa), miscellaneous (M)
      1.2.2. Values Held (Values cluster around)
         1.2.2.1. Work-Recreation (W) -- work as punishment or irksome duty,   work as necessity/human obligation recreation as fun or good for you, cleanliness, order, neatness, rightness
         1.2.2.2. Illness-Health (I) -- illness & death from sorcery-human origin, illness & death from gods, maintaining health
         1.2.2.3. Society (S) -- conjugal family as identity and/or continuity, conjugal family as primary responsibility/provider of security, kin group as identity and/or continuity, kin group as primary responsibility/provider of security, neighborhood village, ethnic group, tribe or nation
         1.2.2.4. Nature (N) -- nature as benefactor, animals & plants as more than natural, nature as enemy, natural catastrophes
         1.2.2.5. Religion (R) -- god(s), spirit(s), ancestors, religious performance (doing repeated rituals), religious institutions, afterlife, observing taboos and prescriptions (food, etc.)
         1.2.2.6. Property (P) -- land, i.e., real property as wealth/prestige, identity; business as wealth/prestige/identity; money or moveable property as

Table 5.2 Continued

wealth/prestige/identity; sustenance (being able to provide food, clothing, shelter on a day-to-day basis; waste, saving, care of

1.2.2.7. Human Attainments (Ha) -- wisdom as associated with experience, wisdom associated with esoteric or specialized knowledge (often in conjunction with certain statuses), classical or literary learning, oratorical or other verbal skills(e.g. repartee), master craftsmanship, artistic skills, military skill, political leadership skill as associated with positions of power, seniority (includes especially respect for old age, physical skills as endurance, strength, effort

1.2.2.8. Persons (Hp) -- individual fulfillment, gender expectations, beauty, grooming, age stage expectations, integrity, achievement

1.2.2.9. Human Relationships (Social Focus) (Hr) -- cooperativeness, harmonious relations, giving and receiving respect, human hierarchies (caste, class), care and nurture of others, generosity, hospitality, sex taboos/rules/expectations, division of labor, competitiveness, aggressiveness

1.2.2.10. Time (T) -- past, present, future, use of mystical

1.2.2.11. Place (Pl) -- dangerous, holy, symbolic of family

2.0   Cultural Settings/Locales -- house/family (H), compound/court year (C), village/neighborhood - face to face daily network (V),wider (W)

3.0   Cultural Information Stored in Social Patterns

3.1. Social Interaction Patterns

3.1.1. Named Institutions

3.1.1.1. Political (A) -- assemblies: generalized functions; courts: formalized function, i.e.,judging, hearing cases; councils: formalized functions, i.e., giving advice; legislatures: formalized functions, i.e., law making

3.1.1.2. Economic (E) -- work groups -- organized corporations, guilds/craft assn./unions, ritualized exchanges, centralized markets, retail businesses, public transport

3.1.1.3. Military (M) -- warrior (external protect.) police groups (internal protect.), ad hoc groups (vigilante, raiding)

3.1.1.4. Ritual (R)

         calendrical (c)

         crisis (cr) -- birth, death, illness/health

         identification-status (i) -- naming, marriage (betrothal, etc.), puberty, age/grade related,

         title confirming-formal

         fertility

         ancestral/family

         revitalization-reintegration (including non-specific fairs and festivals)

         pleasing/appealing powers

3.1.1.5. Religious (r)

         ritual specialist groups

         religious societies -- open membership (as churches); closed membership (as Kivas)

3.1.1.6. Formal instructional (I)

3.1.1.7. Social (S)

         kin (refers only to their meetings or

         formal functioning) -- family, lineage, clan

         cross-kin (refers to meetings or formal functioning) -- age-grades, voluntary associations, residential groups, entertainment groups,

Table 5.2 Continued

informal social (those groups which have a <u>standard, regular,</u> meeting place such as bars, taverns, stores, wells, etc.)

3.1.1.8. Recreational (OR) -- attending public spectacles, e.g., sports events, circuses, movie houses, museums, libraries, etc., participating in organized recreational events

3.1.2. Activities which Characterize the Milieu

3.1.2.1. Converting energy & materials to human use

3.1.2.1.1. Primary conversion (PC) -- providing for food, hunting, gathering, fishing, irrigating, hoeing, plowing, planting, weeding, fertilizing, harvesting (raised crops), herding and feeding animals, milking, marketing/branding butchering, veterinary, looking for water supplies/digging wells, water getting, salt getting/processing, preserving food, providing shelter, heat, light gathering/processing fuel, making/tending fire/heat source/light source gathering building material (lumbering), building shelter (animal or human), providing clothing, obtaining fiber (shearing, cutting flax) or hide, spinning/tanning (preparing for use), weaving, knitting, sewing, (making into clothes), providing mineral resources, mining, drilling, processing minerals (smithing, smelting, refining)

3.1.2.1.2. Secondary conversion or support (SC) -- individual work activity, making tools, vehicles, machines, containers, keeping useful (repairing, mending, cleaning) making objects for household comfort (soap, furniture), transporting/storing, obtaining things made by others (buying, selling, trading, bargaining) doing personal service (maids, servants, hair dressers) group or industrial work activity, working in a factory, supervising work (i.e. on the spot, giving orders,instructions) managing industry or trade (usually from an office) designing (as architects, engineers) owning and possessing, inheriting, dividing goods/property, lending/borrowing/renting/collecting interest, accumulating surpluses or wealth/displaying it, collecting salary/wage/welfare

3.1.2.2. Caring for others (Cf) -- infants, children, aged, ill

3.1.2.3. Maintaining or Changing Social Order and Services (MC) public order -- making/changing/posting laws/rules/regulations, choosing formal role occupants (by discussion or voting, etc.), deciding on/stating goals, determining means, making judgments, settling conflicts, issuing reward/punishment, making restitution (jail, fine, apology, banishment), making contracts/formal agreements, issuing currency, policing, bribing, feuding or rioting, providing military protection (including drilling, warring, making weapons; public services -- building, maintaining communication and transport, maintaining public safety (building dikes, shelters), responding to disasters (fire fighting, rescue), paying tithes, taxes, tributes; private order -- marrying, paying bride wealth/dowry, divorcing, practicing population control (birth control, infanticide, abortion, euthanasia), creating ritual kin (adoption, god parents, blood brothers)

3.1.2.4. Religious & Ritual types of activities (R) -- addressing/sacrificing/manipulating gods/spirits, etc. ritually secluding, making religious objects/symbols, meditating, ritual questing/pilgrimages, ritual cleansing, burying cleansing, wearing ceremonial garb, etc., making oaths/vows, cannibalistic and other ritual eating, contacting

Table 5.2 Continued

spirits/divining/interpreting omens, being in a trance/non-ordinary state, fasting, alms giving/philanthropy

3.1.2.5. Experiencing individual states (I) -- sleeping/resting, dreaming/daydreaming/imagining, eating alone, playing alone, being ill/being in pain, being pregnant/giving birth, having menstruation, having accident, excreting, dying, dressing/bathing/self cleansing/decorating body/cutting hair, modifying body, piecing/scarring/filing teeth, circumcising

3.1.2.6. Multipurpose activities; socializing -- visiting/gossiping/standing around/discussing/watching people, activities (CSo), drinking booze/using drugs (A), sharing meals/feasting (F), gift giving (G), dancing/singing/music making/having a drama, composing poetry/songs/music (Dr), playing, unorganized fun, outings (Pl), participating in/observing organized games/skills contest (OG), orating/speech making (CSO), doing art or decorating things, carving, painting, making jewelry (CSO) joking/teasing/doing tricks/talking sex (CSO) expressing conflict (Cn) -- fighting (physical), fighting verbal (arguing/cursing/daring), doing homicide, destroying property, hiding/avoiding/sneaking out/eloping, listening in/spying traveling (T), walking, travel by beast, vehicle, water travel, air travel, changing residence, exchanging information (E), reading, listening (to person, radio), watching T.V., etc. writing, record keeping, recording, thinking, memorizing, reciting, practicing, studying, sending/carrying/receiving messages, consulting/getting/giving advice, teaching/tutoring

3.1.2.7. Health activity (H) -- diagnosing, curing, giving medicine/setting bones/removing causes, using disease or disaster preventatives, midwifing, making or locating medicines

3.1.2.8. Doing something defined as wrong/committing a crime (W) -- stealing, wrecking (property crime) raping/seducing/adultery/incest (sex crimes), assaulting, murdering/suiciding, lying/doing fraud, not paying debts, doing sorcery (psychological crimes)

3.1.3 Group Size and Composition

3.1.3.1. Group Size -- individual (I), small 2-10 (S), medium 11-40 (M), large 40+ (L)

3.1.3.2. Group Composition (except learner) -- parent/sibling only (P), parent/sibling in a group (S), parent/sibling with formal titled actor (F), kin only (K), primarily one-sex adult (1a), primarily one-sex child (1c), primarily mixed adult (A), primarily mixed child (C), mixed crowd (M), other (O)

3.1.4. Relational-Expressive Atmosphere

3.1.4.1. Competitive (integrated within social structure, e.g., bragging/boasting/daring/risk taking/putting down/doing one better) (Cp)

3.1.4.2. Informal-relaxed (using nicknames, laughing, informal joking, complimentary/praising, relaxing rules) (I)

3.1.4.3. Deferential (formal greeting, formal joking, using formal gestures) (D)

3.1.4.4. Conflictive (threatening to social structure, e.g., fighting, threat-making, quarreling/bickering, expressing envy and jealousy) (Cn)

3.1.4.5. Consciousness altered (trance, using drugs/alcohol, being a medium being possessed) (CA)

3.1.4.6. Judgmental (blaming, shaming, ridiculing, asserting, superiority (haughty, silent, snide) (J)

Table 5.2 Continued

        3.1.4.7. Celebrative (exciting, thrilling) (Cl)
        3.1.4.8. Intimate (kissing, sexual closeness, touching, using endearing terms/using baby talk) (Im)
        3.1.4.9. Sad-Unhappy (crying, mourning, keening) (Sd)
        3.1.4.10. Fearful (screaming, hiding-running away, crying, anxiety) (F)
        3.1.4.11. Serious - task oriented (attentive, all talking and action related to task, focused) (S)
        3.1.4.12. Lethargic (bored, inactive, yawning) (L)
        3.1.4.13. Mixed (no dominant theme relative to individual)
      3.1.5. Objects -- Name them (two most significant)
   3.2. Patterns of control by 1) Adults, 2) Older Children, 3) Peers
      3.2.1. No response (activity just continues) (N)
      3.2.2. Affirming response (A) -- praise child/tell is good, thank child, act on child's suggestion/request/give permission, include in conversation, praise indirectly (comment to other, proverb), give directions/suggestions/instructions (that accept child's effort), more over/make room/share task, smile/nod, touch/pat on back, etc., give child objects needed to participate, give food reward, give money/toys/objects for reward
      3.2.3. Denying response (D) -- deny request/withhold permission, laugh at/belittle/vilify child directly, comment adversely by indirection (proverb, to others), correct child's action/instruct/criticize, warn/threaten, send away, frown at or other gesture or non-acceptance, stamp foot or other gestures of anger/disapproval, shank/slap/shake/push away (minor physical punishment), beat (major physical punishment), ostracize/shun/avoid/leave/ignore, have child think through bad conduct/mistake, withhold objects needed for task, withhold privileges, withhold food
      3.2.4. Mixed (M) -- offer reward or bribe/conditional promise, give in reluctantly/ungraciously/annoyed

in a codebook format in Chapter 8 and appears as Table A.1 in the appendix of this book.

CONCLUSION AND CAUTIONARY NOTE

The guide and coding system provided here can be used for a number of different purposes, but it was designed primarily as a tool for structuring long-term, detailed, cross-cultural studies of the culture acquisition/transmission process. It is best used in cases in which the general cultural context—the conceptual, religious, economic, political, social, familial, and value patterns—are either already understood or are being studied simultaneously. Where the cultural patterns are unknown, general sociocultural observation will necessarily be conducted at the same time as a focused study of culture acquisition/transmission.

The field guide has also proved to be an effective teaching tool for structuring observations in field methods classes. The structured holism connected with solid detail leads students to productive insights about children and the learning process. Many students have been surprised, not always agreeably, by what they saw and learned about adult-child relationships in their own culture. This detailed type of observational system may provide a tool which will, in the long run, make students better professionals in their own fields.

NOTES

1. This is only illustrative. Experienced observers will capture data in even more detail than this.

2. The very best approaches to broad patterns of the sort we are interested in here may be found in Montagu (1978) and Whiting and Whiting (1975). Some other excellent work may be found in the Whitings' other publications (often co-authored) and in the works of the cross-cultural comparativists (holoculturalists) indexed in Levinson (1977). But see also Chapter 4 of this volume.

3. Since the theoretical stances of the majority of the U.S. ethnographers of cultural transmission were generally derived from psychological principles, for example, those of Henry (1960), Hilger (1960), and Whiting et al. (1966), the construction of a classification schema was by no means an easy task. The works of British observers, such as Read, Firth, Raum, and Kuper; of American social anthropologists such as Bohannan; and of the avowedly eclectic T. R. Williams, provided critical aid.

4. Specific letter codes have been developed only for code levels used in analysis completed to date.

6 A Pilot Study of Culture Acquisition in Three Societies: Testing the Method

To test our theory, field guide, and coding system, we obtained data from several cultures in which many different types of activities and multiple learning modes could be observed. Data were gathered from Israel in and around Haifa, from the midwestern United States, and from Zinacantan in Chiapas in southern Mexico. In order to test different data gathering strategies, the method used for each of the three sites varied. The studies were exploratory in that as much attention was given to methodological issues as to theoretical ones. In this chapter, we describe the three sites, detail our data analysis procedures, and summarize our findings. We conclude with an evaluation of the method.

THE HAIFA DATA

Haifa, with a population of 300,000, is Israel's largest port on the Mediterranean. It is a center of heavy industry, international trade, commerce and because of its scenic location on Mount Carmel, tourism. It has two institutions of higher education, the Technion and the University of Haifa. Data from this area were gathered by graduate students participating in a year-long research seminar at the University of Haifa under the supervision of Eisikovits. The children observed

This chapter is adapted from Marion Lundy Dobbert, Rivka A. Eisikovits, Mary Anne Pitman, Jan Armstrong Gamradt, and Kyung-soo Chun, "Cultural Transmission in Three Societies: Testing a Systems-Based Field Guide." Reproduced with permission of the American Anthropological Association from *Anthropology & Education Quarterly* 15:4, 1984. Not for further reproduction. Marion Lundy Dobbert, Rivka A. Eisikovits, Mary Anne Pitman, Jan Armstrong Gamradt, and Kyung-soo Chun were the authors of this chapter.

were primarily middle class and came from families in which the parents were either long-term residents or native-born Israelis. Some of the children lived in homes where traditional religious and cultural values about children's behavior prevailed. Others were observed in urban homes with a less traditional, more egalitarian atmosphere. Still others lived in kibbutz children's houses, spending the greater part of their day with peers and spending "family time" with their parents. Observations were recorded in Hebrew and transferred to the field data sheets (Figure 5.6, Chapter 5). They were spaced up to three hours apart over an average of three days for each child. A total of 230 observations were collected on 33 children.

MIDWEST DATA

Our midwestern data were collected in Minnesota and western Wisconsin in areas settled by Scandinavian and German immigrants who brought with them the northern European work ethic and an emphasis on schooling and formal education. The entire area is dotted with institutions of higher education, ranging from small private colleges to major universities. Educational levels generally exceed the national norms. An economic foundation in soybean, corn, and dairy farming, milling, and high-technology industry creates a general prosperity broken only by small pockets of poverty in river bottoms and in urban areas. Like our Israeli data, the Minnesota-Wisconsin data were gathered primarily in urban areas, though some rural and small-town children were included. Families studied were working or middle class and did not consider their ethnic origins primary determinants of identity. Several families had strong religious fundamentalist or health movement ideologies.

Data for this portion of the study were gathered primarily by graduate students participating in Dobbert's anthropology and education classes. Each child was observed 10 to 18 times at intervals of 10 to 15 minutes during one of the three observation periods. Most of the children were observed at home, in outdoor play, or in shopping centers, but observations were made in other settings, too. The Midwest data base contained 430 observations of 44 children.

ZINACANTAN DATA

Since ultimately we are interested in the possibility of comparing culture acquisition patterns in many different societies, we decided to assess the feasibility of using published ethnographies by re-analyzing their data. We chose the research on Zinacantan, a *municipio* of the highlands of Chiapas, the southern-most state of Mexico, because it is one of the most studied cultures in the world and because one of us had visited Chiapas and had used Chiapas data in a previous study.

Zinacantan lies in rugged mountains where the high altitude creates a temperate climate with hot summers and cold, damp winters. About 9,000 people, primarily Tzotzil speakers of Mayan descent, live in the villages, hamlets, and scattered farmsteads of Zinacantan (Collier 1973). Zinacanteco men raise corn, beans, and squash on small highland plots near their houses and corn in distant lowland river valleys, using hoe cultivation. Tortillas made of maize (corn) are a basic food. Sheep are cared for exclusively by women, and the wool is used extensively. Zinacanteco families live in single-room houses that face a central patio shared with one or more families. These domestic groups are embedded in two other crucial social units, the localized lineage and the waterhole groups, which in turn are grouped into hamlets (Vogt 1970:30–42). Religion is a major focus of modern Mayan life. Sixty-three days each year (Vogt 1970:79–90) are devoted to religious celebration in which Zinacanteco children are involved, both directly and indirectly.

Data were obtained from seven published accounts of Zinacanteco and Chiapas life: Frank Cancian (1965, 1972), Francesca Cancian (1975), Jane Collier (1973), James B. Haviland (1977), Nancy Modiano (1973) and Evon Vogt (1969, 1970). In each account we looked for descriptions of activities, events, or photographs in which children were present and then used the data in the accounts to fill out our field data sheets. Supplementary information was added from general ethnographic descriptions of that class of event or activity. For example, if a text described a boy listening to stories told around the campfire at night in the lowland fields (Vogt 1970:67), then the general descriptions of lowland work were consulted to determine the likely age range of the boy and the probable makeup of the story-telling group.

Data gathering was divided between Chun and a research assistant and coordinated by Dobbert to assure uniformity and comparability. A total of 390 incidents were identified and recorded on an equal number of field data sheets. These represented 100 percent of the detailed statements made about Zinacanteco children of the target age range in the published sources listed previously. Any statement that provided enough data to fill roughly half the categories on our form was employed. As might be expected, the data sheets contained less detail than did those gathered in the field.

DATA INTERPRETATION PROCESSES

Coding

In order to index and thus condense and reduce the data, we relied upon what might be called ethnographic shorthand. Data collected on the field guide sheets were categorized using the subsystem specifications of the code list presented in Chapter 5 (see Table 5.2). Using its definitions and examples, the applicable code words for each data category were identified. We then developed a way to display the codes in a string format based directly upon the format of the field data sheet. Each string consisted of a key word or phrase from the observed incident for each subsystem. The strings, one per observation sheet, summarized the data in each space (that is, each category), as in the example (see Figure

6.1) which summarizes one incident from each of the three cultures. This string technique condensed holistically gathered, context-embedded field notes into a compact format. Great care was taken merely to "shrink" the original data rather than to reduce it by omitting parts. Creating strings was intended to preserve both the cultural processes and ecological contexts of learning data. With this method, the data from an entire sheet of field notes become small enough to view and yet remain detailed enough to recognize. Thus, our method is intended to function as the ethnographic equivalent of reducing on a photocopy machine.

All data were coded by the authors rather than by research assistants, since a primary aim of this exploratory study was to examine the adequacy of the coding system, both as code and as an expression of theory. To facilitate improvements in the coding procedure and in the code categories, we generally worked during the same hours in one large office. When one of us discovered a coding problem, an informal conference was called. During this process, the Ability to Act, Group Size and Composition, and Responding Persons categories (Table 5.2: 1.1.2, 3.1.3, 1.2.1) were completely revised; the Values Held and Patterns of Control categories (Table 5.2: 1.2.2, 3.2) were added to or modified; subcategory labels in other areas were adjusted; and it was decided not to code objects since there was very little comparative literature to guide us. After the project was well under way and about three-eighths of the data coding was complete, an informal test of interrater reliability was performed. Simple percentage of agreement for all coders on a six-protocol sample was 79 percent.[1] At this time, the finished data were recoded, each culture by a new coder, and the remaining coding was completed, again using the conferencing procedure to address problem areas.

We were satisfied that our field samples did represent complete learning incidents and thus had the potential for representing the essence of complex interaction between environments and actors and involved persons. The strings of 13 code words were deemed capable of depicting incidents adequately for analysis and comparison since researchers who worked closely with the data were able to describe the full incident with correct detail upon reading the coded string.[2]

Counting and Ranking

As an initial test of the analytic potential of the coding scheme and of the theory from which it was derived, we performed a frequency analysis based on the coded categories. This analysis was designed to display and compare patterns observed in a subset of our data, the data on older children. The analysis was based upon 323 observations of boys (M) and girls (F) between the ages of 6 and 12: 73 from Israel (43M, 30F), 169 from the United States (94M, 75F), 81 from Zinacantan (23M, 28F), and 30 children, sex unspecified in original source, coded from the works of Vogt, Modiano (Zinacanteco and general Chiapas incidents only), Frank Cancian, and Haviland. In this analysis, we used the data from the three societies as if they were gathered through uniform sampling

Figure 6.1
Sample Strings

C	Lrn	Obs Code	Set	Inst	Activities	Group Size	Compos	Atmos	Ability	Act	RespPers	Resp	Value Expressed	Implied
I	F12	70j	girl's own room: house	none: none	discussing how learner decorated her room: exchanging information	four: small	grandmo, mother, uncle, aunt: kin only	informal, tense	learner reads in room: outside	angry at grandma for violating privacy: conflict	mother: same sex parent	corrects learner's action: deny	"treat your grandmother with respect": human attainment	privacy: place
U	F6	63k	neighbor's home: village	none: none	playing rocket: play	four: small	male 5, male 4, male 2: children only	relaxed: informal	watches boys: outside	make suggestion: play	three boys: children	take her cue: affirm	none: none	none: none
Z	M/F42v	6-14	center: village	church: religious	bringing candles & flowers	immed. family: small	father mother children: parent-sibling only	---: deferential	trail father: participation	joining ritual	parents: same/opposite parent	none, cont. ritual: no response	none: none	importance of religious belief

procedures. This can only be justified by the exploratory nature of our work, in which we were trying to establish whether our categories were functional, where they were functional, and how they functioned. Consequently, our interpretations of findings are conservative. To underscore their tentative nature, we have not employed statistical tests of significance. We have employed Schroeding's standard estimate of error to calculate our observation error,[3] which averaged 6 percent per culture. We then doubled that and rounded it off to 15 percent to avoid accepting insignificant differences as patterns. Thus, only intracultural differences of 15 percent were considered significant in defining pattern variations. For cross-cultural comparisons the observation error was then added to the coding error, derived from the test of interrater reliability discussed above, to establish a basic error level of 30 percent. Only between-culture differences in frequencies above 30 percent were considered significant in pattern analysis.

A second analytical procedure we employed was a ranking procedure. It was necessitated by the lack of uniformity in our sampling which in turn made it difficult to estimate and compare frequencies of occurrence between cultures. Ranking seemed less subject to sampling distortion. Ranks were established within each of the major categories analyzed and a difference of about 25 percent of the rank distribution was considered necessary for significance except in small categories, for which a 50 percent difference was required. We then examined systematic differences between cultures by comparing both rank difference in subcategories and internal rank structure.

We considered analytically significant cross-cultural differences in subsystem categories to be indicative of clearly patterned structures only when they met the test for significance in both analyses, that is, frequency and rank. For example, a cross-cultural difference by sex was considered analytically significant only if the difference appeared in all three cultures, was significant in at least two of them, and also reached significance in the combined totals. Intraculturally, a significant difference by sex was recorded if the frequencies differed by 15 percent or more.

Also, because we were looking for *patterns* of culture acquisition, we developed a concept of *significant similarity*. Subsystem patterns were considered significantly similar across cultures if frequency differences were no more than 15 percent and rank differences were zero for small systems or 1 for large systems.[4] In defining both differences and similarities we effectively create a continuum. It ranges from great difference (considered significant), through moderate difference and moderate similarity, to great similarity (also considered significant). This procedure alerts us to the possibility that patterning exists in culture acquisition/transmission for a particular system and can be tested further by other methodologies.

FINDINGS

Our findings indicate that strongly patterned variations in culture acquisition/transmission contexts and processes do occur. Nine interculturally significant differences were found in 7 out of a possible 12 of our subsystem categories. Significant internal differences were found for all three cultures as well: 15 for the United States, 10 for Israel, 9 for Zinacantan. Specific findings are displayed in Figures 6.2–6.5, below, and are discussed here by category.

Settings

In all cultures, children were most often observed in their homes (see Figure 6.2). The next most common setting was the village or neighborhood. For this age group, no strong cultural or gender distinction emerged by setting. Rather, data seemed to reflect the fact that all children of this age are active and mobile. Overall, the three-culture totals by sex showed slightly greater percentages of home and compound settings for girls, and of village and wider settings for boys, but these differences were not significant.

Institutions

In general, children in the three cultures rarely were observed taking part in institutional functions and were usually involved in informal situations (labeled "none" in Figure 6.2). Cultural patterning could be seen, however, in cases where children were involved in institutions. Children in this age group apparently have access primarily to institutions reflecting strong cultural themes, and have little or infrequent access to institutions that are distant from their culture's central ethos and eidos. For example, our findings show that the Zinacanteco emphasis on formal, institutionalized ritual and religion embodied in the cargo system affects 6- to 12-year-old children quite strongly. For Israel our findings for children show an emphasis on social institutions, such as communal dining rooms and children's houses in the kibbutz, combined with a significantly low emphasis on use of religious institutions.

The overall frequency with which boys and girls participate in institutional patterns and have opportunities to learn about them is similar for both sexes at this age, with two notable exceptions. In the United States, boys are found somewhat more frequently in all institutions than are girls. Although the difference is significant only in the case of economic institutions, the differences mount up so that the presence of girls in noninstitutional settings is significantly greater than that of boys.[5] In Zinacantan, boys are found with significantly greater frequency in institutionalized ritual situations.

Activities

The activities category refers to what people near the child are doing. The model specifies 12 basic kinds of activities (see Appendix Table A.1) from which children can observe and learn. As can be seen in Figure 6.2, multipurpose social activity was the most prevalent in all three cultures (rank 1 in Israel (I)

Figure 6.2
Basic Setting and Activity

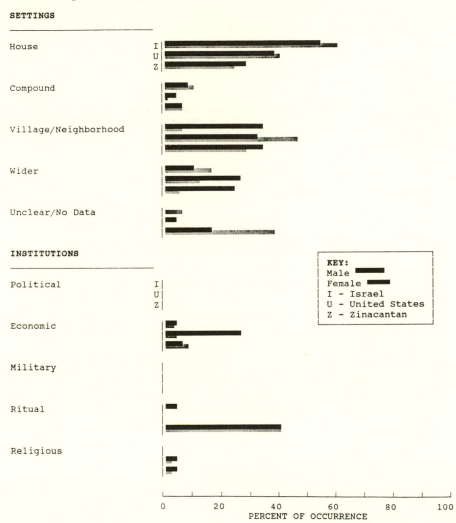

Figure 6.2 Continued

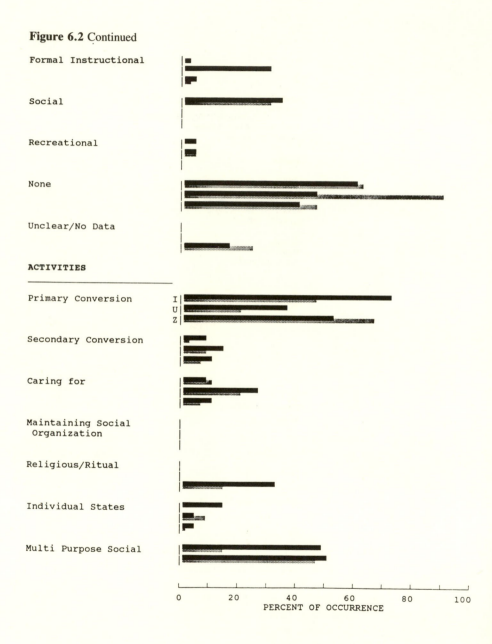

Formal Instructional

Social

Recreational

None

Unclear/No Data

ACTIVITIES

Primary Conversion

Secondary Conversion

Caring for

Maintaining Social
 Organization

Religious/Ritual

Individual States

Multi Purpose Social

0   20   40   60   80   100
PERCENT OF OCCURRENCE

Figure 6.2 Continued

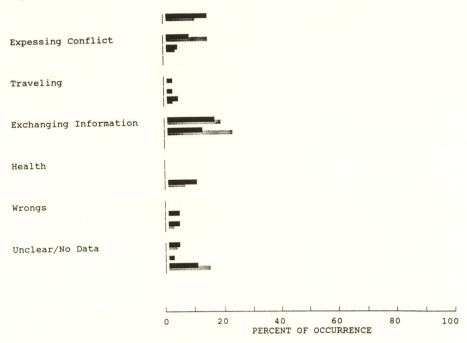

Expessing Conflict

Traveling

Exchanging Information

Health

Wrongs

Unclear/No Data

```
0        20        40        60        80        100
              PERCENT OF OCCURRENCE
```

and the United States (U.S.); rank 3 in Zinacantan (Z)). In both Israel and the United States, exchanging information was ranked second. In Zinacantan, religious and primary conversion activities were most likely to be observed (ranks 1 and 2). As might be expected, our data suggest that access to different classes of adult activity is strongly patterned. The one horticultural society, Zinacantan, has an activity profile significantly different from the two industrial ones.

We take special note of the lower contact with secondary conversion activities noted for Israeli children, which we believe results from inclusion of kibbutz children in our sample. Because they live in children's houses, kibbutz children not only are isolated somewhat from primary conversion activities at this age, which is what we expect to find for Western societies, but, in addition, they appear to be isolated from the types of repetitive maintenance-work activities (chores) that we have listed under secondary conversion. To put it another way, they see even less of the total adult cultural pattern than do U.S. children, who generally see less than the Zinacanteco children. The relatively greater isolation of Israeli kibbutz children was an unexpected finding and is in direct conflict with kibbutz education theory (cf. Spiro 1965; Talmon 1972).

Interestingly, although our sample eliminates formal schooling activities and thus artificially flattens the frequency profiles of the two Western cultures, the profile for Zinacantan still shows a comparatively wider and more even distri-

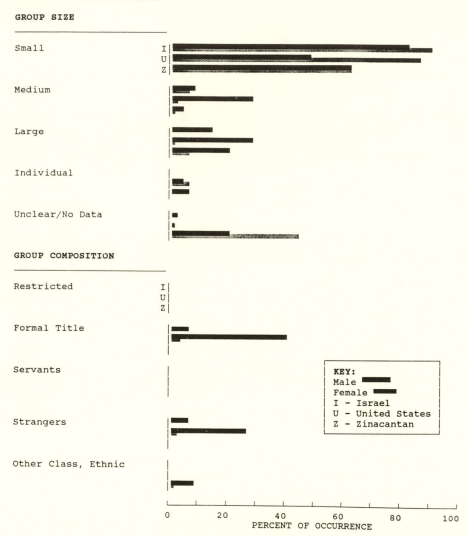

Figure 6.3
Immediate Human Context

GROUP SIZE

GROUP COMPOSITION

KEY:
Male
Female
I – Israel
U – United States
Z – Zinacantan

PERCENT OF OCCURRENCE

Figure 6.3 Continued

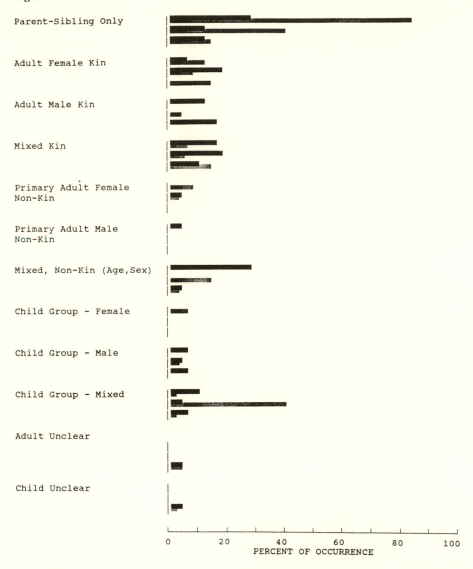

Figure 6.3 Continued

Unclear/No Data

ATMOSPHERE

Competitive

Informal

Deferential

Conflictive

Consciousness Altered

Judgmental

Celebrative

Intimate

Sad

Fearful/Anxious

Serious

0   20   40   60   80   100
PERCENT OF OCCURRENCE

Figure 6.3 Continued

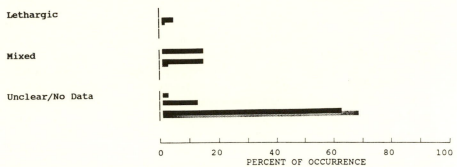

Lethargic

Mixed

Unclear/No Data

0   20   40   60   80   100
PERCENT OF OCCURRENCE

bution of chHthat distribution, too, may be artificially flattened by the normative style of reporting common in ethnography. In fact, if we take settings, institutions, and activities together, the pattern of more and wider distribution of Zinacanteco children is confirmed.[6]

On the whole, differences by gender in access to adult activity are extremely low. Considering the differences in potential adult roles, we might expect them to be much greater. However, since children of both sexes are found primarily at home at this age, the finding seems logical. Significant differences by sex are found in only three cases. In Zinacantan, girls are more likely than boys to be present where primary conversion activities are taking place. But boys have more chances to observe rituals. In the United States, we note that boys more frequently are found in situations in which adults are focused primarily on child care. This is hard to explain, but it appears that when boys are present, adults tend to turn attention to them rather than to some other activity. Some researchers have suggested that cross-culturally boys relate less to home activities managed by females and thus receive more negative attention than do girls (see, for example, Freedman and DeBoer 1979). Our data support this finding only for the United States, and then somewhat weakly; while boys receive significantly more negative responses, they also relate more to adult activity (see Ability).

Group Size

Children in all three societies are seen most often in small groups of 2–10 participants (see Figure 6.3). When the data are examined by sex we note that boys tend to be found more frequently in the larger groups. In the United States, the only society in which the difference reaches significance internally, this is accompanied by boys less frequent appearance in small groups. When taken in conjunction with setting and institution data, this finding is consistent with reports in previous research that cross-culturally boys more often play away from home (see Freedman and DeBoer 1979).

Group Composition

In all three societies, children are active primarily in groups composed of their own parents and siblings (rank 1 for Israel and the United States; rank 2 for Zinacantan). As Figure 6.3 indicates, the only outstanding difference is a contrast between Zinacanteco and U. S./Israeli children's interaction with groups in which some adult acted in relation to the children in a formal role capacity. Outside of school, Zinacanteco children experienced a much higher number of formal contacts, generally with men serving in cargo positions or as shamans.

Two differences in group composition by sex are significant. The higher frequency of boys in groups with formal functions in Zinacantan stems from their greater participation in ritual. In Israel and the United States, boys are found more frequently in groups with nonkin and/or strangers. This is probably true across all three cultures, but because our coding system ranks the presence of occupants performing formal roles higher than the presence of strangers, and we code only one item for group composition, ceremonial occasions in Zinacantan that draw strangers from other *municipios* are ranked as "formal" groups.[7] In Israel, the relatively greater frequency with which girls are found in parent–sibling-only groups is the reciprocal, that is, an artifact of coding. Still, these findings are consistent with sex difference findings in the preceding subsystem categories.

Atmospheres

In all three societies (see Figure 6.3) the most common atmosphere children experience is informal (I, rank 1; U.S., rank 2; Z, rank 2). Serious work-oriented atmospheres are also common (I, 4.5; U.S., 1; Z, 3.5) as are conflictive atmospheres (I, 2; U.S., 3; Z, 5). Although between-culture frequencies differ significantly only for serious atmospheres, the relative importance of atmospheres within cultures, as seen in the rank orders of each, appears quite distinctive. The most frequently experienced atmospheres—Informal, Conflictive, and Fearful for Israel; Serious, Informal, and Conflictive for the United States, and Deferential, Informal, and Celebrative/Serious for Zinacantan—suggest a strong difference in overall emotional-expressive atmosphere between the two Western cultures and Zinacantan and at least a moderate difference between Israel and the midwestern United States.

The influential work of the cultural configurationists, especially Benedict (1934), of Mead and her colleagues on Bali (Mead and Bateson 1942; Mead and McGregor 1951), and research on modal personality all lead us to expect distinctive emotional organizations in unrelated cultures. Our admittedly tentative measures of relational-expressive atmospheres, using behavioral markers, tend to support the concept of cultural character even though our conceptual basis and measurement system are quite dissimilar from those of configurational and psychological anthropologists.[8] Additionally, while it is difficult to be certain (since 64 percent of the Zinacanteco observations could not be scored for atmospheric markers), the profile of subcategory frequencies suggests that Zinacanteco children have somewhat broader experiences of the entire emotional range within their culture than do the children from the other two cultures.

Ability to Act

The ability category describes the child's behavior within the context of the ongoing adult or general activity. According to our model, the learner's behavior may contribute to, interfere with, or remain outside (independent of) those surrounding activities.

The degree and the manner in which children involve themselves in adult activities (see Figure 6.4) across the three societies revealed a surprising and conclusive finding. Six- to 12-year-old children in the midwestern United States related to or participated in adult activities about half as much as did the children from the other two groups. Rather than either assisting adults or watching what they did, U.S. children played or did some alternate task. We expected to find a difference between the two Western societies and Zinacantan on this measure, but were surprised by the U.S.-Israeli difference. We believe this finding must be a real outcome of different attitudes toward children in Israel and in the midwestern United States. Children may indeed be valued differently and treated more as the equals of adults in Israel and in traditional Jewish culture (especially boys) than in the midwestern United States (Goodman 1970, especially Chap. 5; Spiro 1965, Chap. 4; Talmon 1972; Zborowski 1955), where children, although valued, are often excluded. They go or are put to bed earlier than adults; they watch TV; they are not likely to be encouraged to join adult work or conversation with nonfamily members. Our protocols show a great number of these child-excluding situations for U.S. children. In other societies, especially at the higher age levels, children are more often regarded as valuable participants.

Perhaps more surprisingly, we found that girls rather than boys in Israel and the United States were least closely related to adult activity. Cross-cultural studies generally have indicated that girls occupy work roles more often than do boys of this age (Freedman and DeBoer 1979). In our data, this was true for Zinacantan, but not for the United States or Israel. We can only speculate that to the extent that male children are valued more than female children in the two Western cultures, as was the case historically, they may be permitted to relate more directly to adult life.

Acts

This category refers to the activity in which the learner engages as the incident develops. The same 12 subcategories used to classify surrounding adult or group activities were used in this category. As Figure 6.4 shows, in all three societies, the more common acts performed by children were multipurpose social, that is,

Figure 6.4
Learner Role and Behavior

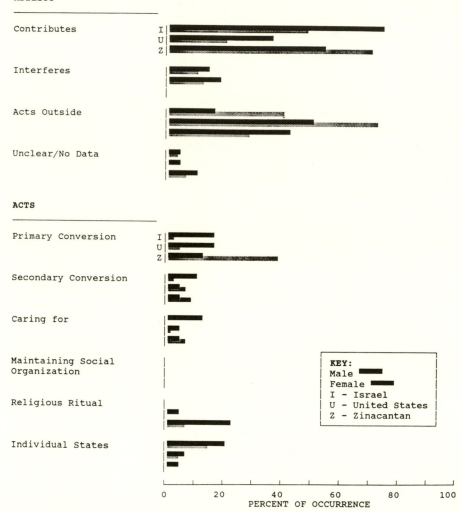

Figure 6.4 Continued

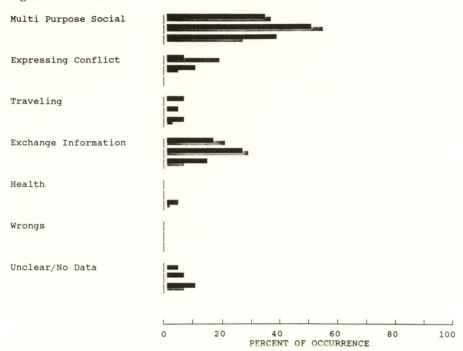

visiting, gossiping, watching, eating, playing, or joking. Exchanging information was also common (I and U.S., rank 2; Z, rank 4) and primary conversion acts were fairly likely to occur (rank 2 in Zinacantan; rank 3 in the United States; rank 5 in Israel).

Expressing conflict was common for children in the two industrialized cultures (ranked third), but was not observed for Zinacantan (or at least was not recorded) for children of this age group by our sources. This finding is consistent with the Whitings' "Dimension A" proposal (Whiting and Whiting 1975). They have suggested a direct relationship between socioeconomic complexity and the likelihood of "dependent-dominant" behaviors in children, such as seeking help, attention, and dominance. The kinds of behaviors we classified as expressing conflict may reflect one aspect of this dependence-dominance cluster. In the United States, for example, children argue and fight more than do the adults surrounding them (in our observations, four times more: 6.5 percent versus 1.5 percent). Because of the data collection method used for Zinacantan, however, interpretations must remain tentative.

A comparison of the Activity category in Figure 6.2 (primarily adult activities, though some are peer activities) and of the Act category in Figure 6.4 shows that the frequency and rank structures of children's acts are not exactly parallel to those in their environments. In the United States and Israel, for example, children are cared for more than they care for others. In Zinacantan, the rank and frequency of care-receiving activities and care-giving acts are similar, but not indicative of reciprocal, interactive behaviors. Rather, children will care for siblings when parents are absent and they themselves are not being cared for. In other cases, children are defined as juniors. In Zinacantan, ritual/religious activity is the first-ranking adult behavior observed by children (23.5 percent), but only the third-ranking act for children (13.5 percent) because Zinacanteco children do not participate fully. On the other hand, the frequency and rank of their multipurpose acts are higher than those of adults, indicating that the children spend more time watching activities than do their seniors.

As with previous categories, the Zinacanteco frequency profile is flatter than the profiles for United States or Israeli children, indicating somewhat fuller participation. The rank profile structure is also unlike that of the two Western industrialized societies, which are almost identical. Religious/ritual and health activities rank higher, and individual states and conflict behaviors have significantly lower ranks.

Looking at all three societies, no significant differences in acts classified by sex were noted. Within societies, the only significant difference was in Zinacantan, where girls were observed than boys doing primary conversion acts at this age more frequently. This means that children between ages 6 and 12 do not, for the most part, seem to be rehearsing potential gender differences through different acts. However, boys' and girls' identical activities may be differentially accepted and responded to by adults according to the child's sex, as our data for responses/patterns of control and appropriateness indicate (see below). Also, although the frequency of acts in most classes is very similar for boys and girls, the relation of these acts to adult activities may be structured differently. The evidence in the Abilities category—namely, that Israeli and U.S. girls engage in more acts unrelated to the primary adult activity surrounding them than do boys, while Zinacanteco girls' acts relate more closely to adults' activities than do boys' acts—suggests this is so.

Primary Responding Person

The primary responder (see Figure 6.5) was often a female parent (first rank, I and U.S.; second rank, Z). Male parents played this role less often (ranks 2, 4, and 3 for I, U.S., and Z respectively). The most noticeable difference in responding persons is the contrast between Zinacantan, on the one hand, and the United States and Israel, on the other. Zinacanteco children receive their primary responses somewhat less frequently from parents and siblings (combined ranks: Z, 6.75; U.S., 4.5; I, 5.5), especially from mothers (frequency: Z, 12.5 percent; U.S., 38.5 percent; I, 38.5 percent) than do Israeli and U.S. children. This is because Zinacanteco boys, particularly, interact more with ceremonial personnel and, when they go to the fields, with male kin in their father's work group. In contrast, in the United States sample, responses from nonkin came from other children. This formed part of a consistent pattern. The U.S. children were the recipients of the highest levels of responses from other children, whether kin or nonkin, with a combined rank of 6.75. In Zinacantan, the combined rank of child responses was 9.75; in Israel, 8. No strongly patterned differences by sex were noted, either within or between cultures.

Patterns of Control

This category describes the character of the response to the child, which may be positive, negative, contain both positive and negative elements, or be absent (coded Affirms, Denies, Mixed, and No Response, respectively). As Figure 6.5 indicates, affirming responses are ranked first in frequency in the United States followed by Denies; in Israel the pattern is reversed; in Zinacantan, No Response ranks first, Affirm second. Taken as a whole, the rank structures of responses and significant differences in response frequencies suggest that between-culture differences are pervasive and significant. This is consistent with theories of culture-personality relationships (see, for example, Whiting and Whiting 1975:108).

Israeli children appear to be a focus of attention for adults. They are almost always responded to either negatively (40.5 percent) or positively (32.5 percent) whereas No Response is extremely rare (1 percent). The level of negative responses is significantly higher than in the other cultures. However, about 10 percent of the time U.S. parents take their children's acts for granted and do not respond at all. For Zinacanteco children, the most common response is none at all (21 percent). When adults in these two societies do respond, it is almost twice as likely to be positively (Z, 17.5 percent; U.S. 49 percent) than negatively (Z, 8 percent; U.S., 17 percent). Although interpretations must be made cautiously, a possible source of response differences may lie in social structure. The dramatic ceremonial structures in which Zinacanteco children are seen (30 percent of the time) are not conducive to a focus upon children. In contrast, the social, economic, and instructional institutions in which Israeli and U.S. children are seen are structured around dyadic and small-group interaction.

All three societies show significant differences in response to boys and girls, with Israeli and Zinacanteco respondents less denying or more affirming of males, while U.S. respondents are significantly more denying toward males.

Values

Looking at the use of values in child-raising transactions (Figure 6.5), we note that in one-half to more than three-quarters of all incidents in each society values were neither expressed nor implied, but that in Israel the rates of both value expression and implication were significantly higher than for the other two cultures. The combined rate of value usage for Zinacantan was slightly but

Figure 6.5
Response Factors

PRIMARY RESPONSE PERSON

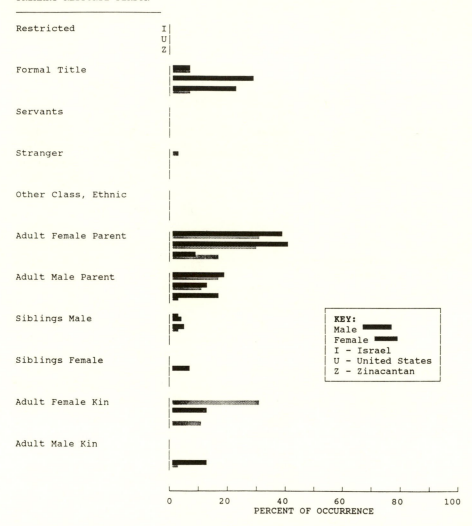

Figure 6.5 Continued

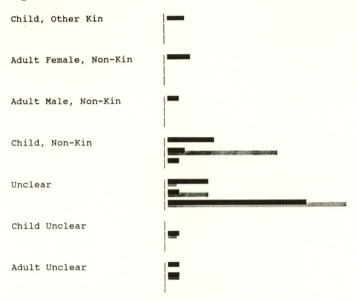

Child, Other Kin

Adult Female, Non-Kin

Adult Male, Non-Kin

Child, Non-Kin

Unclear

Child Unclear

Adult Unclear

PATTERNS CONTROL/RESPONSE

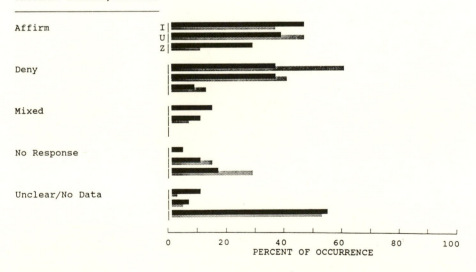

Affirm

Deny

Mixed

No Response

Unclear/No Data

PERCENT OF OCCURRENCE

Figure 6.5 Continued

EXPRESSED VALUES

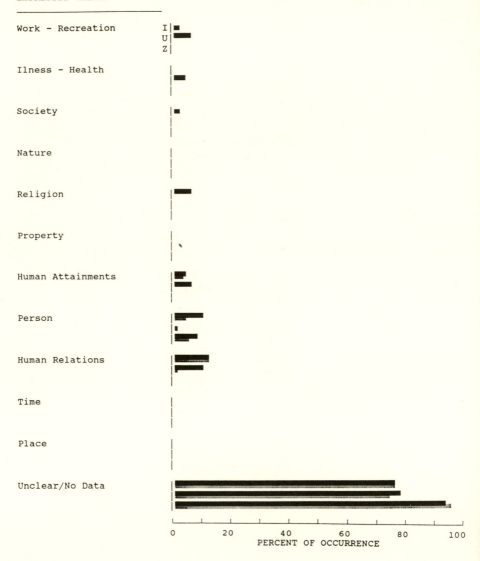

Figure 6.5 Continued

IMPLIED VALUES

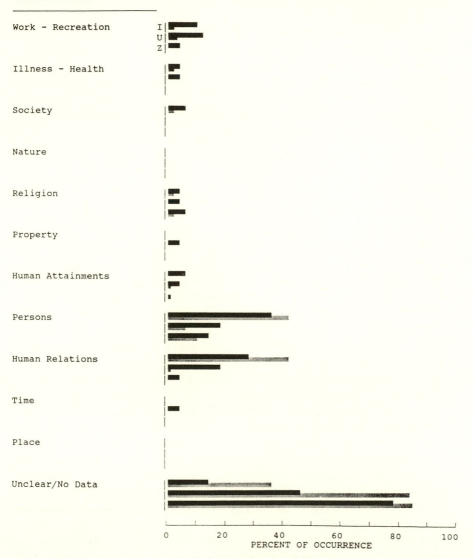

significantly lower. This is consistent with the findings on ability and response. Emphasis on specific values also followed cultural lines but was less well delineated. When the children in our sample were exposed to values by either expression or implication, the values usually related to age stage and sex role/ gender expectations (combined ranks: I, 1.5; U.S., 1.5; Z, 2.25). This tells us that for 6- to 12-year-olds, reminders of their junior status are constant. Only in Zinacantan did the implication of other values, specifically religion and work values, rank highly.

Across the three cultures, girls are the recipients of significantly fewer values than are boys. Although for specific values the difference reaches significance within cultures in only two categories—primarily age-stage and gender references—cumulatively the finding is consistent. Taken in conjunction with the findings on responses, this suggests that boys are indeed reacted to differently than girls, but that the differences are consistent *intra*culturally and not *cross*-culturally.

PATTERNING

Our primary interest in performing this analysis was to search for cultural patterns as processes and as wholes. Using only the frequency and ranking analyses reported above, our findings suggest that cultures are patterned with respect to children's access to cultural wholes and that this patterning follows well-understood economic, political, and religious distinctions between cultures, but that the degree of patterning is not as strong for children as for adults. Similarly, for these three cultures, we found little evidence for universal patterns of differentiation by sex (two significant differences and three strong tendencies across 102 categories). Neither did we find evidence here for strongly differing treatment of boys and girls within cultures. The most strongly patterned society in this respect was the United States, with 15 significant differences in 102 categories. This was followed by Israel with 10, and Zinacantan with 9.

We have hypothesized that sociocultural patterns are learned polyphasically through many simultaneous modalities. Learning necessary future roles may depend very little upon action and much more upon lateral or peripheral vision of the structure of local life. In this, humans may differ from the other primates. We also know at a theoretical level that similar childhoods may be specifically controverted through the use of coming-of-age ceremonies that overtly reject childhood experience and create identity with adults of one's own sex (see, for example, Levine and Levine 1971:194–202) and that child life may stand in stark contrast to adult life, as in Manus, but that children may nevertheless be incorporated efficiently into adult life through the use of structural and value mechanisms (Mead 1930).

INITIAL EVALUATION OF THE SYSTEMS-BASED THEORY
AND METHOD

Our evaluation of the systems-based, holistic field method and the associated data classification schema addresses four issues: (1) Do the field guide and associated code facilitate the gathering of accurate and detailed data and permit adequate characterization of single cultures and fruitful cross-cultural comparison? (2) If they are adequate as a whole, to what extent do they require modification? (3) Do the guide and coding system meet the tests of theoretical adequacy laid out in the previous chapters of this book? (4) What contribution does the systems-theory base of the research make to the study of cultural transmission?

Based on both the data and the analyses presented above, we answer our first query in the affirmative. The theory and field guide together direct the gathering of a body of data that appear to adequately depict the culture acquisition/transmission processes within a single society. They also seem to provide a structure for fruitful cross-cultural comparison. This is true for both data gathered in the field and data compiled from previously published work, though in differing degrees.

Nevertheless, in answer to our second query, we conclude that the subsystem categories will require further and perhaps continued modification. For example, the subsystem Settings was defined along one critical dimension, distance from the *foyer*, the geographical and psychological center of daily life, and coded for four distance levels (see Table 5.2). Settings were easy to code; our agreement level was 88 percent. While this category seemed to distinguish zones that functionally were separate within all three cultures, it did not perform well in distinguishing among cultures. Further, categories such as this one, with few subsets, and those for response/patterns of control and abilities, make examination of the cultural structuring of alternatives impossible. Our experience suggests that three- and four-point scales obscure patterning and that categorical subdivisions of fewer than six to eight items are of marginal utility in theoretical work, no matter how reliable for coding purposes. Thus, categories with slightly more elaborate breakdowns should prove analytically more useful.

In several other cases, the need for modification stems from theoretical considerations. Our ability to code Values and Atmospheres accurately was hampered by definitional and scaling problems. Our initial attempts to produce theoretically justifiable methods for classifying Values, following Kluckhohn and Strodtbeck (1961), Edel and Edel (1968), and Albert (1956), failed to produce functional codes. Although we were moderately successful (our reliability rates were 60 percent for expressed values and 43 percent for implied ones), we do not feel satisfied, and the values subsystem has been revised utilizing some notions from dimensional analysis (see Chapter 8 and Appendix Table A.1). Similarly, although we combed some two dozen ethnographies to define a set of ethnographically distinguishable categories that would classify adequately all the emotional terms we encountered in them and reviewed the psychological literature relating to the classification of emotions (see, for example, Berlyne's brief review, 1971:71–74), this process failed to provide a complete theoretically based system for classifying emotional atmospheres. The ethnographic inductive procedure allowed us to devise a system that worked fairly well, since classification problems arose primarily between pairs or triplets of atmosphere: (1) competitive/conflictive/judgmental, (2) informal-relaxed (only where the presence of children was an adult focus)/serious, and (3) sad/fearful. But this lowered coder agreement to 55 percent. The scaling of emotional atmospheres along two axes appears to provide a promising basis for modification (see Chapter 8).

There is, however, a limit to coding accuracy. Utilizing our own experience and that of the Whitings and of the Human Relations Area Files (see note 4), we suggest that the limits of coding accuracy are independent of category construction and definitional adequacy and that all cultural coding efforts will result in an inherent error of about 15 percent ± 5 percent. Because humans possess the capability for simultaneous activity production as well as polyphasic activity perception, there will be an essential ambiguity in sociocultural data.

An example from the category Activities will illustrate this problem. In all societies, caring for children is a major activity, but in very few do adults do nothing but focus their activity on child care (infant care is not being considered here). More likely they cook, hoe, herd, watch T.V. or visit as they also care for children, creating a multiactivity context in which children simultaneously learn about tasks, about recreation, about the place of children in society, and about proper child care. On the one hand, a system with double codings that can capture multiple purposes and activities rapidly becomes unwieldy. On the other hand, coder disagreement inevitably will arise whenever determination of a primary activity requires a judgment between several feasible alternatives. Unfortunately, employing stricter definitions or better theory will not resolve the basic problem. The multiple purposes and activities of even single actors and the necessity of designating one aspect of them as primary, in conjunction with the necessity of creating categories wide and deep enough to embrace and classify cross-cultural data, create an irreducible degree of coding error in all data-categorization schemes. We make this point not to excuse our own inadequacies but to highlight the definitional and measurement issues and to indicate the inherent limitations of this type of work.

Turning to our third query, we ask: To what extent does our field guide meet the test of anthropological adequacy? Our basic model is founded directly upon an operationalized definition of culture, and our code is a direct expansion and elaboration of that model (See Chapter 5). By including settings, institutions, group size, group composition, and emotional atmospheres in our subsystems, we include specified community dimensions. Through utilization of an 11-category coding scheme (values are considered one category) coupled with a theory of brain function that permits us to define learning as a polyphasic recording process capable of receiving and utilizing simultaneous information in all 11 areas, the systems-based model can code various learning incidents arising from all major primate modes: modeling, group learning, social conflict learning, play, and habitat learning. Additionally, through the illustrative analysis carried out here, the systems-based framework is shown to have the ability to generate data adequate for testing statements related to the differential structure of culture acquisition across societies. Data obtained using the field guide stem from the overall schema in Figure 5.3 (Chapter 5) and reflect overall cultural configurations as displayed in the societies studied.

We conclude, therefore, that the systems-theory base of the model makes an essential contribution to the study of culture acquisition/transmission because it guides us in that endeavor from a holistic perspective. We begin with a series of learning incidents that are recorded globally, that is, as a social, emotional, ecological, ideological interactive whole. We then display these incidents holistically and precisely. We are then able to describe the total, undivided *process/ context* in the way that learners actually encounter it in life. Thus the model presented here should facilitate work that searches for patterns in culture acquisition/transmission.

NOTES

1. This calculation uses the primary subcategory labels (that is, generally, the fourth level in Table 5.2, as, for example, 1.2.2.6). Average interrater reliability in the fine categories was approximately 63 percent. Agreement level for individual primary categories ranged from 100 percent for Learner, Group Size, and Group Composition to 44 percent and 43 percent, respectively, for Activity and Implied Values. This reliability rate is judged to be satisfactory since it is approximately the same as both the 78 percent average reported by the Whitings for the Six Cultures study (1975:55) and the 48 percent to 78 percent reliability rates reported for the Human Relations Area Files for large categories (Bierele 1974; Bierele and Witkowski 1974). It should be noted, however, that high coding reliability does not necessarily imply high theoretical reliability or utility.

2. This has proved to be the case for a body of data of up to 600 sheets of observations, and we expect it will be true for up to 2,000 or 3,000 sheets of personally recorded field notes.

3. For Schroeding's standard estimate of error: $\sqrt{\text{no. of observations}}$ = expected error (see Weinberg 1975). The square root of 323 is 17.9, giving us an observer error of 6 percent, as follows:

No. of Observation	Sheets Analyzed	No. of Expected Errors	Percent in Error
United States	169	13.0	8
Zinacantan	81	9.0	11
Israel	73	8.5	12
Total	323	17.9	6

4. Where two cultural pairs were significantly similar in both frequency and rank and the third culture was dissimilar in rank only, the three cultures were treated as significantly

similar if all frequencies were near zero. This happened in only three cases, in the analysis of infrequently used values, where the percentage of observations for two cultures was zero and for the third slightly above zero. Significant similarities in subsystem usage by gender were defined as a frequency difference of no more than 5 percent across gender within the three societies in addition to a total difference between genders of 10 percent or less in all three societies combined.

5. A systematic observation error of about 14 percent, the result of observing more boys than girls in noninstructional school settings (recesses), inflates the difference slightly but does not affect significance.

6. Its runs through all these basic variables and is seen in the smaller ranges, lower mean frequencies ($\bar{X}$ = I, 64; U.S., 41; Z, 35 for settings. I; 61.5; U.S., 68; Z, 43 for institutions. I, 43.5; U.S., 47; Z, 22.5 for activities) and somewhat smaller number of zeroes in the Zincanteco data.

7. Problems with the coding of group composition are addressed in Chapter 8.

8. For a thorough review of psychological anthropology applied to education see Harrington (1979), whose careful delineation of method facilitates a comparison.

7 Methods for the Discovery of Patterns in Culture Acquisition: Some Comparative Experiments

Through our work with the Israeli, U.S., and Zinacanteco data, we tested the field guide and coding system described in Chapter 5. The work reported on in Chapter 6 indicated that these structured the data gathering and interpretation so as to produce adequate descriptions of learning processes at the level of social interaction. The key factor was the use of strings systematically derived from the data sheets. They permitted researchers to capture process because each string was, in fact, a minidescription of an interactive process, one in which learners encountered a cultural happening, acted within it, and were in turn responded to by others in the setting. However, the systems theory base of the culture acquisition model and the parallel data collection method were designed to explore and compare basic structures in culture acquisition/transmission processes. We continue to be interested in extending the analysis to this level of cultural patterns as processes and wholes. Still, it is a great analytical challenge to develop procedures that reveal the broader sociocultural processes governing cultural continuity and structuring culture acquisition and cultural transmission.

This chapter reports on three analytic experiments. They represent series of attempts to solve the problem of capturing the patterning of societywide processes in a holistic, but precise and detailed, fashion. They were conducted, in particular, to explore the potential of the systems theory basis of the model, a potential not realized in the frequency and ranking analysis discussed in Chapter 6. This chapter describes the methodological procedures of these analytical experiments and assesses their utility. Throughout the chapter, standard statistical procedures

Marion Lundy Dobbert was the primary author of this chapter.

have been avoided even where they might normally be applied. This avoidance has two bases. First, and most important, statistical procedures do not appear adequate for modelling the processes that are at the base of human learning; second, the assumptions of independence for each item (trial) inherent in frequency probability theory underlying many powerful techniques are not acceptable in a systems theory context.

DATA BASE

The pattern discovery experiments detailed in this chapter are based on the data set for 6- to 12-year-old children from Israel, the United States, and Zinacantan, employed in Chapter 6, plus an additional data set for children between the ages of 3 to 6 in all three cultures. The total data set consisted of 578 pages of structured observations of children between the ages of 3 and 12 that were gathered by researchers using the forms and methods described in Chapter 5.

In keeping with the policy of continued improvement of the coding procedures described in the last chapter, the process for creating strings was slightly modified. The 11 essential elements, the coding scheme specified by the theory, were retained (see Figure 6.1 Chapter 6), but the coding for three categories was revised. Group Size and Composition was revised to better capture total group structure, Responding Person was revised to better reflect the multiple statuses adults often occupy, and the Values category was changed to give equal consideration to both stated and clearly implied values.

The codes for each of the eleven string elements or data categories were used in their most reduced form, as single (sometimes double or triple) letter labels.[1] This made string manipulation easier and patterns more recognizable. The result was a very short "11 word" string that replicated the field note sheet in a condensed, miniature form. Each string had a prefix code that identified the culture, observation number, and observer.[2] Some examples of coded strings grouped by pattern are seen in Figure 7.1.

USING DECISION TREES IN THE SEARCH FOR PATTERNING

The patterning in culture can be thought of as resulting from an accumulation of past decisions that are built upon or changed by contemporary decision processes. When decisions are made, they link those cultural elements that influenced them. Over time, this process connects cultural elements into branching structures stemming from specific decision nodes. Each branch will represent a slightly different set of decisions. Research in anthropology has mapped progressive cultural processes in this way, particularly in the areas of kinship classification and economic strategy making (see, for example, Keesing 1970, 1971 and Buchler, Fischer & McGoodwin 1968). Such approaches to the search for pattern in anthropology are usually connected with cognitive process or information-pro-

Figure 7.1
Samples of Strings: 38 Israeli Children in Informal Situations

Cult	Obs#	Obsrv	Set	Inst	Atm	Grp	Acty	Abil	Act	Sex	Age	RP	Rs	V
Young Children Being Cared for at Home															
I	2	K	H	X	I	SP	Cf	RD	PI	F	3	SP	A	X
I	13	L	H	X	I	SP	Cf	O	SC	F	4	SP	NR	X
I	10	K	H	X	I	SP	Cf	RD	I	F	3	SP	A	X
I	39	V	H	X	I	SP	Cf	O	PI	PI	3	OP	A	X
I	33	U	H	So	I	MM	Cf	O	I	M	4	OP	A	X
I	31	C	V	So	I	S1C	I	RD	I	M	6	-	-	X
Joining Talk at Home															
I	45	E	H	X	I	SK	E	RD	E	F	7	SA	A	X
I	47	E	W	X	I	SP	E	O	E	F	7	Sp	A	X
I	44	E	H	X	I	SP	E	O	I	F	7	OP	A	X
I	8	k	H	X	I	SM	E	RD	E	F	3	SP	A	X
I	3	K	H	X	I	S1A	E	RD	E	F	3	SA	A	X
I	38	O	H	X	I	SK	E	RD	E	F	4	OK	NR	X
I	34	U	H	So	I	Sc	E	RD	E	M	4	F	-	X
Talking and Eating															
I	9	K	H	X	I	SP	CSO	RD	CSO	F	3	SP	A	X
I	4	K	H	X	I	SM	CS0	RD	CS0	F	3	SP	A	X
I	7	K	H	X	I	S1A	CS0	RD	DR	F	3	SP	A	X
I	32	O	H	X	I	SK	CS0	RD	CS0	F	4	SP/ OK	A	X
I	49	P	W	X	I	SP	CS0	RD	CS0	F	4	OP	A	X
I	40	O	H	X	I	SK	CS0	O	PI	F	4	SP	NR	X
I	8	R	V	X	I	MC	F	RD	F	M	3	-	-	X
I	25	M	H	So	I	MM	F	RD	F	F	3	A/F	A	X
I	51	Q	V	So	I	SP	F	RD	F	F	3	SP	NR	X
I	27	U	H	So	I	Sp	F	RD	F	M	4	SP	A	X
I	21	M	V	So	I	So	Cs0	RD	CS0	F	3	SP	NR	X
Joining Work															
I	33	O	H	X	s/i	SK	PC	O	PL	F	4	SP/ OK	NR	X
I	12	S	H	x	I	SA	PC	RD	E	M	2	SA	A	X
I	36	U	C	So	I	SC	SC	RD	SC	M	4	F	A	X
Young Children Playing															
I	45	P	H	X	I	SP	PI	RD	PI	F	4	OS	A	X
I	17	L	C	X	I	SC	PI	RD	PI	F	4	C	A	X
I	44	P	H	X	I	SC	DR	RD	DR	F	4	C	NR	X
I	11	L	H	X	I	SC	DR	RD	DR	F	4	SS	A	X
I	1	R	H	X	I	SC	PI	RD	PI	M	3	C	NR	X
I	10	R	V	X	I	SS	PI	RD	PI	M	3	OP	A	X
I	37	V	V	X	I/Im	Sk	PI	RD	PI	M	3	SK	A	X
I	53	Q	H	So	I	MC	PI	RD	PI	F	3	C	NR	X
I	29	U	H	So	I	Mc	Dr	RD	DR	M	4	SP	A	X
I	28	U	H	So	I	Sp	CG	RD	CG	M	4	OP	A	X
I	30	U	H	So	I	Sp	PI	RD	PI	M	4	SS	NR	X

cessing models which were given their modern anthropological formulation by Goodenough, but a branching structure can also be used to model "contingencies in social events leading to certain social outcomes" (Kay 1971:38).

Culture acquisition/transmission processes may be regarded as decision processes in which learners encounter either new or familiar situations and activities and decide how to respond to them. In turn, others decide how to respond to the learner and/or the learner's acts. Figure 7.2 illustrates decision tree analysis

Figure 7.2
Israeli Children Exhibiting Acceptable Behaviors in Informal Social Situations

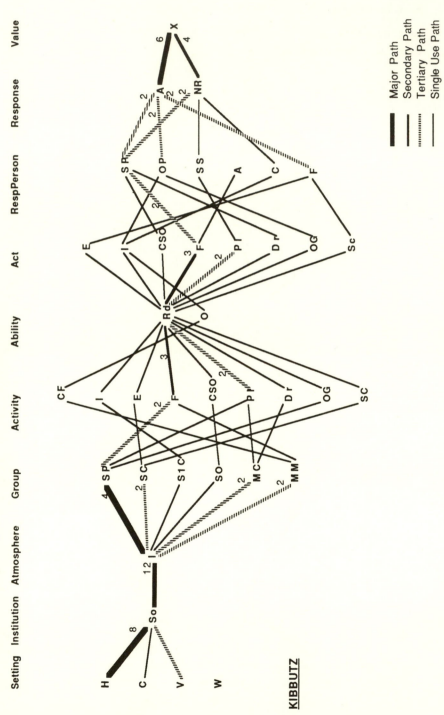

Setting   Institution   Atmosphere   Group   Activity   Ability   Act   RespPerson   Response   Value

KIBBUTZ

Major Path
Secondary Path
Tertiary Path
Single Use Path

120

Figure 7.2 Continued

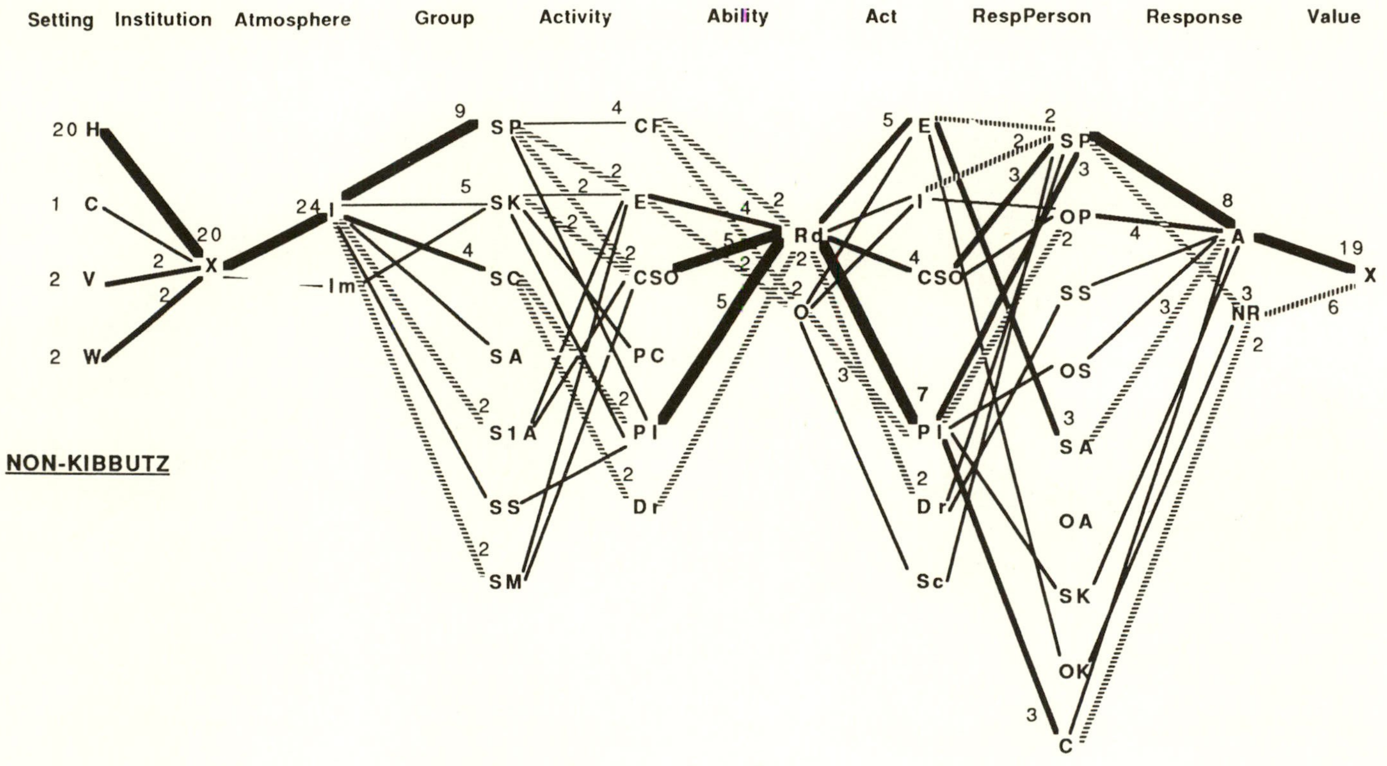

Setting
Institution
Atmosphere
Group
Activity
Ability
Act
RespPerson
Response
Value
20 H
1 C
2 V
2 W
X
I
Im
SP
SK
SC
SA
S1A
SS
SM
CF
E
CSO
PC
PI
Dr
Rd
O
E
I
CSO
PI
Dr
Sc
SP
OP
SS
OS
SA
OA
SK
OK
C
A
NR
X
NON-KIBBUTZ

for highly informal situations such as the data coded in Figure 7.1. The two trees contrast similar situations for kibbutz and nonkibbutz children between the ages of 3 and 7. They were generated from the data in Figure 7.1, which includes all the incidents marked by informal, relaxed atmospheres that are found in the Israeli data set. To construct these trees, each of the elements or cultural category codes in a string was considered a node. There, either a group decision (often historical or tacit, such as the selection of setting or the allocation of groups to setting) or an individual decision (such as selection of an action to perform) is seen as a choice leading to the next element or code in the string. Thus, for each string, a line representing this decision was drawn from the original choice code to codes representing succeeding choices. If subsequent strings repeated a previous decision, each repetition was noted on the line. Because each decision is a choice among multiple possibilities and no decision is strictly determined, the resulting trees contain overlapping and crisscrossing branches of either fewer or greater repetitions. The decision probabilities derived from this data set are indicated both by the number of different branches stemming from each node and by the frequencies noted on all but the single-use path.

A completed tree displays the whole pattern for an observed context. These patterns link social environmental factors; child or learner actions within that context, which are based on its possibilities; and the reactions or lack of reaction of others to that specific contextualized behavior. Figure 7.2 indicates that where the emotional atmospheres are informal and the situation is part of the normal daily structures of child life (for that culture), Israeli children, both kibbutz and nonkibbutz, act in ways that lead to mild approval from those around them; that is, their behavior either evokes no comment but is tacitly accepted, or receives a brief affirmative comment with no explanation attached to it.

The structure of the decision tree also facilitates precise comparison of the structure of learning experiences. We can observe similarities and differences between learning settings and the patterning of behaviors within those settings. The two trees pictured in Figure 7.2 allow us to examine the structuring of informal, positively accepted learning experiences in the kibbutz versus their structuring in urban Israel. The most probable decision paths have been highlighted by the use of wider lines. Beginning under setting and deciphering codes from left to right, we read that for both groups of children these experiences occur primarily at home (H), but for the kibbutz children many home settings are institutionalized (SO). (The children's house, age group, and communal dining hall are coded "SO," while "X" means no institution.) As a consequence, the kibbutz children were seen learning to deal successfully with situations in which there were moderately sized groups of people present (11–14 in MC and MM) in one-third of the observations (See Note 1 for the meaning of code symbols).

The different social structures in turn create distinct contexts for action in the kibbutz and nonkibbutz situations. The urban children had more than half of their positive informal experiences in the contexts of activities conducted by their kin and were cared for only by their parents. The kibbutz children had two-thirds of their successful (affirmed or accepted) informal experiences in the context of almost identical activities, but two-thirds of them were conducted by persons other than parents or kin. When the kibbutz children were approved of by those around them in these informal situations, they were almost always (11 of 12 cases) participating in the ongoing activity (coded Rd), whether it was conversation, eating, or play. In contrast, the urban children observed gained approval for their acts when they did not participate directly but chose to play or do parallel activities, the latter being the case about one-quarter of the time.

The general pattern here suggests that kibbutz and urban concepts about proper contexts and roles for children are structured differently, as the relevant ideologies suggest they would be. It also suggests that kibbutz and urban children are becoming oriented to living patterns that have a measurably distinct structure. Decision trees of this sort, then, are useful in bringing out some of the high-probability patterns in small bodies of data relating to well-defined situations. Clear patterns representing frequently used decision branches become visible. (See Chapter 9 for an illustration of this.)

However, the types of flexible, nondetermined patterns that also appear in these trees require careful study and interpretation by the ethnographer. Even for small bodies of data, to quote Keesing (1971:47), "it should be emphasized that there are not neat 'rules,' amenable to formal description, that govern every possible decision and alternative."

The utility of decision trees is also quite limited. To test their potential for clarifying broader cultural patterns in larger bodies of data for comparative purposes, trees were generated using all of the strings coded for 6- to 12-year-old girls in Israel (n = 29), in the United States (n = 77), and in Zinacantan (n = 53). It immediately became apparent that the decision trees were generating false patterns. If one proceeded along the tree, following, first, all the most frequently used connections between nodes, and, successively, the second and third most frequently used sets of connections in order to generate the three culturally most common decision paths, the decision structures generated either did not exist in even a single data string or were very uncommon. What these connections highlighted were an aggregation of statistically central tendencies, or accumulations, for *individual* connecting decisions taken one at a time. The process of mapping numerous decisions over a fixed structure here has the effect of breaking the strings into sets of paired connections. This destroys the holism of the incidents because the total structures represented in each string, which replicate single decision patterns as wholes, do not consist of separately considered elements, but of a single multifaceted decision. Even small trees require careful interpretation to avoid errors caused by this tree construction process.

SEARCHING FOR PATTERNS VIA PREDICTED CONSTRAINTS AND FUNCTIONS

A second way to conceptualize the processes that create patterns in culture in general and in culture acquisition/transmission in particular is to think of conditioned states or constraints in which the variety in one element of culture has a limiting effect on the variety in another element (Ashby 1968). Constraints or conditioned states occur where the state of "b" (let us say the adult response to a child) depends on the pre-existing state of "a" (the child's actions, for example). This can be written as b = f(a), which reads "b is a function of a." Functional statements such as these are used in systems modeling in order to clarify thought by formalizing the logic in the model, which, in turn, facilitates its testing (Silvern 1972; Weinberg 1975).

The systems model presented in Chapter 5 uses formal functional statements. The labeled input and feedback arrows define those functions (see Figure 7.3). Each labeled arrow indicates constraints that one might expect to find in a culture acquisition process. The functions indicated by the arrows state unambiguously the logic of the conditionality which, it can be hypothesized, governs the culture acquisition/transmission process. The functions are linked into loops of expected constraints. Specifically, the model hypothesizes the following:

1. The deposit of cultural knowledge (DCK) that remains with a learner (L) after some incident in his or her life is a function of specific response (R), setting (S), institutions (I), activity (Ay), group composition (GC), emotional atmosphere (RE), and objects (O).[3]

2. Reponse is some function of the responding person (RP) and the appropriateness (AP) of what the learner does.

3. Responding person is some function of the group present (GC).

4. Appropriateness is a function of who the learner is (L), his/her act (Ac), the learner's ability (Ab), the ongoing activity (Ay), the institutional context (I), and applicable values (V).

5. Act is a function of previous responses, setting (S), institutional context (I), activity (Ay), group composition (GC), the emotional atmosphere (RE), and objects (O) present.

6. Ability is a function of the learner's age, sex (L), and previous knowledge (DCK).

7. Values are a function of setting (S), institution (I), activity (Ay), group composition (GC), and objects (O).

8. Group composition is a function of setting (S), institution (I), and activity (Ay).

9. Atmosphere is also a function of setting (S), institutional context (I), ongoing activity (Ay), and group composition (GC).

10. Objects are a function of cultural milieu, namely, setting (S), institution (I), and activity (Ay).

If we could combine the 10 functions, thus restating functional statement 1 above by saying that the deposit of cultural knowledge that remains with a learner after some incident in her or his life is a function of all the other functions hypothesized, then we would get a complete definition of the nature of cultural knowledge. It would be written as

Figure 7.3
Model of Systemic Interactions in Culture Acquisition-Transmission

Date: 11-19-82	Drawn by: James Gilbertson
Revision 6	Developed by: Marion Lundy Dobbert

A GENERAL THEORY OF CULTURAL TRANSMISSION

3.0

CULTURAL INFORMATION STORED IN SOCIAL PATTERNS

3.1

SOCIAL INTERACTION PATTERNS

Group Size and Composition

Group Size 3.1.31   Composition - Age, Sex, Status, Role 3.1.32   3.1.3

RE = f(GC)

Relational Expressive Atmosphere 3.1.4

Competitive: Bragging, Boosting 3.1.41   Informal-Relaxed Nicknames, Joking 3.1.42 ... etc

Consiousness Altered Trance, Possession 3.1.4.5

GC = f(S)   GC = f(A)   GC = f(I)   RE = f(I)

Objects 3.1.5

Natural 3.1.51   Manufactured 3.1.52

RE = f(A)   RE = f(S)   O = f(I)   O = f(A)   O = f(S)

Named Institutions 3.11

Political 3.1.1.1   Economic 3.1.1.2   ...etc

Military 3.1.1.3

precedent   limit

Activities 3.12

Converting Energy/Materials for Use 3.1.2.1   Caring for Others 3.1.2.1 ... etc   3.1.2

Multipurpose Activities 3.1.2.6   limit

limits

PATTERNS OF CONTROL/RESPONSE   3.2

No Response [O] Continuation 3.2.1   Mixed Response [+/-] 3.2.2

Affirming Response [+]

Praise "you are good" 3.2.31   Give directions that Accept Effort 3.2.35   Promise Reward 3.2.3.12 ...etc   3.2.3

Denying Response [-]

Laugh at/Belittle/Vilify 3.2.41   Spank/Slap/Shake/ Push Away 3.2.48   Withhold Privileges 3.2.4.13 ...etc   3.2.4

CULTURAL SETTINGS/ LOCALES 2.0   limit

limits

R = f(RP)   +/-   (F)

R = f(Ap)   +/-

RELEVANT ASPECT OF PERSONS   1.0

LEARNER 1.1

Characteristics: Age Stage & Sex 1.1.1   limit

Ab = f(Li)   limit

Abilities to Act: Contribution, Interference, Outside 1.1.2   limit

Ac = f(GC,RE,O)   Ac = f(S)   Ac = f(R₋₁...ₙ)   Ac = f(I,A)

Act 1.1.3

deposit

Deposit of Cultural Knowledge 1.1.4   DCK = f(R)

decrease inappropriate Ab = f(DCK)   increase appropriate

OTHER PERSONS/RESPONDING PERSON 1.2

Age, Sex Status & Role 1.2.1   class/weight

RP = f(GC)   V = f(GC)

Values Held [cluster around...]

Work- Recreation 1.2.2.1   Illness- Health 1.2.2.2 ...etc   1.2.2

Property 1.2.2.6

V = f(O)   V = f(A,I)   V = f(S)

Ap = f(V)   precedence

Appropriateness of Learner's Presence & Behavior 1.2.3

Ap = f(A,I)

match

Ap = f(Ab,Ac)

Ap = f(Li)   (F)   match   (F)   match

11. DCK = f(R = f(RP = f(GC = f(S, I, Ay)), Ap = f(L, Ac = f(R$_{t-1...n}$, S, I, Ay, GC = f(S, I, Ay), Atm = f(S, I, Ay, GC = f(S, I, Ay)), O = f(S, I, Ay)), Ab = f (DCK$_{t-1...n}$, L), Ay, I, V = f(S, I, Ay, GC = f(S, I, Ay), O = f(S, I, Ay)))) S, I, Ay, GC = f(S, I, AY), Atm = f (S, I, Ay, GC = f (S, I, Ay)), O = f(S, I, Ay)).

In this circular, looping, mutually interactive set of categories, the primitive, undefined, or basic terms are setting, institution, and activity. There is no way to determine what the numerous repetitions mean, but it is very clear, and very much in accord with the deliberately nonpsychological, nonreductionist position that we took as we carried out the earliest development of the systems model, that the deposit of learned cultural knowledge is radically defined in terms of social structural variables. In this model, culture has been transmitted when the learner deposits in his or her brain information about the social structure with all its ins and outs, of which relevant values and emotional loadings are an integral part. In other words, cultural learning is dependent not solely on what the child does, but on the social-ecological configuration surrounding the child. Children do not come to understand the constraints that create the structure of their society and impose pattern on its daily events by noting and learning the various constraints separately and, over time, eventually linking them into complete structures. Rather, the functional statements suggest the hypothesis that cultural patterns are learned as linked wholes.

Three analytical procedures were devised to test the pattern discovery and clarification potential of the functional statements. First, the statements that described constraints directly related to learning issues were decomposed into simple two-term relationships, such as "response is a function of learner's age and sex" [R = f(L)]. These relationships were then examined to discover whether or not they could be characterized as obvious, clearly patterned constraints. In the second analytic procedure, the constraining functions of the three major social terms—setting, institution, and activity—were compared with the remaining terms contained in the functional statements in order to test the potential validity of statement 11. Third, a number of the simplified two-by-two statements that were used to test constraints were linked to see whether their power to constrain and pattern the successive terms increased, as hypothesized in the original functional statements.

For these tests, a subset of the data base was constructed by removing all cases of repetition recorded by a single observer in a single incident. This eliminated any bias toward accepting as a pattern a constraint that appeared only in a single observation. A set of 516 nonduplicated observations, 153 for Israel, 271 for the Midwest, and 92 for Zinacantan, remained.

Patterning Potential of Individual Constraints

For the first constraint analysis the functional statements were divided into 19 short statements each containing two terms and expressing a single constraint.

Figure 7.4a
Sample Sort R = f(Ay): Number and Percent of Strings in Each Pile, Israel

ISRAEL

Activity	Response & % Expected Total No. [Blanks]	A(49%) A	D(35%) D	M(3%) M	N(9%) N
		Number & % Each Response			
Cf	*20[-]	11(55%)	6(30%)	1(5%)	2(10%)
Cn	8[-]	-(0%)	7(88%)	1(12%)	-(0%)
Cso	*27[-]	15(56%)	10(37%)	-(0%)	2(7%)
Dr	3[-]	2(67%)	-(0%)	-(0%)	1(33%)
E	*21[1]	13(62%)	6(29%)	-(0%)	1(5%)
F	*15[1]	6(40%)	6(40%)	-(0%)	2(13%)
G	2[1]	1(50%)	-(0%)	-(0%)	-(0%)
H	-[-]	-	-	-	-
I	6[1]	2(33%)	3(50%)	-(0%)	-(0%)
MG	-[-]	-	-	-	-
OG	5[1]	3(60%)	1(20%)	-(0%)	-(0%)
PC	10[-]	6(60%)	3(30)%	-(0%)	1(9%)
Pl	*20[1]	11(55%)	3(15%)	1(5%)	4(20%)
R	1[-]	1(100%)	-(0%)	-(0%)	-(0%)
Sc	11[-]	4(36%)	5(45%)	1(9%)	1(9%)
T	3[-]	-(0%)	3(100%)	-(0%)	-(0%)
W	-[-]	-	-	-	-
	-[-]	-	-	-	-

Key: * activity with adequate N
     - significantly above or below
       expectation

For example, response is a function of, or is constrained by, surrounding activity [R = f(Ay)]. Eight constraints on response (L, I, Ay, Ab, Ac, RP, RE, V) were tested. Six constraints on learner's act (L, S, I, Ay, Ab, RE), two on learner's ability or degree of participation (L and Ay), and three on values (S, I, Ay) were tested. The tests were accomplished by resorting the 516 11-word strings similar to those in Figure 7.1 that represented the 516 observations. For each statement, the strings were sorted first by culture and then by the predicted constraints with a separate pile for each possible constraint being tested.

Figures 7.4a, 7.4b, and 7.4c picture the process for the statement R = f(Ay). There are 68 possible specific, state-related constraints and 68 separate possible piles of strings because response has 4 possible codes—affirmation of the learn-

Figure 7.4b
Sample Sort R = f(Ay): Number and Percent of Strings in Each Pile, Midwest United States

MIDWEST UNITED STATES

Activity	Response & % Expected Total No. [Blanks]	A(55%) A	D(24%) D	M(7%) M	N(10%) N
		Number & % Each Response			
Cf	*24[1]	11(46%)	10(42%)	1(4%)	1(4%)
Cn	1[-]	-(0%)	1(4%)	-(0%)	-(0%)
Cso	*44[-]	25(57%)	16(36%)	2(5%)	1(2%)
Dr	4[-]	2(50%)	1(25%)	-(0%)	1(25%)
E	*34[2]	18(53%)	7(21%)	3(8%)	4(12%)
F	*19[-]	7(37%)	10(52%)	1(5%)	1(5%)
G	-[-]	-	-	-	-
H	-[-]	-	-	-	-
I	7[1]	3(43%)	-(0%)	-(0%)	-(43%)
MG	2[-]	-(0%)	-(0%)	-(0%)	2(100%)
OG	9[1]	4(44%)	1(11%)	1(11%)	2(22%)
PC	*20[-]	15(75%)	1(5%)	2(16%)	2(10%)
Pl	*46[2]	31(67%)	6(13%)	3(7%)	4(9%)
R	1[-]	1(100%)	-(0%)	-(0%)	-(0%)
Sc	*50[4]	29(58%)	8(16%)	3(6%)	6(12%)
T	6[-]	2(33%)	3(50%)	1(17%)	-(0%)
W	1[1]	-	-	-	-
	1[1]	-	-	-	-

Key: * activity with adequate N
    - significantly above or below
      expectation

er's behaviors (A), denial of their acceptability (D), mixed affirmation/denial (M), and nonresponsive acceptance (NR)—while activities has 17 possible codes—caring for (Cf), conflict (Cn), general socializing (CSO), drawing and painting (Dr), exchanging information (E), eating (F), gift giving (G), health activity (H), organized games and sports (OG), primary conversion (PC), playing (Pl), religious and ritual acts (R), secondary conversion (SC), traveling (T), and doing things defined as wrong or criminal (W).[4]

To determine whether the strings in the piles of adequate size, that is, those large enough to exceed the expected error of observation,[5] exhibited a proposed constraint, the number of statements in each pile was compared to the number expected if that pile matched the average pattern for the culture. Since this was not a search for theoretical variation from a norm, but for high-visibility con-

Figure 7.4c
Sample Sort R = f(Ay): Number and Percent of Strings in Each Pile, Zinacantan

ZINACANTAN

Activity	Response & % Expected Total No. [Blanks]	A(20%) A	D(6%) Number & % Each Response D	M(1%) M	N(17%) N
Cf	4[2]	1(25%)	-(0%)	-(0%)	1(25%)
Cn	1[-]	-(0%)	-(0%)	-(0%)	1(100%)
Cso	6[5]	1(17%)	-(0%)	-(0%)	-(0%)
Dr	-[-]	-	-	-	-
E	6[3]	2(33%)	-(0%)	-(0)	1(17%)
F	-[-]	-	-	-	-
G	-[-]	-	-	-	-
H	4[1]	2(50%)	-(0%)	-(0%)	1(25%)
I	* 5[1]	1(20%)	-(0%)	1(20%)	2(40%)
MG	2[-]	-(0%)	1(50%)	-(0%)	1(50%)
OG	-[-]	-	-	-	-
PC	*19[14]	1(5%)	1(5%)	-(0%)	3(16%)
Pl	4[3]	-(0%)	-(0%)	-(0%)	1(25%)
R	*21[12]	4(19%)	1(5%)	-(0%)	5(24%)
Sc	3[3]	-	-	-	-
T	2[2]	-	-	-	-
W	1[1]	-	-	-	-
	10[4]	3(30%)	3(30%)	-(0%)	-(0%)

Key: * activity with adequate N
     - significantly above or below
       expectation

straints that could come to the attention of a child or young adult learner, it was assumed that a constraint existed only if the number of strings in the clump varied noticeably from the general expectation.[6] The constraints discovered are displayed visually in Figure 7.5. The stronger constraints are depicted by the thicker lines. The percentages shown are the proportions of eligible string piles that clearly exhibited the predicted constraint. Weaker constraints, those affecting 6–9 percent of the categorical string piles, are indicated by the thinnest lines and the percentages are not given.

When these constraints are described non-mathematically, we learn that the single strongest constraint upon the learning experience of Israeli children (the arrow labeled 48 percent) is the way the child chooses to relate to whatever it is she or he finds going on (labeled "ability"). A detailed analysis of the string

Figure 7.5
Pattern of Constraints

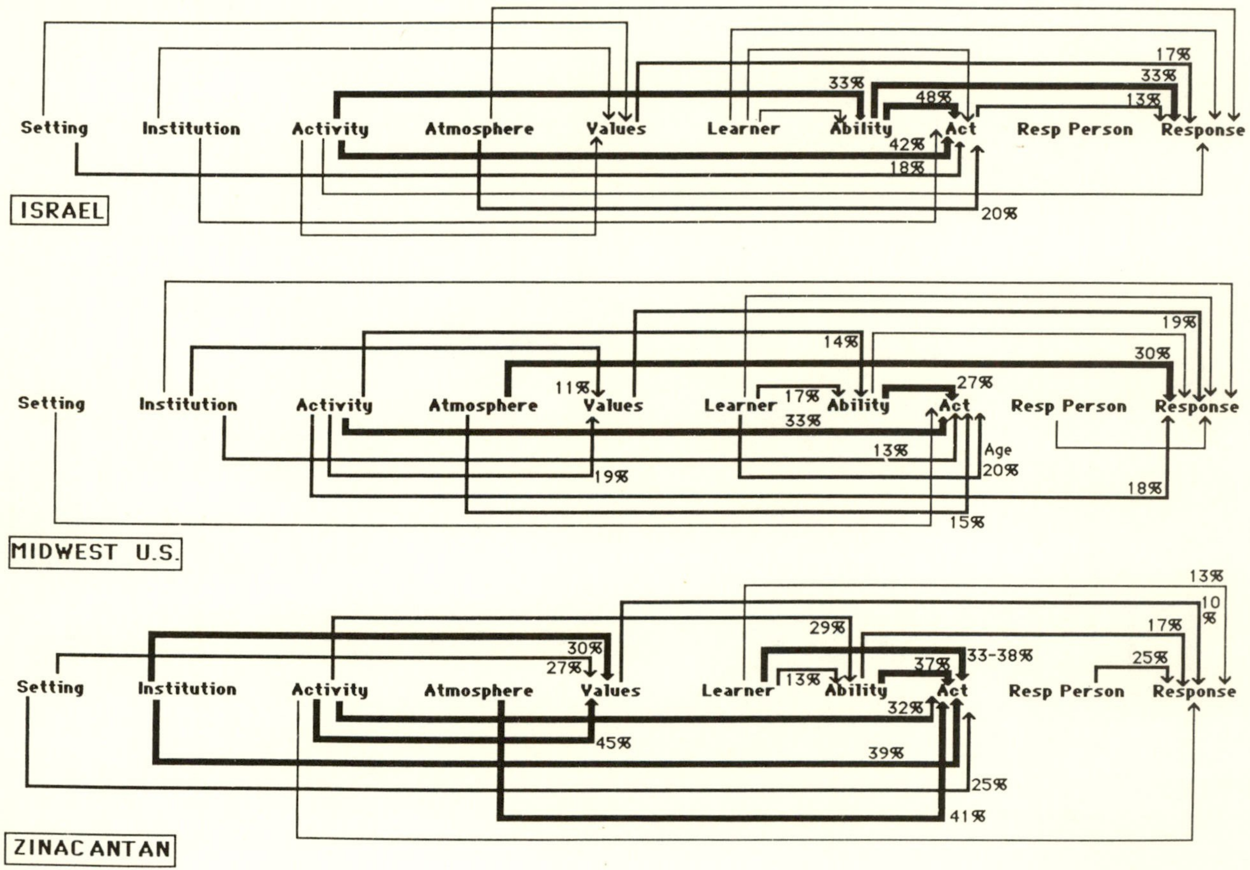

piles shows that interference and nonparticipation on the learner's part are directly and strongly associated with lower rates of positive responses and higher rates of negative ones. For Israeli children, the general ongoing activity also creates a strong constraint upon their learning experiences, so strong, in fact, that nearly one in any two of their acts would be coded in the same category as the ongoing activity. Another constraint, but a moderate one, upon response is values. Examination of the string piles shows that when adults cite values related to age and sex standards, negative responses replace positive ones. However, the citation of values about achievement or worthwhile human attainments is accompanied by a moderately increased level of positive responses. The learning effects associated with the varying emotional atmospheres in which we observed Israeli children are also interesting. Negative social atmospheres, particularly, affect child behaviors, leading to a moderate increase in quarreling but an overall decline in social engagement.

In the United States, too, activity provided a strong constraint on child acts (see Figure 7.5). Thirty-three percent of the activity types led to acts on the children's part that replicated the on-going activity or were coded in the same category. Analysis of the strings in the piles indicated that participation type was moderately constrained by the child's age. As was also true in Israel, older girls were the least likely to participate, remaining uninvolved. Unlike in Israel, in the United States adult response to children was little constrained by the type of participation the children chose. Rather, emotionally charged atmospheres provided the highest cultural constraint upon response, pulling the responses to learners toward the negative and mixed response categories. For example, the data indicated that atmospheres of celebration and quarreling and those with mixed elements increased negative responses. Activity also constrained response. Mealtime activities and situations in which children were being cared for also increased negative response at a moderate level, while work situations such as gardening or cooking raised the positive response level. The U.S. data, too, showed a moderate constraint upon response by values, with 15 percent of all response types exhibiting a specific pattern. When the situation was such that work or health-related values applied, the level of negative responses was raised.

Generally, the acts of Zinacanteco children replicated what the adults were doing but the children's acts were strongly specific to institution and moderately constrained by general setting. For example, string analysis indicated that informal social behavior strongly decreased when children were in compound and house settings and in economic institutions such as markets, and when children were in ritual or economic situations, information seeking decreased. Emotional atmosphere provided the highest constraint on child acts, particularly with respect to the selection of play and ritual acts. A serious atmosphere was associated with an increase in ritual acts by children, whereas a more solemn, deferential atmosphere apparently excluded children from ritual activity, freeing them to engage in more play acts. However, reports exist for only 39 percent of the incidents. Age and sex also constrained learning behavior to a moderate degree.

Younger children participated less, asked fewer questions, and did less work. Girls also asked fewer questions but participated more. They engaged in more work than did boys, but they performed fewer ritual acts. Contrary to trends in Israel and the United States, positive responses increased when children interfered in adult activity. This is probably indicative of an adult tendency to approve of children's attempts at participation even if they fail.

When the constraint patterns are compared across cultures it can be seen that constraint structures themselves differ by culture. Analysis of the specific constraints on responses provides a dramatic example. In the United States emotionally charged atmospheres provided the highest cultural constraint upon responses; 30 percent of these showed clear, specific constraints pulling the responses to learners toward the negative and mixed categories. In Israel, the child's manner of relating to the activity (that is, ability or participation) provided the greatest constraint upon response, 33 percent. This is in itself an interesting finding because Americans do not picture themselves as an emotionally volatile people, whereas they do picture Israelis in that way.[7] In Zinacantan, emotional atmosphere did not seem to constrain the responses given to children at all.

To provide some other examples of cross-cultural differences in learning patterns as displayed in Figure 7.5, we note that in Zinacantan, the role and status of the responding person created the strongest constraint upon response, 25 percent. In Israel, the age, sex, or status of the responding person showed no effect upon response, perhaps indicating a marked overall cultural uniformity in response to children. The constraining effects of the age and sex of the learner were also culturally uneven, with older girls participating less than other children in Israel and the United States and more in Zinacantan. Or, to look at larger patterns, in the upper Midwest, the people we observed tended not to respond to children directly but to the general social situation and to the emotional atmosphere of that situation in particular. In Zinacantan and Israel, however, overall adult responses to children were not as strongly constrained by situational factors. There, more immediate factors, such as the learner's age and sex, the child's choice of participation type, and the applicable values, all provided a greater proportion of the constraints on response.

Taken as a whole, the constraints predicted by the functional statements do seem to exist at some modest level. On the average, 17 percent of the string clumps over the three cultures displayed the effects of the constraints. This is a very mild level of constraint because it measures the cumulative effects of factors that are quite specific, such as whether child interference leads to a positive response and the citation of human relations values or to a negative response and no value citation or to the use of a gender expectation value. But not all of the predicted constraints were found in all three cultures. Two of the constraints— response is a function of learner's act $[R = f (Ac)]$ and response is a function of institution $[R = f (I)]$—were not found in two cultures and three additional ones— that is, response is a function of responding person $[R = f (RP)]$, of atmosphere $[R = f (Atm)]$, and of setting $[V = f (S)]$—were not demonstrated for one culture each. The remaining 14 constraints appeared as predicted in all three cultures, indicating that the functional statements provide a fair description of the culture acquistion/transmission process in general, but require reformulation to achieve accuracy.

The Constraining Functions of Social Factors

The second analytic procedure that uses the 11 functional statements addresses the hypothesized centrality of social structure. The summary functional statement as expressed in 11, above, suggests that the social structural components that create any situation in which a learner is found, namely, setting (S), institution (I), and activity (Ay), are the critical components in the shaping of learning and, therefore, for the understanding of the patterns of culture acquisition and cultural transmission. An examination of the average rank of each of the nine factors as a constraint over all three cultures will provide some evidence to sustain or cast doubt upon this statement:[8]

Factor:	Activity	Ability	Atmos.	Values	Setting
Rank:	8.8	7.7	6.2	5.3	4.7

Factor:	Instit.	RespPers	Learner	Act
Rank:	3.8	3.7	3.5	2.5

The greatest degree of constraint is that created by the ongoing activity in a milieu, one of the major predicted social factors. If we look back at Figure 7.5, we can see that activity constrains children's acts in such a way that over 32 percent to 42 percent of them represent a replication of the general activity pattern of the milieu. Ongoing activities also create moderate levels of constraint upon the way children choose to relate to activity through participation, withdrawal, or interference and upon the citation of values in response to children's behavior. Thus, in one sense the data here seem to support the social bases of the functional statements: the single greatest constraint is created by a social structural factor. However, the major role predicted for setting and institution as constraints is not confirmed. These social structural constraints rank fifth and sixth, respectively. Settings and institutions seem to create strong constraints upon what children do and how adults respond to them only in Zinacantan. This may stem from the fact that there is a sharp division between settings and institutions that belong to the Zinacanteco cultural milieu and those that are foreign; or this finding may be an artifact of the use of ethnographers' reports, in which data have been grouped and patterned by the ethnographer for presentation to the reader.

The second ranking constraint is the child's ability or type of participation. Ability may be defined as a psychosocial factor, since it describes the pivotal stance taken by the child which, at any single moment, relates him or her as an individual to the society at large. Ability was tested only for its constraining effect upon children's acts and upon response. It stood to reason that ability should be highly constraining of act. The effect of ability in constraining response, however, was less predictable and, in fact, is high only in Israeli data.

Because ability is not a social structural factor, a much weaker constraint for ability upon values was predicted, collapsed functional statement 11, where ability appears as a term only once. However, because of the high constraint ability had upon response in Israel and its high average function, the decision was made to check the degree to which ability would constrain citation of values. The hypothesis that the constraint would be weak was not supported. The result, using the sorting methods and minimum size standards described in the preceding section, indicated that ability constrained values cited for 7 percent of the value/ability categories for Israel and the United States and not at all for Zinacantan. When the rankings for constraint factors were recalculated to take account of the constraint exerted by ability on values, the rank of the constraining factor provided by ability was reduced only for Zinacantan but for the three societies taken together it was not changed.

The third- and fourth-ranking constraints are atmosphere and values, which might be characterized as psychosocial and ideological-cognitive constraints, respectively. Thus, the strongly social structural assumptions behind the original functional statements cannot be accepted. Settings, institutions, and the organization of activities do not appear to be responsible for the major constraints on learning factors. However, the picture created by these rankings does generally confirm the utility of a broad sociocultural position over an individually oriented psychological one. Individual factors—who the responding person is, the age and/or sex of the learner, and the learner's specific act—provide the lowest general levels of constraint. Within the separate cultures, in all cases, two of these constraints rank among the bottom three, but one of the individual psychological constraints—but different for each case ("act" in Israel, "learner" in the United States, and "responding person" in Zinacantan)—does seem to provide a moderate (and perhaps culturally pivotal) constraint on the form of children's learning experiences.

The Cumulative Constraining Ability of Linked Functions

The third analytic procedure that uses the 11 functional statements addresses linkages between them. It queries whether the learner's knowledge results from these functions operating in a progressive or cumulative manner. Specifically, it asks whether the multiple constraining factors, which make up the loops between "learner" and "deposit of cultural knowledge" on the systems model (Figure 7.3) and which are laid out in the complete functional statements (1–11 above), create progressively stronger total constraints as predicted in these loops and statements. It is difficult to test this, because the nonduplicated data set contains a total of only 516 strings which reduces the total strings in each pile to a number below the error rate in many categories (see Figure 7.4a–7.4c for examples). Consequently, it seemed reasonable to perform no more than a few sorts designed to test the probable utility of the assumption of progressive, cumulative constraint. A positive result would suggest that pursuit of research based on the functional statements (revised, of course, in accordance with the findings above) would be worth the time and effort.

The first test investigated the question of joint progessive constraint upon learning by institution, one of the weaker constraints (rank 3.8), and by activity, the strongest constraint (rank 8.8). Both of these social structural constraints originally were predicted to have strong effects in the functional statements. A finding of culturally unique patterning for institution/activity combinations would be essential to the maintenance of the radical socially structural learning theory inherent in statement 11.

The strings were first sorted for institution/activity combinations. The three cultures made use of only 55 of the logically possible 144 institution/activity combinations (see Table 5.2 Chapter 5 for lists of all the possible major classes of institutions and activities). Of these, 13 institution/activity combinations were used by all three cultures, 8 were shared by two cultures, and 34 were used by only one of the cultures each. The constellation of institution/activity groups was thus unique for each culture. Since the researchers who collected the Israeli and U.S. data were not limited to particular settings by their data-gathering directives (except that they were asked to avoid schools) and the Zinacanteco data is taken from a number of ethnographies with varying foci, we see no reason to believe that a larger sample would show a patterning that was essentially different from this, although more institution/activity types would be seen for each culture.

Four sorts were then made to test the statements $R = f(I, Ay)$, $V = f(I, Ay)$, $Ab = f(I, Ay)$, and $Ac = f(I, Ay)$, that is, response, values, child's ability to participate, and child's act are each functions of institution *and* activity.[9] Figure 7.6 displays the results of the four combined institution-activity sorts. For one-half of the combined statements tested, the constraining effect of institution and activity taken together exceeds the *sum* of the two effects taken separately. In another five cases, the number of significantly constrained string clumps exceeds the *average* of the separate constraints. In one case, less constraint seems to be indicated for the combination. In other words, when we consider activity and institution together, we find that the result is generally a higher level of constraint upon response, values, child's ability, and child's act than results from either of these separately.

A second test used constraints that were not social-structural and were therefore predicted by the functional statements to have smaller cumulative effects. For this, a sort was performed using Israeli data only. Since previous work had indicated that the constellations of activity, ability, and atmosphere formed culturally unique distributions (Dobbert and Pitman 1983a), the statements selected for this test were response is a function of surrounding activity and child's ability to participate, $R = f (Ay, Ab)$; response is a function of surrounding activity and

Figure 7.6
Multiple Constraint Test for I/Ay

	NEW TEST			COMPARISON WITH SEPARATE FUNCTIONS	
Functional Statement	Culture		% High Level Constraints	Average Constraint (I + Ay/2)	Sum Constraint (I + Ay)
R = f(I/Ay)	I		15%	3%	5%
	U		10%	13%	26%
	Z		13%	4%	8%
V = f(I/Ay)	I		20%	8%	15%
	U		22%	15%	30%
	Z		17%	38%	75%
Ab = f(I/Ay)	I		50%	17%	33%
	U		41%	7%	14%
	Z		17%	15%	29%
Ac = f(I/Ay)	I		46%	25%	49%
	U		37%	23%	46%
	Z		64%	36%	71%

atmosphere, $R = f(Ay, RE)$; and response is a function of surrounding activity, child's ability to participate, and atmosphere combined, $R = f(Ay, Ab, RE)$. For all three statements, sorting revealed that the levels of constraint exceed the *average* for the individual constraints. For $R = f(Ay, Ab)$ and $R = f(Ay, RE)$, the combined constraint for the combined functions also exceeded the *total* for the two single constraints. Israeli responses to children, then, are constrained by multiple factors *taken together*, by activity *and* child's ability *and* atmosphere *and* act. These two tests seem to indicate that the constraints do work cumulatively and that some support can be found in field data for the general manner in which the functional statements are laid out in the systems model.

Taken together, the three analytic procedures that use functional statements suggest that the constraints appear to function in a holistic, systemic manner. The tests also suggest that such functional statements can be linked together and will prove useful in the study of patterning in the culture acquisition/transmission process.[10] But the cumulative constraint tests also seem to be in accord with the single constraint tests in suggesting that the minor role defined in the functional statements for nonstructural constraints (for example, the psychosocial constraints such as ability and emotional atmosphere) is incorrect. The results in both cases indicate that the functional statements require major revision using a broader perspective than the strictly social-structural one that lay behind the original formulation tested here. A new formulation would require greater emphasis upon the constraints supplied by psychosocial and cognitive-ideological factors.

USING A METHOD BASED ON A LINGUISTIC ANALOGY IN ORDER TO CLARIFY PATTERN

The third analytic experiment devised to reveal the precise and detailed diversity of human learning as a holistic systemic process with society-wide patterning is based on a linguistic analogy. Because of the high level of complexity involved in the structuring of natural human language, it seems sensible to suggest that a solution to the search for patterning in culture acquisition/transmission data might be found in the data analytic methods of structural linguists. Methods that are capable of simplifying language structures for pattern analysis might also be useful in simplifying cultural structures.[11]

The following data analysis method uses four major notions constructed as analogies to procedures used in transformational, generative linguistics. First, each data string is conceived of as a sentence in an absolutely positional language, one in which position in the sentence structure defines an absolute grammatical function. Second, the sentences are conceived of as having a basic grammar in which a well-formed utterance requires five elements: an institution, an atmosphere, participation, values, and a response. The remaining elements of the string are then conceived of as modifiers.[12] Third, the idea of bipolarity, in which any element must be defined as taking one of only two possible states (Jakobsen,

Fant & Halle 1956), has been borrowed from the procedural tools of this type of linguistics and used as a *temporary simplification* device during initial data sorting only. Fourth, the idea of "markedness" has also been borrowed. The key elements are then conceived of as existing in either the marked or unmarked state. Thus, a learning situation that takes place in some formal institution is considered a marked element and a learning situation that is informal is considered normal, or unmarked. The choice of formal institution for the marked condition is based upon the fact that increasing levels of formal institutionalization are marks of cultural complexity and are not necessary to the lifeways of *Homo sapiens*. An atmosphere is considered unmarked if it is a common, even atmosphere in which behavioral evidence of moderate or high levels of either adrenalin or parasympathetic system hormone flow is absent. Children's choice of participation type is considered marked only if the child interferes with the ongoing activity, while direct participation and noninvolvement, which was the case in over 80 percent of all incidents, is considered normal and unmarked. Values are considered marked when stated or clearly implied and unmarked if not signaled as part of the response to the child. Responses are classed as normal and unmarked if they are positive and affirming or accepting and neutral because, again, responses in these two classes made up the majority of responses in all cultures. Responses containing decidedly negative elements are classified as marked. Taken as a whole, the marked conditions are indicative of cultural or psychosocial emphasis.

The entire set of strings[13] was then sorted by culture according to degree of markedness. Strings with no marked elements went into one pile; those with only one marked element were placed in one of five piles, a separate one for each element. For each unique combination of two, three, or four marked elements a separate pile was created. Strings with all five marked elements were put into a final pile. The strings ended up in piles that, when sorted by activity class, produced highly uniform groups by age and sex. The patterns were so clear and the strays so few that the configuration of strings in each pile looked as if someone had successfully sorted the data for similarity.[14]

The strings in Figure 7.1 illustrate a sample of the results from the foregoing sort. The figure displays all the nonduplicated strings for completely unmarked, unstressed situations for Israeli children, that is, for situations in which the children are not found in institutional settings (except in kibbutz situations), where atmospheres are even, where values are not cited, and where responses to the children are positive or neutral. Since we have defined the unstressed condition as the neutral or normal case based on the theoretical consideration cited above, analysis of patterns in culture acquisition begins with these incidents and moves outward to conditions of increasing stress or markedness. It is therefore important to determine the relative frequency of this pattern in relation to other, stressed patterns. For the total Israeli set, the proportion of completely unstressed situations is 26 percent. Results for the complete U.S. set are identical: 26 percent of the incidents are entirely unstressed. For Zinacantan, it is a bit more difficult to derive a reliable count of unstressed situations because there are many blanks in the strings, which were derived from published data. Based on the assumption that a good ethnographer would not fail to make note of marked conditions, one can estimate that 47 percent of the Zinacanteco strings were completely unmarked and neutral. A second, quite different figure was derived from a subset of the data that contained only those cases in which responses to children were specifically reported. This subset contained only 46 strings; of these just 14, or 30 percent, were completely unstressed. Both outcomes are considered in the analysis below.

The percentage and number of strings for all conditions of markedness for all three societies are listed in the first row of each response-type entry in Figure 7.7. From this we can see that the completely unstressed condition does constitute the most frequent one in all three societies. The entire distribution, in which the frequencies decrease toward the right and bottom as the degree of markedness increases, tends to support the theoretical assumption that the unmarked situations are indeed the basic or neutral ones from which the others are derived. The distributions also suggest that the cultures' uses of marked situations and responses may be distinct. The second and third most common conditions vary by society. For Israel the second most common condition was related to social situations in themselves unmarked or unstressed, but in which responses were stressed through use of values to underscore them. The condition that had the third highest frequency in Israel was the class of situations with marked atmospheres in which the response was doubly stressed by use of a negative plus a value. For the United States, the second most frequent string type was formalized or ritual situations in which responses remained unstressed. The next most common types represented situations with marked atmospheres but unstressed responses and formal/ritualized situations with values stressed. For Zinacantan, the second and third most frequent types were formal/ritualized situations with unstressed responses and formalized or ritualized situations with marked atmospheres and simple positive responses.

If the actual strings in the piles for each separate level of markedness are examined, they reveal further patterning. The letter notations, the second entry under each condition in Figure 7.7, indicate the age group and sex of the children who are the primary recipients of each class of response in each type of situation. The decimal figures below that indicate the percentage of uniformity of the pattern for that level of markedness. A high degree of patterning in the treatment of children is indicated, since the distribution of the various classes of responses in different kinds of social situations vary systematically by the age and sex of the child.

When the strings within each separate situation pile in Figure 7.7 are sorted by activity, it is quite easy, beginning with the basic informal situation and following the linguistic analogy, to generate the transformational rules behind any given portion of the distribution. For example, the transformational rules for situations in which people are chatting and eating in Israel are as follows

Figure 7.7
Strings by Markedness and Uniformity

Place	Social Markedness	Positive Response W/out Stress	Positive Response w Values	Negative Response w/out Stress	Negative Response w Values
ISRAEL:	Completely Unstressed	26% (41) YG .63	21% (34) YB .82	4% (6) YCH (YG) 1.00 (.67)	6% (10) G .80
	Formalized or Ritualized	4% (7) YCH 1.00	1% (1) --	0 --	1% (2) MX --
	Marked Atmosphere	4% (6) YB 1.00	4% (6) YB .83	1% (2) YCH 1.00	11% (18) YCH .65
	Formalized w Marked Atmos	1% (1) --	1% (1) --	0 --	1% (1) --
	Child Interferes	1% (1) --	1% (1) --	1% (1) --	3% (4) B .75
	Formalized & Child Interferes	1% (1) --	0 --	1% (1) --	2% (3) YB 1.00
	Marked Atmos & Child Interferes	0 --	0 --	3% (5) YCH .80	3% (5) YB & OG .60, .40
	Formal, Marked Atmos & Interf	0 --	0 --	1% (1) --	1% (1) --
	Total Responses This Type	36% (57)	27% (43)	10% (16)	27% (43)
U.S.:	Completely Unstressed	26% (79) G|YG .86|.65	6% (19) YCH .68	3% (8) OG .50	2% (7) MX --
	Formalized or Ritualized	9% (28) YCH .77	7% (20) B (OB) .80 (.35)	2% (6) (YCH, B) .67, .67	4% (11) B|OB .91|.64
	Marked Atmosphere	7% (20) YG .60	2% (6) YB .67	2% (6) G .83	2% (5) (B |OB) 2 observers
	Formalized w Marked Atmos	3% (8) YG .63	3% (8) B|OB .87|.75	1% (2) MX --	2% (6) B (OB) .67 (.50)
	Child Interferes	4% (12) YCH|YB .92|.67	3% (8) B .75	2% (6) YCH (G) .83 (.67)	2% (5) OCH .8
	Formalized & Child Interferes	1% (2) YCH 1.00	0% (1) --	0 --	0% (1) --
	Marked Atmos & Child Interferes	1% (4) YG 1.00	1% (3) (OB) .67	1% (4) YG 1.00	2% (7) OB .86
	Formal, Marked Atmos & Interf	0% (1) --	0 --	1% (3) YCH 1.00	2% (6) YCH|YB .80|.67
	Total Responses This Type	51% (154)	22% (65)	12% (35)	16% (48)

Figure 7.7 Continued

Place	Social Markedness	Positive Response W/out Stress	Positive Response w Values	Negative Response w/out Stress	Negative Response w Values
ZINA-CANTAN:	Completely Unstressed	47% (51) [29%-14] ALL basic	6% (7) [4%-2] mx --	1% (1) [2%-1] --	2% (2) [4%-2] MX
	Formalized or Ritualized	16% (17) [15%-7] ALL basic	3% (3) [2%-1] OCH 1.00	1% (1) [2%-1] --	0 --
	Marked Atmosphere	4% (4) [6%-3] YCH .75	2% (2) [2%-1] (YCH) 1.00	1% (1) [2%-1] --	1% (1) [2%-1] --
	Formalized w Marked Atmos	9% (10) [13%-6] FOCH .90	4% (4) [7%-3] OCH 1.00	0 --	0 --
	Child Interferes	2% (2) [4%-2] (YCH) 1 observer	2% (2) [4%-2] (YCH) 1 observer	1% (1) [2%-1] --	0 --
	Formalized & Child Interferes	0 --	0 --	0 --	0 --
	Marked Atmos & Child interferes	1% (1) [0] --	0 --	0 --	0 --
	Formal, Marked Atmos & Interf	0 --	0 --	0 --	0 --
	Total Responses This Type	79% (85) [67%-32]	17% (18) [19%-9]	4% (4) [8%-4]	3% (3) [6%-3]

KEY:

G = Girl	YG = Young Girl	OG = Older Girl	MX = Mixed	( ) = Possible Pattern
B = Boy	YB = Young Boy	OG = Older Boy	-- = Too Few to	¦ = Especially
CH = Child	YCH = Young Child	OCH = Older Child	calculate	[ ] = Stated Responses

(percentage figures indicate the degree of uniformity for the trait specified as a percentage of all the strings fitting the general class described):

IF chatting and eating take place in an *informal* situation at home or in the kibbutz dining room and the child is a *young girl* (82 percent), THEN the response will be *positive and unstressed*.

IF the *atmosphere* is marked, the situation *formalized*, and/or the child *interferes* AND IF the child is *young* (100 percent) THEN, response will remain *unstressed* and *positive*.

IF the child is an *older girl* (45 percent) OR a girl *outside* (67 percent) the activity, THEN response will be *negative* and stressed with a *value*.

IF the child is a *boy* (69 percent), especially a *young boy* (54 percent), a *value* will be added to the positive response, BUT if the boy *interferes* (100 percent) the response will be *negative* and frequently stressed with *values*.

Comparable rules generated for the United States start at the same point but develop differently:

IF chatting and eating take place in an *informal* situation at home and the child is a *young girl* (73 percent), THEN, the response will be *positive and unstressed*.

IF the *atmosphere* is marked, the situation *formalized*, and/or the child *interferes* AND IF the child is *young* (89 percent), especially if he/she *interferes* (100 percent), the response becomes a simple *negative*. Similarly, if the child is *older* (67 percent) OR remains *outside* the activity the response becomes a simple *negative*.

IF the child is a *boy* (89 percent), especially an *older boy* (56 percent), whether the situation is *marked* or *unmarked*, THEN *values* will be added to the positive response.

IF the *atmosphere* is marked, the situation *formalized*, and the child is a *boy* who *interferes* (75 percent) or *does not participate* (64 percent), especially if the responding person is *not a parent* (43 percent), THEN response becomes *negative* or *negative* stressed with *values*.

IN situations in which the *atmosphere* is marked, the situation *formalized*, and/or the child *interferes*, IF the response remains *unstressed*, the child will be *young* (85 percent), likely a *young girl* (69 percent).

IF the chatting and eating take place in a setting *away from home* (100 percent) OR if the child is a *boy* and the situation is *institutionalized* (75 percent), THEN the response becomes *negative*.

As can be seen, the patterns are quite clear and strongly predictive, but far from deterministic. Further, the specific type of sorting used here, based on a five-element basic "sentence," helps bring out the pattern formation found in the remaining elements, such as the relevance of group size or responding person.

CONCLUSIONS

This chapter has presented three data analysis experiments conducted for the purposes of discovering the patterns that may govern and structure culture acquisition-transmission processes cross-culturally. While all of the methods reported on appear to produce precise, useful results when tested on a small body of experimental data, it is not clear at this point whether any of them is capable of providing clear, vigorous, intuitively elegant results when applied to the larger ethnographic record. Nevertheless, educational anthropologists who follow the canons of science must search for methodologies that produce lawlike statements describing the culture acquisition/transmission process. Educational ethnography, itself, is capable of providing thick description but not lawlike generalizations relating to culture acquisition/transmission. Such generalizations are necessary if we wish to apply the insights we have gained through anthropological research to the amelioration of educational problems, and move the field toward more fruitful theory. The history of science has clearly demonstrated that in the long run, practical utility derives from solid theory. In anthropology and education, we are moving in the direction of theory development.

NOTES

1. Code symbols for the unrevised data categories may be found in Chapter 5, Table 2. The revised group code, an interim one that preceded Table A.1, uses two units, the first letter indicates group size: S = small, M = Medium; the second letter indicates majority composition: P = parents and sibling, M = mixed, C = unrelated children, 1C = children of one sex, K = kin, 1a = adults of one sex, s = strangers, o = other class or ethnic group. The revised code for responding person shows relative sex when it is a two-letter code. The first letter indicates same sex (S) as learner observed or opposite sex (O). The second letter gives status or relationship: P = parent, a or A = unrelated adult, k = kin, F = occupant of formal titled status, S = sibling, C = unrelated child, a "/" indicates a second major responding person. Since the number of possible code combinations per string is so high (over 360 million) only contiguous strings from the same observation set are coded identically, which means that these densely coded strings do not lose individuality.

2. Coders for the data used here were J. Gamradt, R. Eisikovits, K. Chun, and M. Dobbert. The initial analysis, for 6- to 12-year-olds in all three cultures, was designed and carried out by M. A. Pitman. Dobbert completed the 3- to 5-year-old data for the purpose of comparing younger and older children, following Pitman's original analytic organization.

3. The codes in parentheses refer to underlined letters in the category labels or to actual arrow labels, both found in Figure 7.3.

4. The activities classified under each of these terms are defined in the coding categories listed in Table 5.2. Also added for every statement test was a "blank" category for each variable to be used to avoid overestimating pattern strength by including cases in which data were missing. Of course, not all cultures necessarily used all the logically possible constraint types, or if they did, researchers did not observe them.

5. As in chapter 6, Schroedinger's standard estimate of error. See Weinberg 1975.

6. It had to vary by at least twice the error rate, rounded upward to the nearest 5 percent, in small distributions—that is, 20 percent for Israel, 15 percent for the United States, and 20 percent for Zinacantan—or it had to double half the expected rate in large distributions, where there were generally over 100 possible clumps per culture.

7. The data do also explain the apparently self-contradictory U.S. view of Israelis as more volatile than themselves. Activities coded as "having a conflict" and conflictive atmospheres are slightly more common in Israel than in the United States, though by no means very frequent and not a great deal more frequent than in the United States. The rates for conflictive atmosphere are 11 percent for Israeli data and 8 percent for U.S. data; for conflictive activity, 6 percent for Israel and 1 percent for the United States.

8. Average rankings, calculated by listing constraints from highest to lowest percentage for each culture and taking the simple average over the cultures, are used to avoid undue weight created by the high Zinacanteco constraint figures. The latter are the result of our using data taken from ethnographic reports, rather than from raw field observations.

9. The methods of determining significant constraint were similar to those described above for the two-by-two constraint tests except that the clumps accepted as evidence for significant constraint included all those with strings derived from the data of at least three different observers. Additionally, low-frequency acts and values, those that appeared in only 1 percent–3 percent of the observations, were omitted.

10. It is also possible that the use of statistical techniques such as path or causal analysis in conjunction with the structures suggested in the functional statements would help to determine patterning.

11. Eisikovits, in the context of a year-long series of conversations with Dobbert about the nature of science, levels of complexity in physical and human data, and the philosophical implications of varied types of data-coding schemes, originally proposed that the concepts of transformational, generative linguistics might be of use in the search for patterns in culture acquisition/transmission data. Dobbert later developed the methods described here which arose from her experience as a research subject in a foreign language teaching experiment based on the language analysis principles of Chomsky, Jakobsen, Fante, and Halle. For the most part, however, the method is not directly or formally derived from their work.

12. The choice of these five elements as the backbone of the grammar was made on the basis of the results of previous analyses which suggested that these would provide the key elements for comparing culture acquisition processes cross-culturally (Dobbert and Pitman 1983a, 1983b; Dobbert 1984).

13. Five strings from the total set had to be discarded since they did not contain enough information to sustain this type of analysis; hence, the total number of strings sorted was 571.

14. These results were astounding and absolutely unexpected. During the two previous years Dobbert had attempted to sort the strings by similarity several times, basing the similarity sorts on various approaches. Each attempt was a failure. None of the sorts created anthropologically recognizable groupings of similar strings.

8 Facilitating Comparison in Culture Acquisition Research: Developing a Coding System

The several tests of our data collection method and data coding systems indicated that some of the ethnographically derived codes either could not be used reliably or failed to adequately distinguish between cultures (see Chapters 6 and 7). While this is not surprising, scientifically speaking, it does make rethinking of the taxonomy and associated codes imperative. Our taxonomy of human learning tries to order the objective components observed in the numerous adaptions of human communities. As a taxonomy, it does not impose order, but rather attempts to represent it to researchers in a consistent manner. Within any science or area of research, theory can be developed only if the intellectual structure supporting the field permits its data to be assessed within a consistent context. To create a structure capable of supporting rigorous, strictly comparable analyses useful in theory building, classification systems must be based upon a rigorously defined, unifying logic. The existing outlines for coding both general enthographic data (Murdock 1982) and socialization/cultural transmission data (Henry 1960; Hilger 1960; Whiting, Child & Lambert 1966) as well as our own coding system as presented in Chapter 5 do not approach that kind of consistency.

Physics is often presented as a model of a successful, theoretically consistent system. The principles of physics may be examined for their usefulness as a guide for building theoretical consistency in other sciences (Sahal 1977). Such an examination would reveal that to the extent that statements of laws in the physical sciences have been successful it is because the basic variables have

Marion Lundy Dobbert and Rivka A. Eisikovits were the primary authors of this chapter. They were assisted by Mary Anne Pitman.

been defined by a few dimensions; historically, by the three dimensions of classical mechanics—mass, time, and distance (Corrsin, cited by Sahal 1977:42). Spiro (1965) has suggested that an ideal classification system for comparative studies in anthropology would also be based on a typology whose variables designate several strictly defined dimensions. Previous work in the social, biological, and behavioral sciences confirms the feasibility of investigating the structure of complex systems through the use of dimensional concepts (Naroll and von Bertalanffy 1956; von Bertalanffy 1968:65; Zipf 1949; Mayhew, James & Childers 1972; Bowden 1969; Sahal 1977).

To try to formulate lawlike generalizations related to culture acquisition, then, we must first begin to define a workable set of dimensions. We must identify a set of structural equivalents to the dimensions of physics. The theory of dimensions indicates that the actual choice of dimensions is arbitrary, and that consistency and usefulness are the most important criteria for their selection (Sahal 1977:43, 47; Luce 1971:161). This suggests pragmatic derivation based on prior work in the field. Luce notes that the dimensions of physics had their origins in actual physical observation and experimentation and are the products of "the configuration of the system and its observable physical quantities at the time of observation" (Luce 1971:158). Following Luce, we assume that dimensional consistency in the sociocultural systems described by anthropologists will likewise be founded in ethnographic descriptions and observations. We can also assume that some currently existing typologies founded upon real data may constitute protodimensions.

Therefore, we propose that the whole domain of social and cultural life surrounding learners and relating to them be considered a space, and that the entire history of broadly based research in the area of cultural transmission be thought of as defining the dimensions of that space. The dimensions selected for this revision of our coding system, then, are based on logically constructed categorization procedures found in existing ethnographic comparative studies, on experience with dimensional analysis in the study of general cultural structures (see Dobbert et al. 1984b), on structural suggestions derived from the work of anthropologists and psychologists in the areas of values and emotions, and on the results of inductive tests of various proposed dimensions against ethnographic data.

Utilizing the idea of dimensionality in a general way, we have developed an initial set of dimensions to reorganize coding. In the remainder of this chapter, we present the logic and supporting literature behind each subsection of the revised code. However, the revised coding scheme presented here cannot represent a final solution to the issues of coding and scaling in the study of culture acquisition/transmission. This is because the nature of the necessary dimensions has not been defined by broad discussion within the discipline and because the proposed dimensions have not been adequately tested against diverse bodies of data. The work presented here, then, represents an initial attempt to move our existing system toward better-defined dimensions and scales that will promote cross-cultural comparison, but it is a working revision that we expect to evolve further.

THE REVISED CODE

The initial coding scheme and categorizations were presented in Chapter 5 and illustrated in Chapter 6, with specific codes indicated in parentheses in Table 5.2. The suggested revision appears in the appendix as Table A.1.

Learner

Learners (1.1) are coded by sex (1.1.1.1) and appropriate age stage (1.1.1.2). Social age-stage classification is determined by examining the differences in the way the culture treats individuals at different ages, including various responses given at different stages, changes in expectations for behavior, differences in assignment of responsibilities to the growing or aging individual, and differences in definitions of the degree of moral accountability. Our original code assumed that the learners we would observe and study were children, and we divided childhood into four stages. However, contemporary work on age stages and the life course have made this assumption obsolete as anthropologists and other social scientists have undertaken serious studies of learning throughout the life cycle (see Chapter 3). We have therefore expanded our age-stage codes to cover adults as well. Because these stages correspond to common age-stage breaks found in many different societies, there is some overlap in age ranges included in each stage. In some societies, two of these stages may be treated as one. The eight stages include infant (I), ages 0–2; young child (Ch), ages 3–7; middle child (M), ages 6–10; older child (O), ages 9–13; postpubescent child (P), ages 13–18; young adult (Y), ages 13–24/30; middle-aged adult (A), ages 24/30–50; elder (E), ages 50+. For studies that focus on formal learning, the learner's defined stage within the observed program of deliberate instruction will also require coding. Our code (1.1.1.3) includes a space for researchers to enter the specific stages defined by any program.

Because computerized data-base programs will pull learners from any designated age range, it is also useful to code learners by chronological age. This permits researchers to experiment in order to select age stages based on optimal lumping of similarities in behaviors or other aspects of learning incidents. Such experimentation with our own data has enabled us to see that major changes in the range and style of learning experiences for children in Israel and the United States do not correspond with the culturally designated stage change marked by the watershed of school entrance, but occur later, at about age 8.

Ability to Act/Appropriateness

This classification signals the way in which the learner relates to the activity taking place in the setting entered. Unlike the previous and subsequent categories, the code for ability and appropriateness does not derive from a separate category in the structured observation or field guide but rather from researcher judgment about ability and appropriateness based on having observed the learner's activity and the responses to it. The original code used three degrees of participation and proved highly reliable, but the three-category code provided very little range for distinguishing between different culturally programmed learning styles. Test data on older teenagers and Eisikovits's work on young adult learning also showed it to be inadequate for studies beyond childhood.

The revised coding categories are now classified along two dimensions, participation and self-direction. These are organized along two axes. The horizontal axis builds upon our original code and ranges ability and appropriateness along a scale from no participation to skillful participation, but introduces a greater number of degrees of skill and involvement. The new vertical axis is concerned with the learner's degree of self-direction and dominance within the situation observed and has "learner gives direction" and "learner follows direction" at its two poles. Figure 8.1 pictures these dimensions and the types of participation and abilities that characterize a wide range of learners in many varying situations. The two dimensions combine to create a 10-category code for 1.1.2, Ability to Act/Appropriateness of Act, that has the following range: 1.1.2.1, No participation (N); 1.1.2.2, Leaves during observation (L); 1.1.2.3, Plays (Pl); 1.1.2.4, Does other work task (O); 1.1.2.5, Interruption or interference (I); 1.1.2.6, Unskillful participation (U); 1.1.2.7, Watches or asks questions (W); 1.1.2.8, Junior participation (J); 1.1.2.9, Full skillful participation (F); and 1.1.2.10, Learner initiates/directs task in setting (D). Sample behaviors associated with each category are included in Table A.1.

Responding Person

Those who respond to the learner are classified according to their closeness to or distance from the learner in terms of kinship, sex, and relative authority. The familiarity dimension and relationship factors used to build this subsection of the code are based on the same concepts as those described below for classifying the composition of the group (Figure 8.5). Characteristics of Responding Person (1.2.1), see codes along the familiarity scale in three comprehensive groups: 1.2.1.1, Parent or sibling (P); 1.2.1.2, Kin (K); and 1.2.1.3, Nonkin, and by five possible authority relationships to the learner: junior (j), client (c), equal (=), respected senior (r), and formal authority figure (f), as well as by relative sex: same (s) or opposite (o). This creates a code that will retain and display structured information about the status of the respondent in relation to the learner. It will also allow researchers to examine issues related to the way different types of individuals respond to various classes of learners, thus providing information that may be used in conjunction with data on activity, responses, and values to investigate cultural conceptions of teaching roles and

Figure 8.1
Ability to Act/Appropriateness

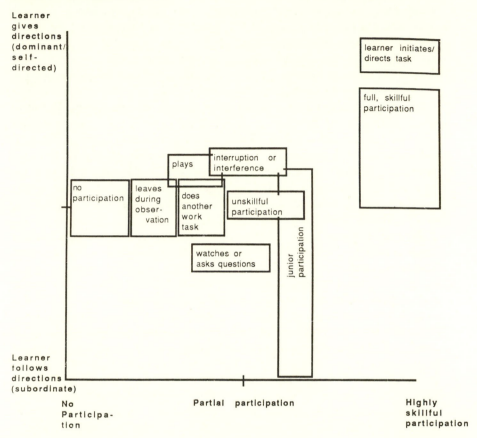

content pertinent to learners at different stages. The organization of the code may be seen in Table A.1.

Values and Explanatory Statements

Values in use or explanations revealing a world view or particular judgment standard governing a specific incident are ascertained from statements made by the participants or, using the ethnographer's knowledge of the culture, are inferred from strong implications made by gestures or indirect statements of any kind. In order to derive a coding system for this type of statement, we have employed a combination of ethnographic and logicodeductive methods. We first examined ethnographies of many societies and noted all the values mentioned by the anthropologist authors. Our original code was based on this study, but, as we indicated in Chapter 6, the result did not lead to a reliable coding system. In order to revise the code, we reviewed classic statements related to the topics of cultural or human universals and world views (Beals, Spindler & Spindler 1967; Edel and Edel 1968; Hoebel 1972; Kluckhohn and Strodtbeck 1961; Kroeber 1909; Maslow 1954; Mead 1970; Miller 1978). We then used Kluckhohn and Strodtbeck's idea of value orientations, with some modifications, as a heuristic device to bring together values, worldviews, and cultural universals from ethnographies and to generate a more complete list of major common value statements. Following that, we classified our derived value/judgmental statement sets or clusters along two axes, a good/evil axis referring to basic judgments about the fundamental nature of all things, and a materiality/immateriality axis that measures relative orientation to the concrete earthly present versus some more intangible and distant space-time frame, whether in the far past, in the future, or in the spiritual realm. Finally, we located and named the values clusters that the process generated. The resulting clumps with their relations to the two axes are shown on Figure 8.2.

The coding system lumps all related values into ten loose clusters. Because values proved to be very difficult to code, even the smallest sub-subsystem terms have been scaled and assigned their own scale position. This allows coders to make positive classifications of all value, explanatory, and incentive statements, coding them within the correct range and facilitating comparative study. For cases in which no values or explanatory statements are given or implied in an incident, the code provides a special class, "no statement made . . . ." This category is not residual; the majority of learning incidents in all the cultures we have studied so far fall into it. The "no values" category permits analysis of incidents for purposes of determining where and when values and explanations are given to learners and what factors lead to responses containing evaluative remarks. A category is also included for mixed and unclear statements. The major coding categories and code letters for 1.2.2, "Values" (including ontological-epistemological statements or explanations, as well as related motives and incentives to action) are listed below. For each category, the range of specific values along the Goodness/evil, (G) and Materiality/immateriality (M) dimensions, are also indicated.

1.2.2.1 A highly pessimistic world view that focuses on the presence of *evil* in a harsh environment—from G.0.0 to G.2.0. and M.0.0 to M.2.5 (E)

1.2.2.2 World views that emphasizes *material gain* in a context of scarcity—from G.3.0 to G.4.0 and M.0.5 to M.1.5 (M)

1.2.2.3 World views that emphasizes *achievement* or personal accomplishment—at G.4.0 and from M.3.0 to M.4.5 (A)

1.2.2.4 World views that emphasizes the necessity of strong *social control*—from G.3.0 to G.4.0 and M.6.0 (C)

1.2.2.5 World views that are based on *technological*, objectivized visions of an impersonal nature—from G.4.0 to G.5.0 and from M.3.5 to M.8.5 (T)

Figure 8.2
Values and Worldview

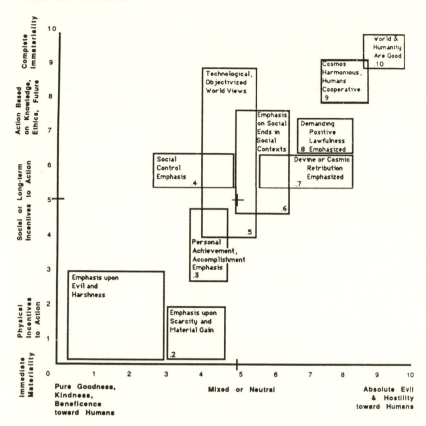

1.2.2.6 World views that emphasizes *social* ends in a context of social balance—from G.5.0 to G.6.0 and from M.5.0 to M.7.5 (S)

1.2.2.7 World views that emphasize divine or cosmic *retribution* upon those who violate a divinely established order—from G.6.0 to G.8.0 and at M.6.0 (R)

1.2.2.8 World views that picture life and the gods as good but as demanding high standards of behavior and that regard positive *lawfulness* as the critical factor for a successful society—from G.7.0 to G.8.0 and at M.7.0 (L)

1.2.2.9 World views that envision a naturally *harmonious* cosmos in which humans are cooperative, active partners—from G.8.0 to G.9.0 and from M.8.0 to M.9.0 (H)

1.2.2.10 Viewpoints that define the world as good and humanity as *good* in connection with an otherworldly orientation—from G.9.0 to G.10.0 and from M.9.0 to M.10.0 (G)

1.2.2.11 No statement made or given (X)

1.2.2.12 Values, ontological-epistemological statements, explanations, or incentives that cannot be classified (U)

The list of specific value statements classified within each category, along with their codes, may be found in the complete code given in Table A.1.

Institutionalization, Setting, and Objects

Data about general cultural settings provide important ethnographic information essential to culture acquisition/transmission incidents, and it is important to record them for use in interpreting findings. Nevertheless, detailed analyses of our data indicate that codes for setting are redundant and that institutionalization codings provide an accurate measure of the influence of setting on a learner. Therefore, the setting code has been dropped from the scheme and the institutionalization code (see below) has been revised to better and more consistently reflect the influence of settings on learning. Similarly, the coding of objects may be considered redundant when objects are seen as a structured part of both institutions and activities. Therefore, this code has also been eliminated. By dropping these two categories, we exponentially decrease the number of logically possible patterns for the data strings, thus increasing our chances of locating patterns.

The degree of institutionalization is now classified along two dimensions. The horizontal dimension is derived directly from the definition of institution and refers to the *degree* of formalness, fixity, definiteness, and regularity of the named entity, which may range from the low (left) end of the scale, unfixed and informal, to the high or right end, strictly fixed and formal. The inclusion of settings characterized by low formalness and fixity required the addition of a new set of coding subcategories, 3.1.1.1, "noninstitutionalized" (~), to cover settings at the lower end of the scale—house/family (H), porch/veranda/patio (P), courtyard/compound/yard (C), neighborhood (N), open spaces in local village or town (V), and open spaces far from point of origin (F). (Each subcategory in the new scheme, such as "noninstitutionalized," continues to be numbered with respect to its position on the theoretical systems diagram, Figure 5.3. Hence this subcategory is numbered 3.1.1.1. Each is assigned a shorthand code symbol as noted in parentheses.) The second, vertical dimension for degree of institutionalization refers to the degree of sacredness of the institution. Figure 8.3 depicts this schematically for ten types of organizations scaled along two dimentions. The actual classification will have to be adjusted by utilizing the religious or ritual areas of the dimension system to capture the main features of such institutions as private religious schools, initiation bush schools, or the sacred foot races found among Native Americans.

To reflect their relative positions in the two-dimensional schema, the major coding subcategories within 3.1.1, Degree of Institutionalization, have been renumbered beginning at the bottom left with the least fixed, most secular cat-

Figure 8.3
Degree of Institutionalization

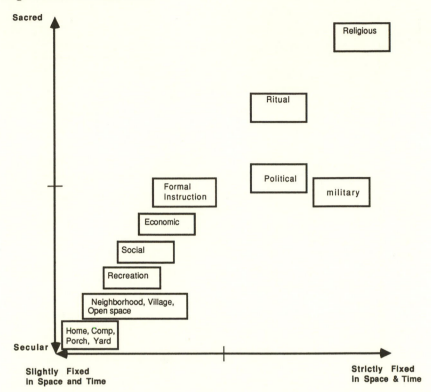

egories. The categories with their codes are 3.1.1.1, Noninstitutionalized (~);
3.1.1.2, Recreational (OR); 3.1.1.3, Social (S); 3.1.1.4, Economic (E); 3.1.1.5,
Formal instructional (I); 3.1.1.6, Military (M); 3.1.1.7, Political (A); 3.1.1.8,
Ritual (R); and 3.1.1.9, Religious (G). The complete, detailed code, including
any minor alterations, appears in Table A.1 in the appendix.

Activities and Acts

All types of actions, whether they characterize the learning environment or
the learner's acts, continue to be conceived of and categorized using a single,
identical sector of the coding system. The original code for activities and acts
was inductively derived from ethnographies. It was designed to characterize
human economic, political, and social activities in such a way that data from
societies organized upon differing principles, such as hunter-gather societies
versus industrial ones or work-oriented societies versus more socially oriented

Figure 8.4
Surrounding Activities and Acts

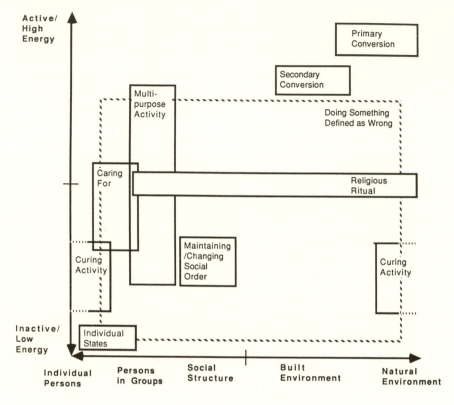

ones, would be coded in a fashion that would equally reflect their differences and similarities. In the two-dimensional scale shown here (Figure 8.4), the vertical energy/activity dimension encompasses a range of activities extending from those tending to involve large muscular movement requiring heavy caloric expenditure to those utilizing smaller, finer, or fewer muscles. The horizontal dimension relates the energy expenditure to defined parts of the environment beginning with an orientation toward the individual at the left and ranging through an orientation to the social environment at center to a broad ecological orientation on the right.

The revised coding scheme for 3.1.2, "Activity Clusters That Characterize the Milieu and Learners' Acts" (see Table A.1) continues to be organized by classes of related activities. The code is organized with the lower-numbered categories representing activity classes characterized by narrow foci and lower energies. The major subcodes include 3.1.2.1, Experiencing individual states (I); 3.1.2.2, Giving/receiving curing activities (H); 3.1.2.3, Caring for others/

receiving care (Cf); 3.1.2.4, Multipurpose activities, with 17 separate codes (see discussion below); 3.1.2.5, Maintaining or changing social order and services (MC); 3.1.2.6, Religious and ritual types of activities (R); 3.1.2.7, Converting energy and materials to human use, which includes 3.1.2.7.1, Primary conversion (PC), and 3.1.2.7.2, Secondary conversion or support (SC); and 3.1.2.8, Doing/suffering something defined as wrong/committing a crime (W).

Within this framework, four of the coding subcategories have also been modified. First, because our data indicated that people spend very large amounts of time in what we have labeled "Multipurpose activities" (3.1.2.4), we have assigned a number of subcodes to this area in order to distinguish the various types of social, oral, physical, and creative activities that fall into this category and better reflect the broad variety of deliberate information exchanges used in training and formal education. These finer descriptive details and their subcodes are:

socializing (So)

visiting/gossiping/standing around/discussion/watching people activities (VW)

joking/teasing/doing tricks/talking sex (J)

drinking alcohol/using drugs (D)

sharing meals/feasting (F)

gift giving (G)

art and entertainment activities—doing or watching (A)

playing, unorganized fun, outings (Pl)

participating in/observing organized sports, games/skills contests (OG)

expressing conflict (Cn)

physical movement (ph)

deliberate information exchanges (E)

oral teaching/learning as giving/ attending lectures giving/getting instruction, tutoring (L)

electronic or media-aided teaching/learning (Md)

involved or operational teaching/learning, as showing/demonstrating or watching same, practicing, lab exercises, etc. (Dm)

record keeping/communicating, as writing, recording, entering data; sending/carrying/receiving messages (Rk)

studying, memorizing, reciting, thinking (St)

consulting, getting/giving advice, briefing, asking information-seeking questions (BQ)

Second, the modification occurred in the "Caring for others" (Cf) subcategory (3.1.2.3). It has been reoriented away from the recipient of the care and toward classes of caring activities. It now includes physical care such as cleaning people up, making people comfortable, and giving medications, as well as the mental care and cognitive activities involved in enhancing well-being, empathic listening, counseling, giving information, and so on. This makes the subcoding of this subcategory more consistent with the action-oriented focus of the dimensions for this part of the activities code system and allows us to see how learners acquire caring behaviors. A third subcategory, "Health Activity" (3.1.2.2), has been renamed "Giving/receiving curing activities" (H) to better reflect its original focus on actions.

The process of plotting activities along two dimensions (Figure 8.4) suggested the fourth subcategory modification. Category 3.1.2.8, "Doing/suffering something defined as wrong/committing a crime" (W), required conceptual broadening. The original code for this class of activities listed a number of acts that are defined as major crimes in many societies. The space occupied by this type of crime activity fell into an area characterized by moderately high energy levels with an orientation range stretching from the individual through the social. However, if one looks at the diagram with the idea of wrongdoing in mind, it is immediately clear that wrongdoing can occur in most of the other coding areas. For this reason, the way wrongdoing is plotted has been expanded so that it underlies and shadows the other code areas (dotted large box), and the code has been revised to include new areas of wrong, such as violating religious laws or taboos and harming self or others through neglect or carelessness, and to expand the definitions of other areas of wrongdoing, for example, violations of the social order such as lying or committing fraud. The dimensional concept suggests that this category could be dropped altogether, and all crimes and wrongs could be treated as negative cases of the positive acts coded in the other seven categories. A reconceptualization of this order, however, is probably premature because codes in anthropology have historically been formulated as positive content lists that suggest areas an observer should attend to.

Group Size and Composition (People)

The code for 3.1.3.1, "Group size," unchanged from the original, is broken down into four levels: individual (I); small, 2–10 (S); medium, 11–40 (M); and large, 40+ (L), which scales groups by size range. The composition of the groups of people surrounding the learner is now coded by a single two- or three-term code that uses three subcodes to classify the group by relative size, familiarity, and type of relationship to the learner.

The codes classify groups with reference to the particular dimension that our studies have shown are most likely to have an effect on the learner and on the learning taking place during the incident being coded. The first term codes the familiarity of group members. Familiarity is scaled so that the subcodes lie along a continuum from very familiar types of groups, such as immediate family, to unfamiliar types, such as strangers. This is depicted in Figure 8.5 on the vertical

Figure 8.5
Group Composition

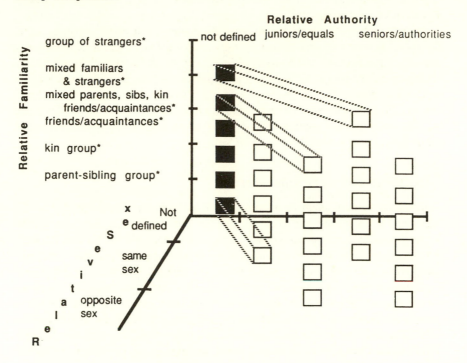

* Mixed age/sex/seniority/authority
  unless characterized by a dominant relationship factor

scale. The subcodes for familiarity contain the six categories indicated by the black boxes (see the classification of 3.1.3.2, "Group composition," in Table A.l). These include 3.1.3.2.1, Parent-sibling group (P); 3.1.3.2.2, Kin group (K); 3.1.3.2.3, Friends and acquaintances (F); 3.1.3.2.4, Mixed group of parents, siblings, kin, friends, or acquaintances (MC); 3.1.3.2.5, Mixed group of familiars and strangers (MF); and 3.1.3.2.6, Group of strangers (S).

In addition to familiarity, a second and, possibly, third dimension is coded when group composition is noticeably uniform or dominated by a single sex (front to rear axis) or status (left-right axis) relative to the learner. Thus groups that are composed primarily of individuals of the same or opposite sex as the learner are noted, as are groups composed primarily of the learner's equals or of persons with seniority/authority over the learner. The possible intersections of these features are indicated by a series of boxes in Figure 8.5 representing the dominating relationship factors that might be marked for any group. Potential connections have been partially sketched in for groups of strangers dominated by same-sex females, mixed groups of familiars and strangers dominated by the opposite sex, and parent-sibling groups, such as a group of the learner's sisters, dominated by the same sex.

Because groups are classified by specific features that affect learning, other details of structure are not coded. For example, a family group standing in a crowd is classified as "large group/mixed group of familiars and strangers"(L/MC) because the mix is the feature that dominates the incident. If a girl and her mother are sitting together in the evening and talking with a group of a dozen women, three of whom are her aunts and the rest her mother's friends, the group will be classified as "medium/mixed group of parents/siblings, kin, friends or acquaintances/same sex/senior" (MMCsa).

Relational Expressive Atmosphere

Research on nonhuman mammals and on humans has suggested that we all learn best when we are in relaxed, happy, or slightly excited, alert states. This suggests that the general emotional atmosphere is very likely to affect learners' psychological receptivity to information by influencing their personal emotional state. Historically, too, anthropologists of the configurationist school (for a good example see Benedict's *Patterns of Culture*, 1934 and, more recently, Chagnon 1968) have suggested that the emotional organization of sociocultural life varies greatly cross-culturally. These differences are thought to impinge upon both what is learned and how it is learned (see, for example, Mead's *New Lives for Old*, 1956). In addition, emotional atmospheres dominating any particular setting will have a strong influence on the responses of adults and seniors to learners. Our recent exploratory research indicates that, for some cultures, atmosphere has a stronger effect on responses to learners than do adult activity, the learner's actual behavior (good or bad, approved or disapproved), the identity of the respondent, or the values applicable to the situation.

To explore issues of this type, accurate coding is essential. Our original code, derived from terms used to describe emotional states and atmospheres in a large sample of ethnographies that were then lumped by similarity, proved difficult to use. Our new system for categorizing expressive atmosphere is based on the body of psychological research on the classification of emotions (Berlyne 1971; Fantino 1973; Kleinginna and Kleinginna 1981; Plutchick 1980) and on Chapple's (1970) work on hormones in relation to personality and temperament. Our system uses two dimensions derived from a thorough sifting of that work to select the dimensions most useful for comparison at the most comprehensive level. The first dimension, the varied levels of activity associated with differing hormonal outputs, is scaled along the horizontal axis. The second dimension, measured along the vertical axis, has a negative-to-positive range representing the tendencies for withdrawal and attraction. Figure 8.6 depicts 14 emotional atmospheres arranged within the four quadrants created by the intersecting scales. This dimensional representation of emotions facilitates accurate coding of

Figure 8.6
Relational Expressive Atmosphere

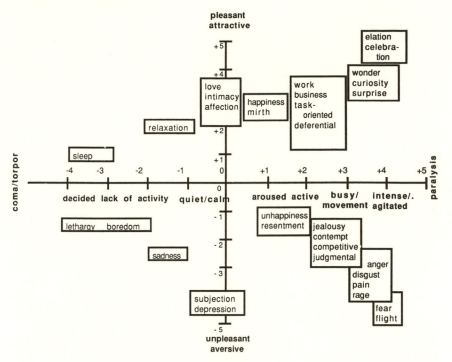

relational-expressive atmospheres. The revised coding scheme indicates the characteristic behavioral markers for each emotional orientation. Codes for 3.1.4, Relational Expressive Atmosphere, are numbered from least active to most active, with positive and negative pairs placed together: 3.1.4.1, Sleep (M); 3.1.4.2, Boredom/lethargy (B); 3.1.4.3, Relaxation (R); 3.1.4.4, Sadness (S); 3.1.4.5, Love (L); 3.1.4.6, Depression/dejection (D); 3.1.4.7, Happiness (H); 3.1.4.8, Resentment/unhappiness (U); 3.1.4.9, Task oriented (T); 3.1.4.10, Judgmental/competitive (J); 3.1.4.11, Wonder/surprise (W); 3.1.4.12, Elation (E); 3.1.4.13, Anger/disgust (A); and 3.1 4.14, Fear (F). Behavioral markers for each are given in Table A.1.

Patterns of Control/Response

This code category refers to the type of responses, overt or covert, intentional or unintentional, that learners receive from people around them during a learning incident. Responses are scaled along two dimensions. The horizontal axis expresses the degree of instructional deliberateness of the response. It ranges from "no instruction" to "deliberate instruction." The vertical axis expresses the

Figure 8.7
Patterns of Response

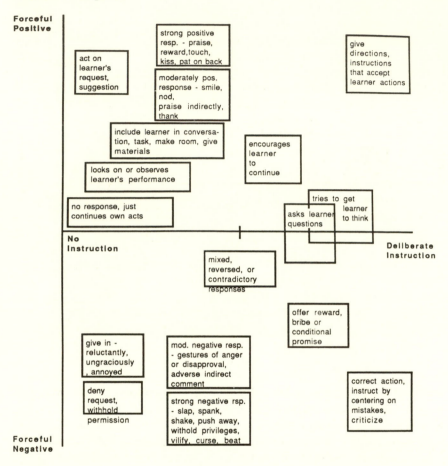

degree to which the response is positive/confirming or negative/denying toward the learner's act. This axis is broken into degrees registering the general level of positive or negative forcefulness in the responding person's reaction to the learner, with the midpoint representing a minimum of definiteness or a lack of forceful deliberateness.

The major response types shown in Figure 8.7 are grouped for coding purposes into six classes along the deliberateness-of-instruction axis. Within each code class, responses are further coded for degree of positive or negative forcefulness: + + or − − (forcefully positive or negative), + or − (moderately positive or negative), no code (minimally positive). In some cases, those in emotionally restrained or exuberant cultures, for example, cultural style differences will change the class to which a response belongs, and this must be reflected by adjusting the code along the scale to reflect the way concepts of affirmation or denial are perceived within the particular tradition. The six response classes are 3.2.1, Accepting Noninstructional Responses (A), such as including the learner in the conversation, giving the learner materials, or observing the learner's performance; 3.2.2, Implicitly Instructional Reactions (I), coded as strongly positive responses, such as praising, giving rewards, or kissing; strongly negative, such as spanking or withholding privileges; moderately positive, such as a smile or nod; and moderately negative, such as gestures of disapproval; 3.2.3 Responds to Learner Initiatives (L), by acting on learner's suggestion (+ +), reluctantly giving in to the learner (− −), and denying learner requests; 3.2.4, Purposeful But Indirectly Instructional Responses (P), which encourage the learner to continue (+) or to think (+), for example; 3.2.5, Mixed, Reversed, or Contradictory Responses (M); and 3.2.6, Directly Instructional or Directive Responses (D) that accept learners' actions (+ +) or correct or criticize actions (− −).

The Coding Scheme as a Whole

The codes presented here and in our previous work have been developed hierarchically so that they begin at the macro level but also contain lists of elements or subcategories for more detailed analysis. Thus this coding system may facilitate the linking of macro- and microanalysis in ethnographic research. The nondetailed, high-level coding may be used for broad cross-cultural comparison. For the analysis of specific contexts, such as schools, workplaces, religious settings, the more subtle and detailed subsystem classifications may be used, modified, and further developed, or new subsystems may be fitted into the code to cover additional areas. Macro- and microanalysis can then conceivably be linked into a single theoretical structure.

CONCLUSION

To demonstrate the comparative potential of a dimensionalized approach, all statements about the child-raising and child-life systems for children from ages three to approximately seven in five ethnographies (the Spindlers' study of the Menomini, Ward's study of Rosepoint, Hostetler and Huntington's description of socialization in Amish society, T. R. Williams's work on enculturation in Dusun society, and Leis's study of the Ijaw) were scaled along eight of the dimensions developed above: (1) energy and arousal in activities and emotions; (2) materiality/immateriality and (3) good/evil for values applied to children; (4) deliberateness of instruction by adults; (5) child participation in terms of degree of skill and (6) level of dominance or submission; (7) positivity and negativity for responses and emotions; and (8) people (individuals) versus nature as a focus for activity.

Figure 8.8 plots these dimensions by putting ethnographically related orien-

Figure 8.8
Five Cultures, Eight Dimensions

Figure 8.8
Five Cultures, Eight Dimensions

5 Cultures,
8 Dimensions
Figure 8.8

162

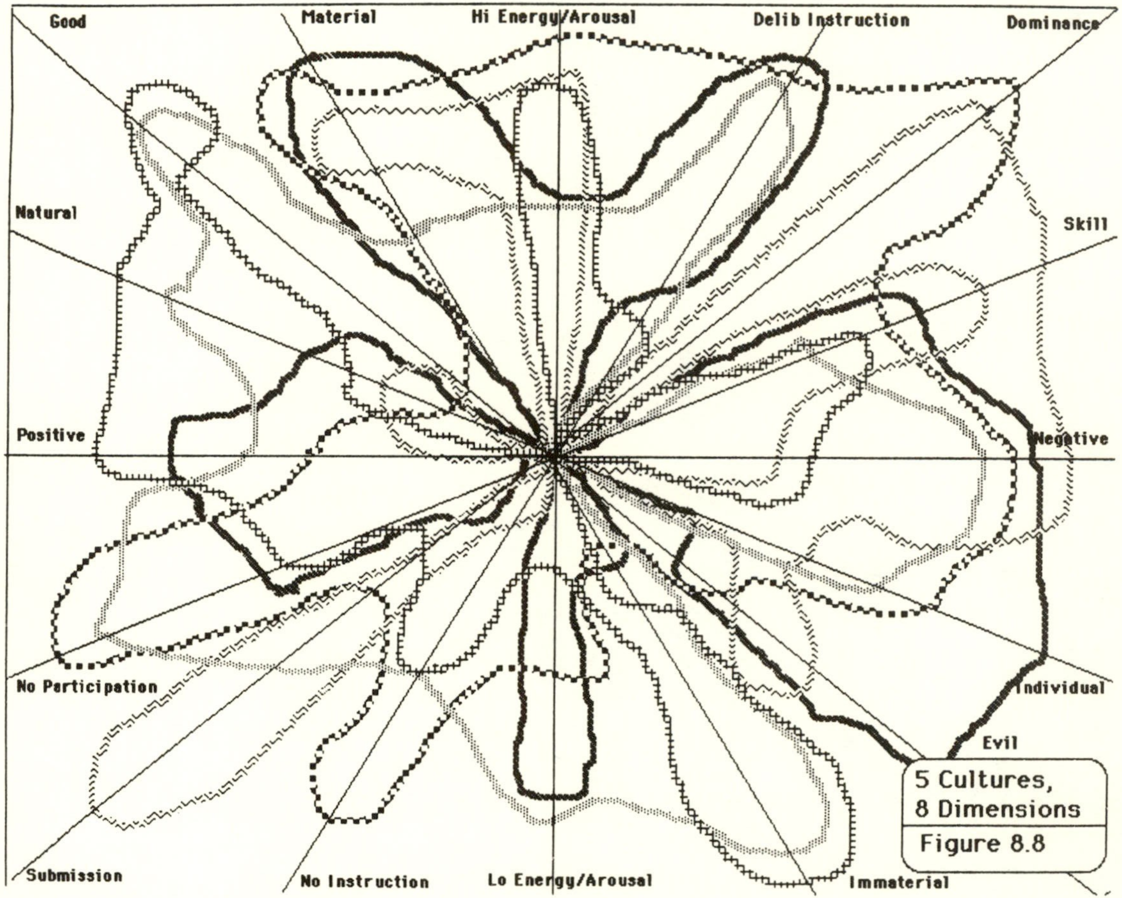

Figure 8.8 Continued

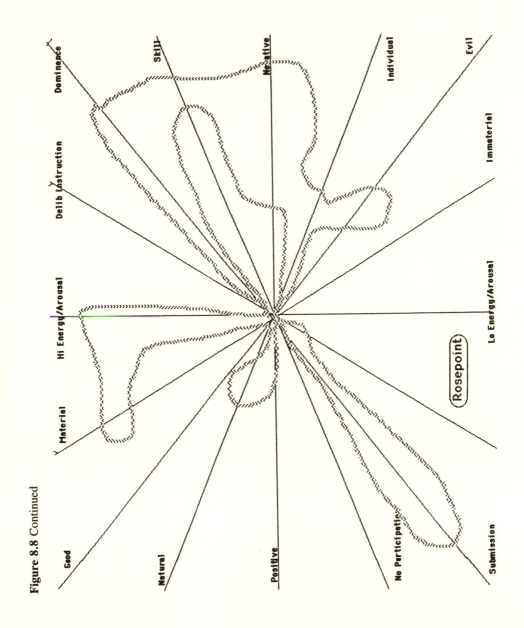

Figure 8.8 Continued

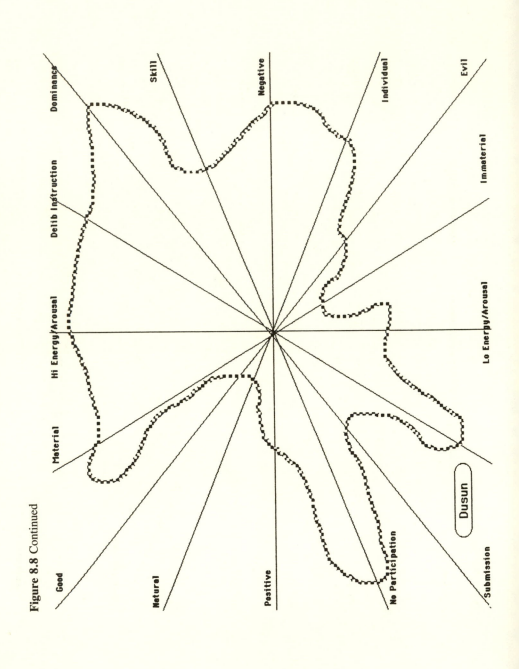

Figure 8.8 Continued

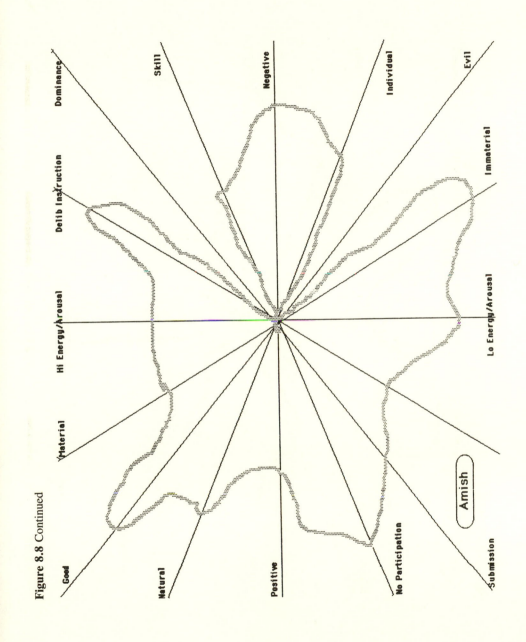

Figure 8.8 Continued

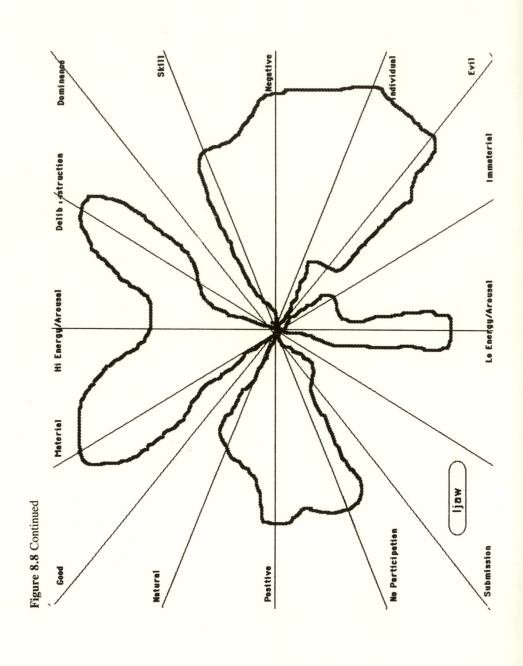

Figure 8.8 Continued

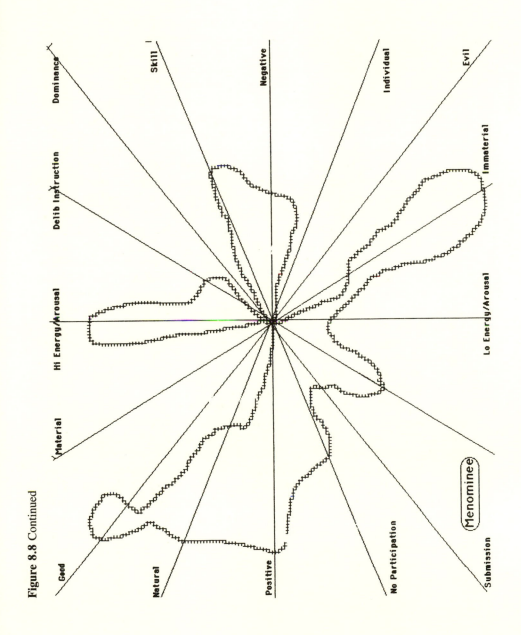

tations adjacent to each other to depict the culture acquisition/transmission spaces for each of the five societies. Each culture's use of the dimensions, and consequently its space, is distinctive. The Ijaw space shows a well-developed pattern in which opposite ends of the scales are differentially utilized. Deliberate instruction, for example, is used frequently while noninstructive methods are very seldom used, and values emphasize the evil aspects of the universe but not the good ones. The Rosepoint space is more fragmented and shows an even greater orientation toward the far ends of the scales, with very little use of the midrange; responses are negative, and there is a strong emphasis on materiality, skill, dominance, and energy. The Dusun space has the same general orientation as the Ijaw and Rosepoint spaces, but shows greater use of the moderate middle parts of the scale. Children are also permitted to be dominant and often receive no instruction. Neither good nor evil is strongly emphasized; both high and low energy levels are common. The Amish space provides quite a contrast to the previous three, being more strongly oriented to the left and lower portions of the space as a whole, indicating a quieter, less energetic style, with an emphasis on goodness and nonmaterial values. The similarly oriented Menomini space also indicates an emphasis upon non-materiality, positiveness, and goodness, but is more energetic and has a greater focus on the natural environment. The spatial patterns suggest that the five societies represent at least two different classes of culture acquisition/transmission types or structures. The first type, oriented to the upper and right portions of the space and occupied by the Ijaw, Rosepoint, and Dusun systems, is relatively energetic, materialistic, negative, and focused on evil. In contrast, the second type, represented by the Amish and Menomini spaces, is oriented to the left and bottom, emphasizing goodness, nature, and nonmaterial values. This type is also more positive and less individually oriented when taken as a whole.

Burton (1978) has suggested that, in order to achieve the theoretical objectives of our discipline, anthropologists of education should construct linkages between children and culture via utilization of universal patterns. A well-conceived coding system designed to guide the collection of data about those linkages would in itself function as an informal statement of theory. Because the subsystem codes presented here are roughly scaled along one or more broad dimensions, the revised coding system does contain elements of a primitive universal framework for future comparison of acquisition/transmission structures across cultures. Learning interaction incidents coded by this system can be analyzed not only for frequency of occurrence of various types of environmental, interactional and learning elements, but also for structural position of those elements in a universe of possible positions.

9 Cultural Transmission and Culture Acquisition in a Korean Village: The Systems Model in Ethnographic Terms

Kyung-hak Kim and Kyung-soo Chun

The research reported in this chapter was conducted for the specific purpose of studying learning processes in rural Korea, with a focus on children between about 6 and 12 years of age. We also wished to study the process of culture acquisition and transmission by applying the systems-based model described in this volume to a Korean community. In so doing, we hoped to discover some of the model's strengths and weaknesses. Finally, we wanted to try to illustrate the model's quantitative aspects with the use of thick, descriptive, ethnographic, qualitative data.

In order to accomplish these objectives, Kyung-hak Kim traveled to a village in rural Korea to gather the necessary data. He lived in the community for three months, doing standard anthropological fieldwork via in-depth participant observation and informal informant interviewing and conducting structured observations using the format described in Chapter 5. The resulting 191 completed data gathering sheets were coded and eventually grouped in terms of locations: living room or *anpang* (34), courtyard (21), workplaces such as rice paddies and highlands (24), play spaces (64), church (22), elementary school (7) kindergarten (11), and the market (8). The analytic framework used to structure the observation and coding was based on the holistic, systemic theory of human learning as a multi-modal, interactive process constrained by the cultural milieu. The format for data gathering was based on a draft version of the field guide (Dobbert and Eisikovits 1984) which represented a mid-point between the original

Mary Anne Pitman and Marion Lundy Dobbert assisted with the writing of this chapter.

and final versions presented in Chapters 5 and 8.[1] The format for analysis was based on a decision tree technique similar to the one described in Chapter 7.

THE VILLAGE OF SAEMINAE

The community where this research was conducted is called Saeminae and is located in the southwestern part of the Korean peninsula. The general character of this community and its entire area are both typical of rural Korea. It takes about two hours, if one is lucky, to reach the local bus terminal from the main city of Kwangju, provincial center of the area. From there you ride a local bus over an unpaved road, suffering numerous jolts and a thorough shake-up until the bus lets you down in a calm, cozy corner of the paddy fields. Snakelike lanes and passes lead you on foot to the village through hills dotted with pine trees and highlands packed with tobacco plants and vegetables. On rainy days, you must fight the muddy slopes to keep a good balance. The coastline is not very far from the village, but one does not see any signs of marine landscape. Administratively speaking, this village is a part of Pobsong-myon (subcounty), Youngkwang-gun (county), Chollanam-do (province), and is located about 20 minutes' walking distance from the local bus stop.

The villagers have a geomantic interpretation of the shape of the land surrounding the community, which is said to look like a shallow basket. Therefore, once a family (surname group) completely fills the basket, in terms of population and richness, the basket is going to start emptying out. Interpreted historically, this means that the surname group that founded the village became bankrupt and was replaced by another surname group, the Ch'angwon Hwang lineage (which was a kind of localized patri-kin group 200 years ago). Today the residents of Saeminae and the neighboring villages recognize Saeminae as the Hwang lineage's. Out of a total of 43 households in the village, 21 are Hwangs. In short, the dominant lineage group of the village is the Hwang.

Like its neighbor villages in the region, Saeminae is experiencing the general impact of the nationwide urbanization and industrialization trends, which lead to outmigration from the rural areas and a shift of population to the main cities. Population growth tends to have slowed and, even more important, there are not many young married couples with children in comparison with urban sectors. Table 9.1 shows the village's population and age structure.

Traditionally, the lineage organization is a social group that serves to lead political and economic activity at the village level in Korea (Chun 1984). Currently, this tradition is changing due to the impingement of general social change. In addition, internal integration forces that hinge upon lineage activity have been slowly decreasing in Korea in general. We expect to see evidence of that process in this examination of socialization itself.

The basic subsistence economy of the community relies on small-scale agriculture, including rice cultivation and cash-crop production, mainly tobacco. Total cultivated land in the village covers 58.4 hectares, including 37.8 hectares

Table 9.1
Population Structure of Saeminae

Age \ Sex	Male	Female	Total
70 and above	6	7	13
60-69	6	2	8
50-59	1 3	1 1	24
40-49	9	1 6	25
30-39	7	8	15
20-29	1 3	8	21
10-19	2 0	1 5	35
0- 9	1 9	1 2	31
Total	9 3	7 9	1 7 2

of rice paddies and 20.6 hectares of highlands. The average amount of cultivated land for each household in the village is 1.2 hectares, comparable to the national average of 1.02 hectares (Hwang 1984). Although the size of the village is smaller than that of the national average, Saeminae seems to be an average, rural Korean village, and like others is experiencing modernization in terms of social organization and economic structure. For these reasons we selected it as our research site.

CULTURE ACQUISITION IN FAMILY AND INFORMAL SETTINGS

This analysis focuses on issues of cultural transmission and culture acquisition in the setting of the wider village rather than in the formal public school setting. The places where children may be found and seen learning in the village can be divided into two conceptually different settings, which may be termed institutional and noninstitutional (see Chapters 5 and 8). Noninstitutions include here the living room (called *anpang*, meaning, literally, inner room), courtyard, workplaces (rice paddies and highlands), and the play spaces that are dominated by peer groups; institutions include a church, a school, and a market.

The following description of patterns of interaction by setting are derived from a decision tree display that was constructed for each setting from codes for the categories on the data gathering form. Figures 9.1a and 9.1b provide a sample of a display that was constructed from the 34 structured observations recorded in the setting of the anpang or living room. The thick line represents the primary

Figure 9.1a
Anpang: All Links Observed

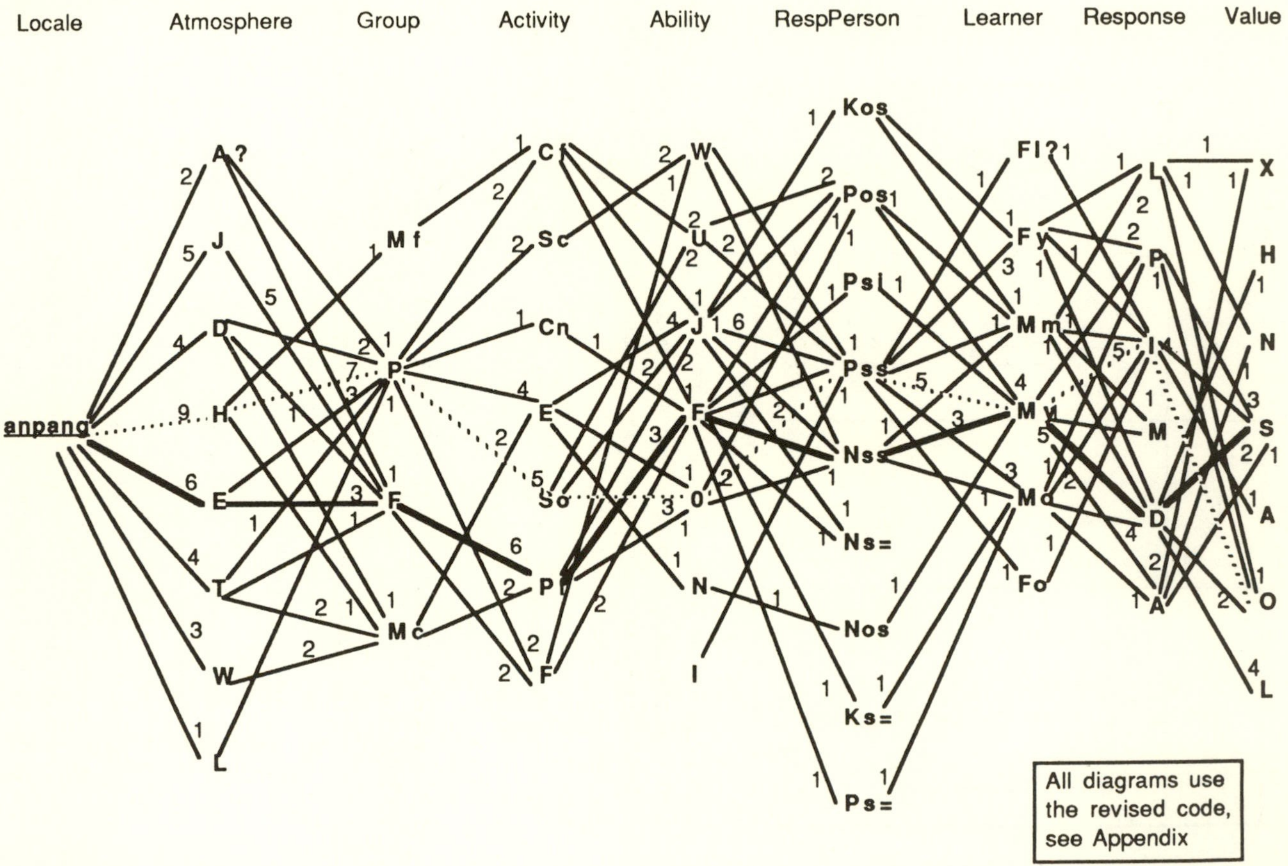

All diagrams use
the revised code,
see Appendix

172

Figure 9.1b
Anpang: All Links Observed More Than Once

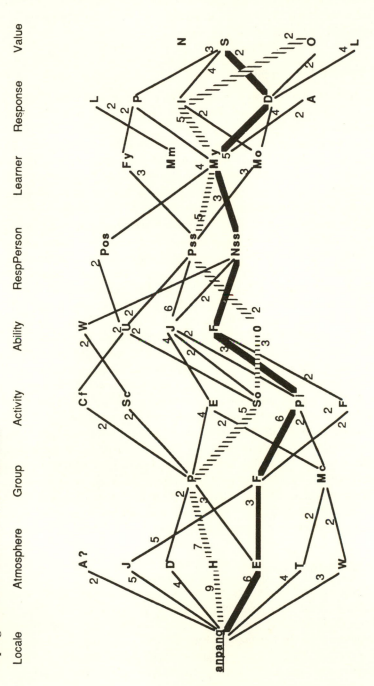

patterns; the dotted line represents the secondary pattern; the thin lines suggest pattern variations. These decision codes and frequencies were then interpreted to produce the descriptions that follow.

Living Room (Anpang)

Traditionally, this part of a house was exclusively occupied by the women of the household and their young children. One may still sense this atmosphere in the anpang even in these days of change and modification in the traditional behaviors related to the sexual division of spaces in rural Korea. Most of the time, young children share this room with both their parents. These days, the anpang is a center of the family's home life. Usually all family members get together here during mealtime and after work. Consequently, the primary bonds among the family members are clearly displayed and various situations involving children can be observed. Families in Saeminae observe their ancestral rites here, and they also invite their kin and close friends into this room. Guests are customarily not allowed into the anpang without the hosts' guidance. On these occasions, while the parents talk with their friends and relatives, the hosts' children play around in the room with the guests' children.

There is a television set in the anpang around which the family group relaxes after work and supper until bedtime. The children spend most of their time watching various kinds of TV programs, sitting beside their parents. The children like to watch cartoons and war dramas. Later, when they meet their friends to play outside their homes, or sometimes in the anpang, the children will imitate the TV programs. Here, too, brothers and sisters sometimes fight a little with each other or a big brother teases his little one. Their father may shout at them for this childish activity with anger and abusive language. In this setting, right or wrong behaviors of children are noted and disciplinary action is taken during mealtime as well as during the various ritual activities. In the anpang we find children interacting mainly with *groups* of family members.[2] In terms of their own *abilities*, the children tend to get involved in the *activity* of the adults or behave indifferently to that activity. In the anpang adults talk, care for, or educate children. These kinds of activities are associated with relevant *values*. In the anpang, brotherliness, table etiquette, and related values are emphasized.

Courtyard

The courtyard is the place where children can play simple games and all members of the family get together for joint work while enjoying an exchange of stories about ordinary everyday life. Children sometimes bring in their friends for games after the parents go to work.

In the courtyard the most frequent *activity* people engage in is work, such as repairing tools and preparing crops for delivery to a warehouse or to vinyl houses for storage. Animals are cared for here as well. Children between the ages of three and six do not *participate* in these activities but observe, while children over seven usually participate and perform a part of the whole job. The *group* consists primarily of family members and their intimate neighbors who participate in the activities that take place in the courtyard. However, it is generally parents who *respond* to the children's behaviors, interacting with their own offspring and making the courtyard a particularly good place to observe parental control patterns that shape children's behaviors. Here children are taught how to deal with tobacco leaves and are shown methods for repairing some machines. Attitudes toward livestock and *values* about repairing tools are also taught here.

Workplaces: Paddy Fields and Highlands

The setting of the paddy fields and highlands and the nature of the *activities* that take place there makes the *atmosphere* of the learning event work-oriented for children. The type of work activity needed in specific workplaces determines who can participate in work as well as the atmosphere of the work, setting the limits of the range of children's behavioral patterns. The kind of work in which children *participate* in Saeminae varies according to their age. The usual workplaces where children may be seen participating are primarily in the highlands. It is quite rare for children to go out to the paddy fields, because most paddy work is too complicated and sometimes too difficult for children. With respect to "work," the activity of children most often coincides with that of adults.

In Saeminae, a work *group* is usually composed only of family members. Children accompany their parents to the workplaces beginning at ages three to four. However, before ages four to five, children do not work but instead sit aside, either simply observing their parents and older siblings at work or playing by themselves with some farm machines. While four- and five-year-olds do not usually work, they are often asked to run simple errands such as delivering water and beverages to a work site. Beginning at the age of six or seven or above, though fairly unskilled, children become involved in some minor part of the work with their parents and often show somewhat active and skilled *participation*. But at other times they may get in the way and interfere with the adults' work. As they become older, they begin to take part in more complicated kinds of work, so that by the time they enter junior high school, they sometimes are full participants in paddy field work.

Work activity specifies a set of applicable *values*. Parents usually teach their children that work is an inevitable part of rural life, what kind of work can be expected from the children according to their age, and how to finish work with ease. Within these settings, parents often show positive *responses* to children's behaviors that are appropriate for the age and gender. Inappropriate behavior is usually followed by some negative response. By repeatedly telling their children the importance of work, adults in the village emphasize the fact that working is an important part of life in rural areas.

Due especially to the recent outmigration of the younger segment of the population to cities, with the resulting lack of able workers, many children are expected to help whenever possible. Tobacco particularly needs lots of small touches, which requires that children go out to the fields. Because of this, children may sometimes earn a little money by helping other families with their work.

Children thus acquire culture in family, home, and work settings through their polyphasic capacities by watching, thinking about, being exposed to, and participating in many activities in everyday life.

Play Spaces

The play space is where children of similar ages get together and play around outside the anpang, courtyard, or workplaces. In the setting of the play space the surrounding *group* is usually composed only of children. The play group is divided by age into two subgroups, one of children under age 5 and another of ages 6 to about 12. While gender does not appear to make any difference in the younger group, it does in the older group: Boys usually play in a wider range of places than girls, who play in a courtyard or a side street.

The *participating* learners differ in their *ability* to perform according to age, according to the complexity of rules for the ongoing game, and according to the degree of acquired skill. As they play, the older children intentionally or unintentionally teach youngsters the rules of games. Those between the ages of 10 and 12 show skilled behaviors and occupy the leading positions in the play group. Though age is not a crucial factor in that it does not determine a rigid status relationship of obedience, youngsters by and large follow their older siblings. The children are often involved in quarrels, but these usually break out within an age group.

Playing enables children to form their social bonds. In the play spaces, the peer bond plays a particularly important part in establishing relationships. Lineage bonds are no longer so important. Due to the shrinking number of young parents in the village (caused by the nationwide trends toward urbanization and industrialization and the associated outmigration), the number of children has been declining. The subsequent lack of potential friends has led the children to play together regardless of lineage differences.

CULTURE ACQUISITION IN INSTITUTIONS

In Saeminae there are three institutions[3] in which children can participate: the church, the primary school, and the market, and from each of these we have collected structured observations.

Church

Established in 1975 as a branch of a larger Presbyterian church, the Saeminae church has been led by one preacher for years. Ever since its establishment, the church has been consistently unpopular with the villagers. The most important conflict between the church and villagers has centered around the issue of ancestor worship. While the preacher has been trying to prevent people from performing the ritual observances of ancestor worship, the Confucian tradition has remained quite strong for most of the villagers. Consistent with this tradition, the older village people believe that ancestor worship is one of the most important rituals that must be performed by the living descendants of the lineages. Due to the reluctance of the church to sanction ritual performances of ancestor worship, there are only four adults who attend the church. All are women who are also mothers and wives. But even those parents who do not go to church do permit their children to go. This practice arises from the parents' belief that it may be better for their children to go to church for singing and dancing than to play outside in the hot weather or to play on the banks of a stream where there is some danger. Most of the villagers in Saeminae seem to consider the church as one of the good places for their children to go to have fun.

In general, the number of children attending church on weekends is correlated with the farming cycle. Because of the shortage of labor arising from the absence of young families, children usually have to help out. Thus during the busy season for farmers, the adults are unlikely to allow their children to go to church and require instead that they help with the work.

In church, the children can learn not only Christian doctrine but also interesting games and songs. It is not usually Christian belief but the games and dancing learned for fun that attract most of the children who attend. Especially on Sunday, going to church enables them to play in a *group* with other children from neighboring villages. They feel that it is much more fun to play games in church than to work at home.

Activity in church includes praying, the singing of hymns and other songs, dancing, game playing, and listening to fairy tales told by the preacher. In church, the children *take part* in these activities in a halfhearted and unskilled manner. Most of the children at times interfere with the ongoing activities such as the preaching or hymn singing just by behaving somewhat inappropriately.

Despite their behavior in church, some learn, intentionally or unintentionally, at least some of the rules of behavior expected in church. The institution of the church sets limits on children's behavioral patterns, and their behaviors are usually reinforced by praise or various negative *responses*. A set of *values* based on either Christian morality or the ordinary ethics of daily life is also taught in a way that may not be questioned. The value of following prescribed church rules is always emphasized. In addition, the value placed on work by most adult villagers is frequently in conflict with church emphases.

School Settings

Since children in rural areas spend most of their time in their community (with the notable exception of time spent in school) they learn a great deal through a series of everyday life processes that help them become adults. School knowledge alone is not enough to enable children to become adults in Saeminae society. Without doubt, school-based, instructed learning is only one part of the whole process of cultural transmission and culture acquisition, but the school performs a primary function in educating children, specifically in transmitting particular, defined forms of cultural knowledge and skills. The school as a formal organization is unlike family or peer group and has its own sets of specified rules. Here, while children must be able to learn many things in the regular curriculum, they learn things beyond the hidden curriculum as well. One of the most important lessons is learned through traditional actions that reinforce the value system of popularity in society.

For those children of Saeminae on whom this research focused, there were two school settings, an elementary school and an affiliated kindergarten, both of which give the children experience with institutions for formal education.

Kindergarten

When we conducted our fieldwork, the kindergarten had just been approved by the local government and was newly established in June 1984. As a consequence, there was no licensed nursery teacher. A female staff member (age 24) from the elementary school was temporarily obliged to teach the kindergarten class in addition to her own class, and facilities were still inadequate. The total number of children enrolled in the kindergarten *group* was 40, 5 of whom were from Saeminae village.

Kindergarten children of ages 4–5 together with their teacher were seen engaging in the *activities* of singing, dancing, and the playing of games. Here the children simply try to imitate their teacher's behaviors and actions in singing and dancing, though they cannot do it perfectly.

The kindergarten, as an educational institution, prescribes a set of behaviors for the children. For example, they are supposed to be good listeners and attentive to their teacher, they are not to fight with their friends, and they are expected to form a line when necessary. In addition, sets of *values*, such as using proper words and maintaining order all the time, are also emphasized. It is the teacher who most frequently interacts with the children and is the most influential figure. For this reason, the children try to elicit words of praise from their teacher and make efforts to get their teacher to pay personal attention to them.

Elementary School

Children from Saeminae and its neighboring villages attend a single school. The total number of students has been declining due to outmigration of the local rural population. At the time of our study, there were only 11 teachers, including a principal.

By and large, most of the villagers tend to think that the school is solely responsible for the formal education of their children. Frequently when village parents see their children playing outside, they complain that the teachers do not assign sufficient homework. From the teachers' perspective, based on their experience, it is not very useful to give heavy homework assignments because, as a rule, more than half of the children come to school with their homework unfinished. This is particularly true during the busy seasons for farmers, when one sees increasing numbers of children leaving school early without the teachers' permission, or not coming to school at all. During these periods, there are noticeable differences between the attitudes of parents and those of the teachers. The children experience a great deal of embarrassment because of this as they are caught between the parents' and the teachers' expectations.

Although the children can learn a great deal in terms of knowledge and behavior through formal schooling, the knowledge accumulated affects only a small part of their lives as a whole. The more important elements shaping children's ways of thinking and modes of behavior are very likely the things that they have seen, heard, and felt before entering school. This conclusion is supported by ethnographic observation in art classes. The most common and favored themes for drawing in all grades are usually mountains, trees, the students' houses, paddy fields, highlands, cattle, work with farmers, and so on.

Two main types of *activities* occur at school, attending classes and playing on the school playground. In class, the children are usually passive *participants* in relation to the teacher while they simultaneously interact with their friends, taking great care to hide this from their teacher. After school, the children spend a couple of hours playing on the school playground with their friends rather than going straight home. The school playground thus functions as an outing place for Saeminae children. This means that play must be assessed as a major component of formal schooling and one that provides important social role learning for children. Because the concept of extracurricular activity has not been developed in these rural areas, however, this extracurricular social learning takes place through unsupervised, informal play among friends who are enjoying themselves in a pleasant pastime.

Market

The villagers of Saeminae generally go to a periodic market (called *pobsong*), which is held every five days. The buses that go through Saeminae on the way to this traditional market are more crowded than usual on market days. During the busy summer farming season, which requires heavy agricultural labor, villagers visit the market less frequently than in winter. Villagers from Saeminae generally sell a variety of produce harvested the previous year in order to obtain cash with which to buy what they need. When parents, especially mothers, go to market with their children, they may buy cookies for the children or purchase necessary goods such as tableware, clothes, and shoes. The children who accompany their parents to the market cannot avoid observing certain kinds of cultural scenes—buying and selling negotiations (haggling) between their parents and the merchants; the somewhat noisy, impromptu advertisements put forth by many merchants; and the merchants' arguments for better prices. Too, there are often many kinds of humorous and entertaining showmen the children enjoy watching. Thus children in the periodic market, amidst its crowded and clamorous *atmosphere*, observe the numerous bargaining *activities* of *groups* of people consisting of strangers as well as their parents. In this setting, it is usually the mother who *responds* to the children's behavior. For example, she may provide an answer when they raise questions about the names of items displayed. The value set that child learners encounter in the market includes *values* about how to make a good deal or how to maximize profits.

FUNCTIONS OF THE MAJOR ELEMENTS OF CULTURE ACQUISITION

So far, by dividing the descriptions of children's lives in Saeminae into categories based on noninstitutional and institutional settings, the former including anpang, courtyard, workplaces, and play spaces, and the latter including the church, school, and market, we have selectively discussed how culture is transmitted and acquired. The constituent elements of these descriptions include all aspects of the settings in which children are found, the atmosphere of the settings, the age, sex, and behavioral patterns of the learners, the individuals responding to the learners, the patterns of responses, and relevant values. While all these elements with their mutual constraints are closely related, some appear to exert a pivotal influence on the process of cultural tranmission and culture acquisition in Saeminae.

First, in considering the total configuration, the very fact that the setting and surrounding activities *include* children is significant. The participation of children in the setting determines some of its features, especially group structure and, according to the setting and activity, the atmosphere that dominates the learning events. It is this total configuration that determines the children's behavioral patterns and the values emphasized in dealing with them. A good example is provided by the activity in which all family members get together in the anpang for meals or TV watching: the necessity for educating the children in correct behavior dominates the accompanying atmosphere. In the market we see a very different configuration. One feature of the surrounding group here is that it consists primarily of strangers, but it also includes children. The activity of negotiating prices for goods in the market is in large part responsible for the fact that the entire atmosphere is quite noisy and exciting. Children rarely participate actively in bargaining and instead simply watch or ask questions of their parents, but this kind of "watching" or "asking" is, from the children's perspective, an equally important mechanism for the acquisition of culture. The family-oriented setting and the activities that take place in the anpang are also closely associated with the values of brotherliness, good table manners, and respect for the elderly. In contrast, the institutional setting of the market and the activities within it limit the values observed to those related to buying and selling or the pursuit of profit. In the workplace, although the setting and activities are also dominated by the fact that the main feature of the group is its familiar composition, the total configuration is nevertheless altered by an atmosphere which is mostly work oriented.

The elements of setting and activity discussed so far are closely connected with Saeminae's sociocultural environment. We note that a different type of function, the adults' economic activity, also has a particularly strong impact on the configuration of other components of the process of cultural transmission and culture acquisition for children. The absence of a full labor force, for example, often leads children to become involved in varied economic environments which, on the one hand, reduces the time shared by parents and their offspring, and, on the other hand, increases the time children spend with their peer group. In Saeminae, as the number of people involved in small-scale farming declines, it becomes more and more difficult to mobilize an effective labor force from among the small group of villagers. In theory, each worker has to spend more time in the fields and paddies if the work is to be completed. Thus, the value frequently emphasized by parents in workplaces or in the context of daily activities is that of hard work. They say, ''It is only work that entitles you to eat meals.'' The emphasis on this value is related to the children's behavior—being absent from school or leaving school early—during the busy season for farmers. In addition, the settings of paddy field and highlands and the activities there emphasize for children the value and necessity of work in rural life through the structures of those activities themselves.

In institutional situations like the church, school, and market, the total learning configuration is dominated by rules of behavior that children are expected to follow. For example, in church children are supposed to behave quietly. In school, they are also supposed to obey the school rules; in kindergarten it is emphasized that the children must follow their teacher's instructions and not fight with their friends. Institutional configurations are also dominated by organized ongoing activities—prayer and praise of God along with singing and games in church, formal instructional learning in school, and negotiation of the price in the market. In each case, the organized activities define the dominant atmosphere and determine the value emphasis. These include a prohibition on alcohol and smoking and a rigid observance of weekend prayer in church, and the pursuit of maximum profit through negotiation in the market.

The institutional and informal home-related contexts are often in conflict. The children experience confusion when there is a conceptual difference between their schoolteacher and parents or when differences exist between church and home with respect to value emphases. For example, while alcohol and smoking (tobacco) are considered a sin by the church, parents think of the tobacco plant as an important contributor to the household economy and ask the children to help them by working in the tobacco fields. Also, as a part of their normal errands, children are frequently sent out to buy a bottle of an alcoholic beverage for their parents. The children find themselves caught between two different and opposite theories of morality, the preacher's and their parents'. A school-related conflict, which was discussed above, centers around the issue of getting home-work done, a school priority, versus the need to take children to the workplaces, a parental economic priority. As the above examples illustrate, children in rural villages frequently experience conflicts, not only on the superficial basis of behavior, but also with respect to the deeper value system. The values emphasized in church and school conflict with those of the home and do not provide the children with any consistent value set. In short, in these examples we can see that the setting and activity are not the only important elements in the config-uration of the process of cultural transmission and culture acquisition for children in Saeminae, but that values related to economic activity like the cultivation of the tobacco crop have a profound effect too.

Unlike the above factors related to types of settings and activities, the learner's characteristics and ability to perform, though closely connected with the other elements in a total learning configuration, appear to be very weak elements in the structuring of the cultural transmission and culture acquisition process. Cer-tainly the age of the learner is closely connected to both the learner's ability to perform, as our data have shown, and to settings in which the learner may be found. For example, children are not allowed to participate in meetings of the village council or in adult drinking parties. However, such constraints are rare in Saeminae where our qualitative data contain evidence of few cultural settings in which learners are constrained simply due to their age. But at this point, we have not gathered enough age stage data, as the age range 6 to 12 might be homogeneous with respect to cultural transmission and culture acquisition. Sim-ilarly, our current data do not permit a detailed analysis of the effect of a child's sex on cultural learning, although, in comparison to age, sex appears to exercise a greater effect, and we do know that sex seems to be a critical element in the socialization process in the general Korean picture. Another characteristic of learners, membership in a lineage group, does not exert much influence on the process of cultural transmission and culture acquisition. For example, even in play groups, children from the Hwang lineage always get together and play with children from other lineages. Moreover, when children from two different groups quarrel with each other, it is very difficult to find a clear behavioral pattern in which children are seen taking the side of their own lineages. This phenomenon is very different from what those who are now young adults (ages 20 to 30) in Hwang's lineage probably experienced during their childhoods. They would have associated primarily with children of their own lineage and would have favored children from their own side in a quarrel and rejected the other children with different surnames, regardless of right or wrong.

REFLECTIONS ON THE DATA GATHERING AND INTERPRETIVE PROCESSES

This chapter attempts to shed light on the way in which children in Saeminae become adults in their society. Too often, research in this field does not consider the cultural context surrounding the children or if context is considered the detailed relationships between constituent elements of the context is not taken into account. Therefore, we have not been able to generate consistent explanations about the processes of cultural transmission and culture acquisition as they occur in the everyday lives of Korean children. In order to address this fundamental question, we have employed the systems-based approach with its specific technique of data-gathering that employs a field guide (see Chapter 5). The data gathering sheet enabled the researcher to collect complete information on all the elements of culture learning. But, more importantly, the elements are systematically interrelated and allow us to analyze the systemic configurations of the culture learning process in this specific field setting. In this study, the field guide was used as a primary data gathering tool and proved helpful in identifying the various elements at work in the cultural transmission and culture acquisition process as children in Saeminae experienced it. However, the following points should be carefully considered by others before they try to use the guide.

First, if cultural transmission and culture acquisition processes involving children in a particular community are to be studied, as in this research, the social, economic, and ecological environments of the community should be examined in detail. These three environments are closely connected with the way of life of the community's residents. Unless these environments are examined in detail, it would be very difficult to properly perceive the meanings of the behaviors of either the adult residents or their children.

Second, the recording of information on the data gathering sheets, which are a part of the guide, should be accompanied by interviews with the learners and other people interacting with them. Without this general ethnographic approach, the meaning of the ongoing learning events cannot be reasonably understood. In this study, because the field-guide sheets were employed as the major device for gathering data on children, it was necessary for us to depend on inferences made from the observer's perspective in order to make judgments about the values emphasized in learning events. When analyzing exchanges, whether in the form of dialogues or behaviors, between participants in a learning event, the connection between the exchanges and the wider sociocultural context in Saeminae had to be inferred. However, the validity of this inference remains a problem.

Third, the level of description requires careful consideration. The relationship between elements relevant to the process of cultural transmission and culture acquisition should be depicted using concrete behaviors and dialogues, so that the exact nature of a particular learning event can be described appropriately. Thus, field notes may have to be transferred to the data gathering sheets at the rewrite stage of data collection.

Fourth, all elements of children's lives should be studied with equal emphasis. In this chapter, for example, the analysis is somewhat unbalanced because its initial purpose was to understand the processes of cultural transmission and culture acquisition that affect children outside of school. Processes occurring in

school received relatively little attention. But for a more comprehensive understanding of the patterning of cultural transmission and culture acquisition of
children in that society, a study such as this would also have to investigate the
processes in school in greater detail.

Fifth, in sorting data according to the data classification framework of the
field guide (see Appendix Table A.1), the classification frame must be properly
modified and supplemented in accordance with characteristics of the study area.
To provide an example from this study, when a child from one lineage group
does not consider another child from the same lineage group as a relative but
instead thinks of him or her in just the same way as another child from some
other lineage group, it is unclear from the point of view of the classification
codes whether the second child should be categorized as kin or nonkin. The
ambiguity should be resolved emicly. In this study, since children usually regard
children closer than cousins as relatives, the grouping was done accordingly.
However, this problem of degree of kinship can be quite different across cultures
and even between individuals.

With the above points given proper consideration, we are convinced that the
model has the potential for describing the prevalence of certain interactive variables in specific cultures and for illuminating the actual process of cultural
transmission and culture acquisition.

NOTES

1. Therefore, the codes that appear in Figures 9.1a and 9.1b do not have an exact
one-to-one correspondance with the codes that appear in either Table 5.2 or Table A.1.
Nevertheless, readers of the previous chapters will recognize the basic conceptual frames
as well as adaptations in coding which occurred after this study was completed.

2. Categories that are found in the systems model and field guide and that were used
to structure coding and display of data are italicized here.

3. The term ''institution'' is used here as defined operationally for the field guide (see
Chapter 5).

10 Becoming a Social Worker: Applying the Culture Acquisition Concept to a Professional Context

Empirical evidence underscores the tenet that although differences exist in the content, context, degree of superficiality, and effective quality between child and adolescent learning experiences and those that occur during adulthood, the two processes are not qualitatively discontinuous (Brim 1966; Csikszentmihalyi 1981; Elder 1974; Fendrich 1976; Inkeles 1969; Mass and Kuypers 1974; Mauer 1980; Moss and Kagan 1972; Newcomb 1967; Thomas 1982). Social scientists tend to relate to childhood learning as phenotypical because children constitute a most salient group readily available for observation and research. Furthermore, learning is considered their major social responsibility in preparation for future group membership and participation.

The concept of social learning can and must be extended forward through the human lifespace (see Chapter 3). Professional education constitutes one of the pivotal contexts for such learning. Learning a profession or learning to become professional is one of the main domains of adult learning. In the course of professional training and initiation, adult learners are exposed to numerous contexts of deliberate instruction. In other words, a heavy emphasis is placed on the transmission of a body of knowledge. Conversely, the acquisition end of the continuum receives less emphasis. As no intrinsic differences between child and adult learning processes have been demonstrated, this chapter will claim that the more characteristics of childhood learning adults are encouraged/enabled to exercise in the process of their professional education, the more closely will that education approximate the depth and holistic quality of culture acquisition.

Rivka A. Eisikovits was the primary author of this chapter.

The expression "professional culture" has become almost a cliche in organizational theory and professional socialization literature (Becker et al. 1961;
Greenwood 1957; Fox 1957; Ritzer 1972). However, a closer look reveals that
"culture" is colloquially used and from an anthropological perspective often
denotes little more than an empty metaphor. Culture theory per se has not been
systematically applied to the elucidation of processes and phenomena occurring
within professional groups. Consequently, professional learning, rather than
being conceptualized as enculturation or culture acquisition, is most commonly
perceived as a process of socialization: considerably narrower in scope (Mead
1963a) and clearly outcome oriented.

Although age-stratification theorists (Dombeck 1983; Faherty 1983; Riley,
Johnson & Foner 1972; Tallman and Ihinger-Tallman 1977) posit a more active
role for adult learners, the classic literature (Dager, Hines & Williams 1976;
Kanter 1977; Proctor and Davis 1983) has treated them as passive due to the
emphasis on learning subject matter. The entire process has been presented as
occurring on a bipolar communication continuum mostly involving a socializing
agent and a socializee—a transmitter and a receiver. Underlying this approach
is a reified, cognitive, static perception of professional knowledge.

Our contention, presented in this volume, is that learning is a process that is
dynamic, ongoing, interactive, automatic, and multi-modal. Therefore, an anthropologically adequate theory of education, including adult education, will
consist of at least five characteristics. First, it will start with the concept of
culture—basic to anthropological inquiry—as its initial frame of reference.
Hence, the framework for education is broadly defined as culture acquisition/
transmission. Because of the predominant application of the narrower socialization model to professional learning, institutions of formal instruction have been
considered the main context for such studies. This is true of the classic works
(Becker et al. 1961; Bucher and Stelling 1977) that explore the way neophytes
become physicians, psychiatrists, and practitioners of other medical subspecial-
ties. These authors regard the socialization process as separable from a holistic
study of the "professional culture" the candidates are preparing themselves to
join. The systems theory of culture acquisition/transmission posited in this volume states, instead, that the concept of culture must frame the study of learning,
that education can be meaningfully studied only as a subsystem of a larger cultural
framework, a complementing relationship in which the parts and the whole
mutually define each other.

The second aspect of an anthropologically adequate theory of education is a
focus on community as both the source and context of learning. The implication of this tenet for the area of adult professional learning is to suggest a research and programmatic need to offset the usual emphasis on deliberate
instruction by highlighting the considerable portion of professional learning
that occurs in natural (that is, nondeliberately designed) community settings.
It also calls attention to the fact that such learning does not cease with formal
training but rather continues, in different forms, throughout the professional's

career. This focus on community precludes conceiving of "professional culture" within the traditional socialization model, in which the educative role or function is ascribed to institutions of formal instruction alone (Greenwood 1957).

Third, in addition to the inclusion of culture and community, an anthropological theory of education as culture acquisition/transmission has to take into account all phylogenetically important types of learning, such as modeling, group learning, social conflict learning, and play, in addition to direct instruction. Professional education tends to disregard some of these universal modalities of knowledge acquisition, particularly group learning and play. Peer group learning is most commonly used for drilling or routinization. Its potential for developing innovative problem solving is underestimated. The same is true of the play element that is largely untapped as a resource for the development of heuristic thinking. The impact of the absence of this skill is seen here as one of the reasons for the impasse within which the profession of social work is presently found. However, its roots are deeper and its consequences more pervasive. This deficiency stems from the earlier mentioned narrow model of professional socialization (in general, one not unique to the field of social work) and constitutes a paradigmatic insufficiency. According to this model, the socializee's role is perceived as largely passive, emphasis is on transmission rather than acquisition, and learner feedback is de-emphasized.

The dominant cognitive-deliberate-instruction orientation in professional training not only loses sight of the other important forms of learning mentioned above, but also disregards the fourth aspect of an anthropologically adequate theory of education, the polyphasic nature of human learning (Henry 1960:268). The fact that humans process information through all their senses simultaneously is taken in this volume as a basic tenet of culture learning theory that must be extended to adult learners.

Finally, an anthropologically adequate theory will be comparative. It will provide the framework for the comparative analysis of different sets of culture acquisition/transmission data to enhance comprehension of this vitally important human process.

The purpose of this chapter is to discuss the gains to be made by applying a cultural theory of education, such as the one proposed in this volume, to the context of professional learning. Illustrative materials will be drawn from a study of social workers that focuses on their perception of their profession and the way the latter is transmitted.

While our operationalized model facilitates all stages of the research enterprise from the design and systematic collection of data through its analysis and interpretation and on to theory construction and generalization, the data collected for this particular study predated the operationalization and testing of our field method and thus precluded its application at that early stage of the research. Nevertheless, the application of culture acquisition to this study's findings will demonstrate its paradigm enriching potential.

THE STUDY

This study was of social workers' attitudes toward change, their perceptions of their profession, and how these attitudes and preceptions are transmitted. The choice of social workers for a study of change orientation and its transmission was motivated by the profession's manifest and pervasive change ideology. By looking at how such a profession adapts to macro social changes, one can presumably encompass a whole gamut of change processes from the individual through the social-organizational and on to the larger cultural level. This seems to be one possible avenue to the operationalization of the study of culture change, a methodological conundrum with which anthropologists have grappled for some time. A detailed ethnographic interview guide was chosen as the main research instrument. This was preceded only by a brief period of unstructured observation at each setting by members of the research team.[1]

Sixty veteran social workers (five years or more in practice), 60 junior social workers (less than five years in practice), and 60 last-year social work students constituted the research sample. The ethnographic interview guide included both similar and specific questions directed to the three categories of informants. Familiarity with many of the informants helped researchers construct a culturally appropriate interview guide and aided in interpretation of the data.

Social work education at Haifa University, as in Israel in general, occurs on two main levels. The B.S.W. (Bachelor of Social Work) is a professional degree quite similar to the M.S.W. (Master of Social Work) in the United States in terms of syllabus structure and content areas, except that the former is more time intensive. In Israel, the B.S.W. is the level at which practitioners are prepared, whereas the M.S.W. is primarily a research degree. In general, similarity between professional orientations and training programs in Israel and the United States is high. Although addressing social issues specific to the respective national scene, the programs' common core of professional values probably supersedes such context-engendered differences.

Field instruction is concurrent with formal academic instruction throughout the period of training, with equal time allotted to each in the second and third years. During the first year, the balance is slightly in favor of theoretical subject matter. It should be noted that among the human service professions, social work is the only one that starts field instruction at the very earliest stages of formal training. In other professions, such as law, medicine, and teaching, field instruction takes place either during the last stages of training or upon completion of training, in a sequential order. However, because a few innovative medical training programs are experimenting with early simultaneous practicum and theoretical learning—at Macmaster University in Canada or Ben Gurion University in Israel, for example—the matter is becoming a salient issue in the design of curricula for professional education.

Specializations in social work include such areas as the family, children and youth, geriatrics, community development, correction, health, mental health, and rehabilitation. In the first two years, students take generic courses and related field work. In their third year, students concentrate their courses in one of the above domains. Field placement and ongoing supervision also occur in a specialized topic-related agency. Emphasis is placed on exposing students to theoretical and experiential learning in treatment techniques such as individual case work, group-work techniques, and community level intervention. The entire process of formal training is marked by a bipolarity between the theoretical and the clinical components of the program. All participants, both those on the transmitting and on the receiving ends, are constantly comparing and evaluating their relative contributions.

To allow for the emergence of a variety of opinions, informants included in the sample came from a wide range of work settings, from traditional relief oriented social service agencies to more innovative settings providing counseling and educational services, such as an adolescent sex education center, to name just one; from organizations that employed only social workers to those in which social work was a secondary service; from practitioners engaged in intraprofessional work contexts to those participating in interdisciplinary teams. Some of the questions dealt specifically with the formal aspects of training; others addressed issues of common concern to the profession at large. However, the depth of professional enculturation was made a central dimension of the study as a whole. Time spent in the profession was built into the interview guide by virtue of the categories of informants selected: veterans, juniors, and students.

FINDINGS

In the remainder of this chapter, findings related to culture acquisition/transmission are briefly outlined and data are brought in selectively for illustrative purposes. The study indicates that in spite of its professed dedication to social and individual change, the social work profession, both in its social structure and its dynamic of cultural transmission, is organized as a traditional post figurative culture (following Margaret Mead's 1970 classification). The fieldwork supervisor, for those in training, and the on-the-job supervisor, for those in professional practice, are considered the repositories of all relevant knowledge and, hence, the highest authority figures and role models. One would expect Gearing's transactional model (1973) to be evident, at least partially, because of the pervasiveness of dyadic learning situations. Instead, the authoritarian apprenticeship model of socialization dominates. The study could not discover any indication of provision for change based on input from learners. The transmission of culture is designed to be just that: unidirectional, from masters to novices, with few feedback processing mechanisms built into the supervisory encounter.

The earliest evidence of this transmission orientation is found in the participants' reasons for choosing social work as a career: The more veteran the social workers, the stronger their wish to account for a rational choice. Some explanations given mention previous experience in voluntary activities, previous work in the army as personnel officers or in charge of military service conditions, and personal acquaintance with social workers who recommended the profession or whose work seemed interesting and a model worth following. The wish to treat people—"do therapy"—is also frequently mentioned. To others, their choice appears to be a more practical alternative to psychology because one reaches the stage of clinical work sooner. In other words, it is considered a short cut to becoming a clinician.

While the veterans give more ideologically positive answers, the junior social workers do not refrain from presenting their decision to become social workers as negative choices: They say that they did not want to become teachers, that they had switched from sociology and other less applied fields, that social work was a second choice to psychology because they had not been admitted to psychology programs. The juniors' answers are also vaguer; they mention, for example, attraction to human relations work, saying that social work was the first idea that came up in this context, or describe entry into the field based on mere curiosity. In general, their responses to career choice questions made it appear that this is an unprocessed issue for them. The students' answers are quite similar to those of the junior social workers. Understandably, the students' accounts are often related to their current stage of formal instruction. Some were attracted to social work because it was popular with their peers, others because it was hard to get admitted, and thus a challenge.

Researchers have claimed that not only career choice but also expectations of particular work settings should be oriented toward what is already known. Some have claimed, for example, that successful socialization is to a great extent determined by the visibility of the new role to candidates. When neophytes have correct or realistic images of the professional role they are preparing to enter, their performance in formal training is viewed as superior to that of candidates who have held unclear or mistaken perceptions of their future occupation (DaBassis and Rosengren 1975; Wright 1967). The majority of the informants in this study reported having arrived at the school of social work with reasonably realistic expectations. This makes their later reported lack of role clarity hard to explain on the basis of positive role anticipation theory, leaving our research team with the challenge of looking for an alternative explanation.

Veteran social workers often claim to have selected their specific jobs because of the expectation of finding good supervision, innovative intervention methods and, again, the opportunity to "do therapy"—all viewed as possibilities for professional self-development. The service population was of no particular interest except in highly specialized agencies devoted to a restricted age group such as the very young or the very old. For example, hospital social workers generally reported having opted for this work setting out of interest in short term treatment and work with multidisciplinary teams. Only one informant referred to helping sick people as a value. There is no marked difference between veterans and juniors in this respect. However, an apparent discrepancy between the two choices discussed thus far emerges, at least for the veteran group. Their stated reasons for preferring the profession were predominantly other-directed, while their choice of a specific career was determined by professional self-interest.

The focus in the literature on formal training places heavy emphasis on the importance of on-the-job supervision as the main vehicle of cultural transmission. Our findings suggest that this focus diverts attention away from what is really happening. What emerges from the responses of the veteran workers is that important skills such as defining boundaries between professional, personal, and family identity subsets, and ways of overcoming high burn-out rates (characteristic of the human service professions), were not learned in the school of social work but were informally acquired in supervisory encounters in the course of practice or through peer group learning in both directly and indirectly work-related contexts.

When asked to describe their specific career and provide role definitions, the social workers we interviewed ended up providing detailed, descriptive task analyses. Hardly anyone, veteran or junior, offered substantive role definitions. The ones provided were phrased in normative cliches from the professional literature, such as "community change agents" or "help people change." This lack of a distinct professional identity can be regarded as a deficiency resulting from the narrow model of socialization employed. Only a sense of rootedness in the larger cultural system will allow the neophyte to develop an identification with the profession.

In answer to the question "What is special about social service agencies that employ only social workers as compared to settings where social work is a secondary service?" both veteran and junior workers expressed the expectation that professional stimulation would arise from sources outside of one's self. Although there was a high level of agreement on the challenge of working with professionals from other disciplines, the advantages of an all-social-work team also found many advocates. The latter preferred not to spend their energy on interprofessional power struggles. They indicated that social workers have a high capacity to cooperate pragmatically and reach hard decisions based on a common core of values. Most informants, however, enjoy the stimulation inherent in working in interdisciplinary teams. Both experienced and inexperienced workers are attracted to specialized or innovative agencies in the hope of becoming part of their "exciting projects." But they become disillusioned upon realizing that to bring about effective change, one has to be among the initiators. The recurrent cultural theme of viewing others as the initators of change can be attributed to the passive style of formal socialization that social workers have been exposed to which also does not provide them with sufficient opportunities to develop heuristic thinking.

When asked "What changes occurred in your professional role perception in general and your job perception in particular?" veterans report a broadening of scope, a new realization of the nature of their work, that therapy is not "the be all and end all," and that social workers also have crucial mediating and teaching functions. While many spoke about the necessity of undergoing changes in professional self-identity in nonspecific normative terms, none addressed the focused question about role definition. As expected, juniors and students did not relate to such changes.

In response to questions about the future of social work in their particular setting, an inability to envision or design even middle-level structural changes emerges among all categories of informants. There is no awareness of contradictions between various short-range instrumental goals that have gradually acquired the status of telic values. For example, a typical goal was to "Reach out more to the community and give therapy to the entire community." The antithetical nature of the two parts of this statement goes unnoticed. It is derived from the prestigious source of the psychiatric model. The unquestioned value of therapy is related to the social workers' quest for professional status. They cannot reconcile it with their desire for independent change in social work. The tension between "therapy" and the holistic tendencies of social work that call for relating to individuals in their wider social context has not been resolved. Because a large part of the course work is taught by clinicians, and field experience is also supervised by them, the theoretical components of the curriculum are under emphasized and the conceptual fuzziness described above is transmitted to the students.

Although unburdened by habit or tradition, the students are no more imaginative or innovative than the veterans in suggesting improvements. Changes they advocate are often short-range and self-interest oriented, such as lowering the caseload for students. Others call for changes in prevailing proportions of the various treatment methods and work areas—all quantitative rather than qualitative proposals. For example: "It is important to devote less time to organizational arrangements and more to methods for inducing in-depth change in patients." A few students brought up the possibility of a more radical change. They expressed the belief that the need for social service agencies, as we know them, would disappear in the future, and they proposed, in vague terms, to transfer workers to other community services.

In answering the questions "Do you believe in what you are doing?" and "Do you feel it is part of a social worker's job?" evidence of self-doubting is more common among veteran social workers. Changing the institutional realities is hardly seen as possible. Junior social workers talk openly about being psychotherapists as their "real job" and look down on paperwork. Many informants, both juniors and veterans, see difficulties in the definition of interprofessional boundaries as well; however, they do not consider it their task to actively define the boundaries. Sometimes informants disagree with institutional policies but mostly accept them as givens. The informants' general status quo orientation and their perception of institutional frameworks as immutable may be partially explained by the focus of their education on the individual; only a few specialized in community-level intervention.

Although there is a consensus on the importance of theory, which according to Greenwood "serves as a base in terms of which the professional rationalizes his operations in concrete situations" (1957:47), our findings indicate that traditional authority, as embodied by the supervisor, fulfills this rationalizing function while little more than lip service is paid to the role of theory for the improvement of practice. Thus, when asked about the structure of the curriculum, students explained that fieldwork provided their most meaningful learning experiences. Greenwood (1957) maintains that early field instruction encourages the belief that practice does not presuppose previous knowledge. The responses of the students in our sample corroborate his contention. Most were of the opinion that theoretical, policy, and evaluation courses were not very helpful and they would have liked even more treatment methods courses instead.

This is not the first study to distinguish between a training and an educational approach in professional instruction (see, for example, Gartner 1976). While training emphasizes skill development through repetitious work, education fosters the development of knowledge and judgment, using case learning only to illustrate theoretical class learning. The student attitudes evident in the informant data (summarized above) stem from student exposure to a training orientation that is congruent with the prevailing model of socialization.

CONCLUSION: IMPLICATIONS OF THE CULTURAL PERSPECTIVE FOR PROFESSIONAL EDUCATION

In his widely quoted 1957 article, Greenwood establishes a ground rule still devoutly followed today: "One of the principal functions of the professional school is to identify and screen individuals who are prospective deviants from the professional culture" (p. 54). However, a 1982 statement regarding major curricular trends in graduate social work education, which was issued by the deans of the leading schools on behalf of the Council of Social Work Education, singles out the present pluralism in careers and diversity of practice among social workers. The document views pluralism in social work education as a natural and desirable consequence of this state of affairs. In spite of such liberal policy statements, the narrow socialization of neophytes continues as if absolute clarity prevailed about the future professional scenarios they will have to enact. The contributions of such "prospective deviants" or misfits as potential innovators who could expand the boundaries of the profession and move it out of the stagnation portrayed in this study are lost.

This model of professional instruction can be conceptualized as cultural transmission. Little room exists for peer socialization as a formative influence. As in law school (Philips 1982), professional instruction in social work is mainly used to enhance routinization, rather than as a heuristic tool with culture-enriching potential. The main difference between the ethos of the two professional cultures is, however, that while legal professionals are primarily trained to serve as norm-maintaining defenders of the status quo, social workers are supposedly devoted to the promotion of change. Anchored as it is in such a narrow view of culture, the transmission construct of social work education has been shown in the present study to be maladaptive. Instead of preparing "reflective practitioners," to use Schon's (1983) coinage, it produces unimaginative technicians who do little to construct the rituals and role structures of a change-oriented professional culture.

Although this study was not designed as longitudinal observational research and it relied primarily on interviews to create its data base, in some respects it is more holistically conceptualized than the previously mentioned studies of professional socialization (Becker et al. 1961 and Bucher and Stelling 1977). While the latter concentrate on the socializing institution or training program and consider the professional communities as "external structural variables" (Bucher and Stelling 1977: 277), our frame of reference in this study has been the climate of ideas prevailing in the profession at large—made up of a wide range of practitioners—in the light of which students' views and the formation of their professional identities are considered.

In spite of its limitations, this study has demonstrated the limiting effect for the profession of applying a transmission-oriented paradigm of professional education. It should be noted that qualitatively similar assumptions underlie occupational socialization practices in general. According to most writers, the hallmark of professionalism is that it becomes a total life context for the practitioner. Greenwood compares the degree of commitment required to the act of joining a religious order. A fragmented, isolative perception of training as a self-contained process is incapable of preparing the candidates for this kind of future vocation. However, the holistic culture acquisition/transmission model proposed here bestows an enculturative role on all professional-cultural activities, structures, and interactions, formal and informal, that the neophyte, if exposed to them, will polyphasically absorb. From an anthropological standpoint, professional education, like childhood enculturation, is a teleological process best conceptualized, designed, and examined contextually.

The meaningful application of this cultural perspective to the study of professional groups and processes carries a paradigm-enriching potential. Considered as human adaptive ability and defined as a set of skills for living in an environment derived from social learning and acquired through membership in a social group, the holistic culture acquisition/transmission model offers a positive solution to the stalemate in the professional culture of social workers described above. The consequence of a cultural definition of professional training will be that individual members will interact to construct and improvise skills and abilities that suit their needs. The adoption of such a cultural perspective is apparently contingent upon effective professional enculturation that encourages neophytes to construct a sense of cultural identity. Our findings, however, suggest that not only students and juniors but veteran practitioners as well, lack such a clear professional identity.

The systems-based field guide and outline we offer provide both a most suitable instrument and an interpretive scheme for the systematic ethnographic study of the professional culture acquisition/transmission process. An initial short-term fieldwork period, however, would be required for an in vivo adjustment of some of the categories to a professional enculturation context. Thus, for example, "learner" and "age stage" would need to be reconceptualized according to the level of professional advancement, spanning all the stages from first-year studenthood throughout professional practice. "Setting" and "institutions" should be replaced by an exhaustive list of service delivery organizations, formal and informal collegial contexts, etc. To redesign "acts" and "activities," a detailed preliminary ethnographic task analysis is required in a wide range of "settings" and "institutions." Focused participant observation would be needed to check and adapt the "group size and composition," "response," and "atmosphere" subsystem labels.[2] The processual elements of professional learning could be captured by our observation schedule through a context-suited time-sampling method.

Proposing a future research agenda in the concluding section of their extensive literature review on adult socialization, Mortimer and Simmons single out the need for studies that "link the specific aspects of the socialization experience and the requirements of the role that is being learned" (1978:447). The operationalized culture acquisition/transmission model presented in this volume is optimally suited to that scientific endeavor, and its applied value is expected to manifest itself in improved professional education as well as service delivery.

NOTES

1. The team consisted of a principal investigator (Eisikovits) and ten advanced graduate students. The fact that we did not perform systematic observations of social workers in their various activities instead of relying on interviews as the primary source constitutes a considerable methodological limitation. Systematic collection of participant observation data with the aid of our field guide would have added a wealth of descriptive materials against which the interviews could have been tested. See below for further consideration of the issue of sturdy design.

2. As stated in the concluding section of Chapter 8, the codes presented in this volume begin at the macro level but also contain lists of elements or subcategories for more detailed analysis. Thus the coding system facilitates the linking of macro- and microethnographic research. For some specific settings, however, such as schools, workplaces, etc., subsystem classifications may be in need of further modification or development. That is the case here.

Appendix: Complete Revised Code List

1.0 Relevant aspects of Persons
   1.1 Learner
      1.1.1 Characteristics
         1.1.1.1 Sex
            Female (F)
            Male (M)
         1.1.1.2 Age Stage
            infant (I), age 0-2
            young child (Ch), age 3-7
            middle child (M), age 6-10
            older child (O), age 9-13
            post pubescent child (P), age 13-18
            young adult (Y), age 13-24/30
            middle aged adult (A), age 24/30-50
            elder (E), age 50+
         1.1.1.3 Stage in program of formal/deliberate instruction
      1.1.2 Ability to Act/Appropriateness of Act
         1.1.2.1 No participation (N)
         1.1.2.2 Leaves during observation (L)
         1.1.2.3 Plays (Pl)
            models another activity
            informal play
            organized sports
         1.1.2.4 Does Other Work Task (O)
            works on another activity
            obeys instruction of senior member not related to activity at hand
         1.1.2.5 Interruption or Interference (I)
            asks about things unrelated to task/activity
            suggests change in activity
            refuses adult/senior request not related to activity
            gets underfoot with private acts of own
         1.1.2.6 Unskillful Participation (U)
            does it incorrectly, poorly, ineptly
            gets in the way while trying
            does not do task/share/requested part/refuses instruction
         1.1.2.7 Watches or Asks Questions (W)
            (if very young, explores, exhibits curiosity)
            models activity
         1.1.2.8 Junior Participation (J)
            does child or junior role
            tries it
            does simple partial task
            does part of it
            included by special arrangement like apprenticeship work
         1.1.2.9 Full Skillful Participation (F)
            participates fully as partner or coworker
         1.1.2.10 Learner Initiates/Directs Task in Setting (D)
      1.1.3 Act (same as 3.1.2)
   1.2 Other Persons Responding Person

1.2.1 Characteristics of Responding Person
    1.2.1.1 Parent or Sibling (P)
        Sex
            same (s)
            opposite (o)
        Seniority/Authority
            junior (j)
            client (c)
            equal (=)
            respected senior (r)
            formal authority figure (f)
    1.2.1.2 Kin (K)
        Sex
            same (s)
            opposite (o)
        Seniority/Authority
            junior (j)
            client (c)
            equal (=)
            respected senior (r)
            formal authority figure (f)
    1.2.1.3 Non-Kin (N)
        Sex
            same (s)
            opposite (o)
        Seniority/Authority
            junior (j)
            client (c)
            equal (=)
            respected senior (r)
            formal authority figure (f)
1.2.2 Values (including ontological-epistemological statements or explanations, as
    well as related motives and incentives to action)
    1.2.2.1   A highly pessimistic world view that focuses on the presence of <u>evil</u> in a
           harsh environment (E)
        1.2.2.1.1   Values scaled on the good-
                evil dimension

Society is an evil to be done away with (G.0.0)

The only good in life comes through a rare fluke or bit of luck or by chance (G.1.0)

An abundance of evil spirits constantly make people ill and ruin crops (G.1.0)

A major spirit/god is evil and of equivalent strength to the good god(s)/spirit (G.1.0)

        1.2.2.1.2   Values scaled on the
                materiality/im-materiality
                dimension

Indulging in orgies (M.0.0)

Preventing others from getting things wanted (M.0.5)

Rituals are situational, pragmatic, performed to meet an immediate need (M.1.25)

Avoiding jail, fines, arrest, lashings, etc. (M.2.0)

Giving punishment, arrest, judgment, etc. (M.2.0)

Humans are evil, malicious, out to do everyone in (G.1.0)

All illness and death come through sorcery (G.1.0)

Illness is seen as a punishment (G.1.0)

Work is a punishment inflicted on humans (G.1.0)

Social life is a necessary evil, it is bad but prevents what is worse (G.1.0)

Many taboos are required to prevent harm, many talismans to ward off evil (G.2.0)

Many places are evil or dangerous (G.2.0)

Work is hard, to be avoided, toil to escape (G.2.0)

Most people are evil if provoked (G.2.0)

Sorcery is suspected at every death (G.2.0)

Evil must be severely punished to stamp it out and keep it from spreading (G.2.0)

Getting or avoiding revenge (M.2.0)

Protecting one's self from immediate harm, avoiding danger (M.2.0)

Displaying/proving machismo, courage, one's aggressiveness (M.2.5)

Tricking someone (M.2.5)

Displaying fact that one is cleverer, sharper than another (M.2.5)

Tricksters are admired, to be emulated (M.2.5)

Confrontation is valued, urged (M.2.5)

1.2.2.2   A world view that emphasizes material gain in a context of scarcity (M)

1.2.2.2.1   Values scaled on the good/evil dimension

All the gods/spirits have evil, hostile sides/elements (G.3.0)

Gods are easily offended/ capricious

Gods can/must be bribed to soften them up and win care for humans (G.3.0)

Humans can be caught in the god's rivalries and get hurt (G.3.0)

Gods are weak, easily manipulated, but jealous and demanding (G.3.0)

Nature is niggardly, it never produces enough (G.3.0)

Certain specific happenings portend evil and must be counteracted (G.3.0)

Life is a struggle, nature is hard but can be made to produce (G.4.0)

1.2.2.2.2   Values scaled on the materiality/ immateriality dimension

Getting goods or property, specific items (M.0.5)

Increasing output, crop, or preventing loss in enterprise (M.0.5)

Healing the body now (M.1.0)

Gaining wealth over time (M.1.5)

Making/avoiding debt balance (M.1.5)

Avoiding future scarcity, being prepared for future (M.1.5)

Perpetuating an exchange situation that benefits you (M.1.5)

Entrepreneurship, results of work, acquisition (M.1.5)

Illness/crop failure/etc. are part of
the normal tribulations of life
(G.4.0)

Work is a chore, it is required to get
results (G.4.0)

1.2.2.3   World views that emphasize achievement or personal accomplishment
(A)

1.2.2.3.1   Values scaled on the
good/evil dimension

Human goodness is defined as
cleverness, quickness, competitiveness
to make good outcomes occur (G.4.0)

Preventing waste, to save/ preserve
(M.1.5)

Traders and business people are social
ideals pointed out to imitate (M.1.5)

1.2.2.3.2   Values scaled on the
materiality/ immateriality
dimension

Improving social rank/position (M.3.0)

Acting in accord with social rank, age,
status, class (M.3.0)

Getting promoted, elected, appointed
(M.3.0)

For pleasure (M.4.0)

For long term health, endurance
(M.4.0)

To achieve leisure time (M.4.0)

Utilizing nature, exploiting it,
dominating it because its purpose is
to supply human needs (M.4.0)

For personal fulfillment (M.4.5)

Producing personal psychological or
moral growth (M.4.0)

Improving -beauty,
skills, athletic
prowess (M.4.5)

Gaining -fame, power,
authority, managerial
ability, education,
knowledge, learning
(M.4.5)

Improving speaking ability, oratorical
skills (M.4.5)

Improving luck, fate or avoiding bad
luck or fate (M.4.5)

Seizing opportunity to win (M.4.5)

Personal attributes are thought of as
utilitarian (M.4.5)

Admirable qualities are individualism,
achievement, personal
accomplishment, self direction, self
reliance (M.4.5)

Asserting one's rights, insisting upon
fulfillment of expectations (M.4.5)

1.2.2.4   World views that emphasize the necessity of strong social <u>control</u> (C)

1.2.2.4.1   Values scaled on the good/evil dimension

Ritual performance is essential to ward off evil, exacting performance is essential or disasters will follow (G.3.0)

Innovation will make the already bad worse (G.3.0)

People are weak and easily go wrong (G.3.0)

Humanity through its own actions brought evil into the world (G.3.0)

Obedience is defined as good (G.3.0)

People only remain good if there are many rules regulations defining behavior and if someone constantly supervises and checks (G.3.0)

Justice is based on punishment to control populace and assert the right (G.3.0)

Strong police and military are essential (G.3.0)

Only <u>our</u> way is good, way of others is bad (G.4.0)

Orderliness is critical or the social fabric will break down (G.4.0)

1.2.2.4.2   Values scaled on the materiality/ immateriality dimension

Incentives based on legalistic attitudes, exacting standards of rightness which are enforced by gods or gossip mechanisms (M.6.0)

Avoiding bad gossip (M.6.0)

Conforming (M.6.0)

Protecting one's reputation (M.6.0)

One must... (M.6.0)

Everyone else does (M.6.0)

1.2.2.5   World views that are based on <u>technological</u>, objectivized visions of an impersonal natural law (T)

1.2.2.5.1   Values scaled on the good/evil dimension

Innovation is desired because it makes life better (G.4.0)

Nature works on automatic laws (G.5.0)

Illness comes from natural disease agents and is overcome by technological means (G.5.0)

1.2.2.5.2   Values scaled on the materiality/ immateriality dimension

Improving the item, strain, product; stewardship reasons (M.3.5)

For reasons of care, cleanliness, neatness, good order (m.3.5)

Demands of good craftsmanship (M.3.5)

Innovation is valued (M.3.5)

Progress in materials, technology is desired (M.3.5)

Accumulated experience indicates that this is the way it works (M.5.5)

The data tell us to do this (M.5.5)

Efficiency (M.5.5)

From motives oriented toward actual, chronological future (M.7.5)

Because that is what science tells us, it
is scientifically correct (M.8.5)

Scientific training and knowledge are
valued as such as are the larger
attitudes based on them (M.8.5)

Because it is good to have knowledge,
to possess information (M.8.5)

1.2.2.6   A world view that emphasizes social ends in a context of social balance
(S)

1.2.2.6.1   Values scaled on the
good/evil dimension

Some spirits/gods are good, some are
evil (G.5.0)

Whether law is good or bad depends
on viewpoint, on its function
(G.5.0)
Wrongdoing creates a social
imbalance which must be
rebalanced (G.5.0)
Goodness is defined as a return to
balance (G.5.0)
Fairness is emphasized (G.5.0)

Human nature is mixed or neutral,
good but corrupted (G.5.0)
How you judge a person depends on
your viewpoint (G.5.0)
A major good is the achievement of
knowledge of human nature,
through experience, seniority
(G.5.0)

Ancestral way is valued because it
provides for order and social good
and is our way (G.6.0)

1.2.2.6.2   Values scaled on the
materiality/ immateriality
dimension

Protecting the group (M.5.0)
Enhancing the reputation of the group
(M.5.0)
Because we are the chosen people
(M.5.0)
Because I/we are the (name of people),
reasons based on assertion of
identity (M.5.0)

Self identity based upon membership of
family lineage or clan, upon whom
behavior reflects (M.5.0)

Classical or literary learning as a
desirable mark of "culture" or class
(M.5.0)

Fulfilling duties to others, completing
obligations (M.6.5)
Doing one's share (M.6.5)
Being fair (M.6.5)
Teaching someone what they need to
know to be a good citizen, neighbor,
person (M.6.5)

Becoming a skillful leader, developing
leadership qualities (M.6.5)
Emphasis on sex and gender functions,
division of labor, age stage
expectation for responsibility (M.6.5)
A theory of generalized socio-economic
reciprocity (M.6.5)
Working is seen as a contribution to
society (M.6.5)

Bringing about utopia on earth - in

future (M.7.5)
For the sake of future generations
(M.7.5)
Improving quality of life (M.7.5)

1.2.2.7   World views that emphasize divine or cosmic <u>retribution</u> upon those
who violate a divinely established order (R)

1.2.2.7.1   Values scaled on the
good/evil dimension
Gods are good but they relate to
humans through punishment and
chastisement (G.6.0)
Illness is seen as a punishment (G.6.0)

If you violate social law or bring social
discord someone becomes ill
(G.8.0)
Other humans, while wrong, are like
us, not to be feared as evil (G.8.0)

1.2.2.7.2   Values scaled on the
materiality/ immateriality
dimension
Avoiding causing natural disasters which
the gods visit upon bad people
(M.6.0)
Avoiding punishment from the gods
(M.6.0)
Satisfying the gods so they won't bring
retribution (M.6.0)
Avoiding pollution (M.6.0)

1.2.2.8   World views that picture life and the gods as good but demanding high
standards and which regard positive <u>lawfulness</u> as the critical factor for
a successful society (L)

1.2.2.8.1   Values scaled on the
good/evil dimension
Humans are good because they obey
law and are controlled, lawlessness
is rare (G.7.0)
Human goodness is expressed in
performance of duty (G.7.0)
When people do their duty good and
right order prevail (G.7.0)
Goodness and social order stem from
law which must therefore be
enforced (G.7.0)
Justice occurs when the law is fulfilled,
satisfied (G.7.0)

Strenuous ritual is required to satisfy
good god(s) and get results (G.8.0)
God(s) are stern, hard, just
fathers/kings (G.8.0)

1.2.2.8.2   Values scaled on the
materiality/ immateriality
dimension
Obeying commands of gods, goddesses,
ancestors, sacred law (M.7.0)
Being in accord with tradition (M.7.0)
Avoiding breaking taboos (M.7.0)
To get to heaven (M.7.0)

Because orderliness is essential, rituals
are fixed, calendars defined, ritual
specialists and special knowledge are
required (1.7.0)
Seniors are to be listened to because
they have a better knowledge of
tradition and right (1.7.0)
Seniority, respect, lineal order, to carry
out defined duty (1.7.0)

1.2.2.9   A world view that envisions a naturally <u>harmonious</u> cosmos in which
humans are cooperative, active partners. (H)

1.2.2.9.1   Values scaled on the
good/evil dimension
Humans are capable of becoming
good, true, honest and wise,
serving society and self through
proper behavior (G.8.0)
Humans are essentially good if left

1.2.2.9.2   Values scaled on the
materiality/ immateriality
dimension
Acting out of pity, kindness, generosity,
humility (M.8.0)
Being of service, helpful (M.8.0)

alone and not corrupted (G.8.0)
Humans are a harmonious part of
nature that fit in naturally but can
cause disruption (G.8.0)
Harmonious, cooperative, present
active spirits/ gods/ goddesses that
activate natural forces (G.9.0)

Cosmos is a harmonious eco-system in
which humans have a good niche
(G.9.0)
Nature is beneficent and abundant and
provides all humans need (G.9.0)
People can go to holy places and get
blessings (G.9.0)
Work is a natural, fulfilling human
activity (G.9.0)
If one follows nature's rules and stays
in harmony, health and happiness
result (G.9.0)

Humans help the gods/nature create
and maintain order (G.9.0)
Rituals that are well performed, with
good hearts/intentions bring the
good to humans (G.9.0)
Social law is of human origin, but
essentially good and rarely to be
questioned (G.9.0)

Because it is the right season,
everything has a due time and
season (M.9.0)
Conforming to nature and natural law
(M.9.0)
Because all life is sacred, is our sister/
brother (M.9.0)

Remaining in harmony with nature
(M.9.0)
Doing our share to keep nature in order
(M.9.0)

If you violate nature's rules it creates
existential disharmony (M.9.0)

Obtaining a spiritual guide (as through
a vision quest) (M.9.0)

From motives of collaterality,
brothers/sisterhood, cooperation,
equality, sharing, communality of
goods (M.9.0)

1.2.2.10   Viewpoints that define the world as good and humanity as good in
connection with an other-worldly orientation (G)

1.2.2.10.1 Values scaled on the
good/evil dimension
Good god(s) are in everything and
infuse goodness into it (G.9.0)
Gods respond immediately to prayers
by filling requests (G.9.0)
Rituals are easy, nondemanding
(G.9.0)
God(s) are indulgent fathers/mothers
(G.9.0)

Humans are perfectible or were once
perfect (G.9.0)
Humans are capable of becoming
completely unselfish moral, ethical,
giving only to others (G.9.0)

Unchangeably good and pure god(s) -
above all created things in
goodness (G.10.0)

1.2.2.10.2 Values scaled on the
materiality/ immateriality
dimension
Obeying the sacred rules of the gods
(M.9.0)
Because it is right, truthful, ethical,
moral (M.9.5)
Because it is beautiful (M.9.5)

Honoring, worshiping or serving the
god(s)/spirit (M.10.0)
Achieving nirvana or spiritual escape
from earthly life (M.10.0)
Reaching an aesthetic ideal (M.10.0)
Hearing or communicating with god(s)
(M.10.0)

> The ancestral ways are sacred,
> absolute best (G.10.0)
> Society's laws are god-given (G.10.0)
> Wrongdoing is a sin (G.10.0)

1.2.2.11   No statement made or given (X)
1.2.2.12   Values, ontological-epistemological statements, explanations, or
incentives that cannot be classified (U)
3.0 Cultural Information Stored in Social Patterns
3.1 Social Interaction Patterns
3.1.1   Degree of Institutionalization
3.1.1.1   Non-institutionalized (N)
house/family (H)
porch/veranda/patio (P)
courtyard/compound/yard   (C)
neighborhood (N)
open spaces in local village or town (V)
open spaces far from point of origin (F)
3.1.1.2   Recreational (OR)
attending public spectacles, e.g., sports events, circuses, movie houses
museums, libraries, etc.
participating in organized recreational events
3.1.1.3   Social (S)
kin (refers only to their meetings or formal functioning)
family
lineage
clan
cross-kin (refers to meetings or functions)
age-grades
voluntary associations
residential groups
entertainment groups
information social (those groups which have a standard, regular meeting
place, such as bars, taverns, stores, wells, etc.)
3.1.1.4   Economic (E)
work groups -- organized
corporations
guilds/craft assn./unions
ritualized exchanges
centralized markets
retail businesses
public transport
3.1.1.5   Formal instructional (particularly modern state schools) (I)
3.1.1.6   Military (M)
warrior societies (external protection)
police groups (internal protection)
ad hoc groups (vigilante, raiding)
3.1.1.7   Political (A)
assemblies: generalized functions
courts: formalized function, i.e., judging, hearing cases
councils: formalized functions, i.e., advice giving

legislatures: formalized functions, i.e., law making
3.1.1.8   Ritual (R)
calendrical (c)
crisis (cr)
    birth
    death
    illness/health
identification-status (i)
    naming
    marriage (betrothal, etc.)
    puberty
    age/grade related
    title confirming-formal
    fertility
    ancestral/family
revitalization-reintegration (including non-specific fairs and festivals)
pleasing/appeasing powers
3.1.1.9   Religious (G)
ritual specialist groups
religious societies
    open membership (as churches)
    closed membership (as kivas)
3.1.2   Activity Clusters that Characterize the Milieu and Learners' Acts (Categories should be conceived of as reciprocal wherever appropriate, so that "making judgments" includes being judged and "gift giving" includes receiving gifts.)
3.1.2.1   Experiencing individual states (I)
sleeping/resting
dreaming/daydreaming/imagining
eating alone
playing alone
being ill/being in pain
being pregnant/giving birth
having menstruation
having accident
excreting
dying
dressing/ bathing/ self-cleansing/ decorating body/ cutting hair/ modifying body/ piercing/ scarring/ filing teeth/ circumcising
3.1.2.2   Giving/receiving curing activities (H)
diagnosing
treating/ operating/ giving medicine/ setting bones/ removing causes/ giving psychotherapy
using disease or disaster preventatives
midwifing
making or locating medicines
3.1.2.3   Caring for others/receiving care (Cf)
physically
    cleaning people up
    dressing
    protecting, sheltering, monitoring
    feeding, giving liquids, medications
mentally/enhancing well-being

empathetic listening
providing advice, counseling
directing people to help or giving services/needed information
providing/setting direction, permissions
providing goods and services (money, food, shelter, etc.)

3.1.2.4   Multipurpose activities

socializing (SO)
visiting/ gossiping/ standing around/ discussing/ watching people, activities (VW)
joking/ teasing/ doing tricks/ talking sex (J)
drinking alcohol/ using drugs (D)
sharing meals/ feasting (F)
gift giving (G)

art and entertainment activities -- doing or watching (A)
dancing/ singing/ music making/ composing; organizing, watching, performing drama; story telling, watching t.v., listening to radio
doing art or decorating things, carving, painting, making jewelry
playing, unorganized fun, outings (Pl)
participating in/ observing organized sports games/ skills contests (OG)

expressing conflict (Cn)
fighting (physical)
fighting verbal (arguing, cursing, daring)
committing homicide
destroying property
hiding, avoiding, sneaking out, eloping
listening in, spying

physical movement (ph)
leaving setting
changing residence/ moving
doing exercises
walking
land travel by beast, vehicle
water travel
air travel

deliberate information exchange (E)
oral teaching/ learning as giving/ attending lectures; giving or getting instruction, tutoring (L)
electronic or media-aided teaching/learning (Md)
involved or operational teaching/ learning, as showing/ demonstrating or watching same, practicing, lab exercises, etc. (Dm)
record keeping/ communicating, as writing, recording, entering data, sending/ carrying/ receiving messages (Rk)
studying, memorizing, reciting, thinking (St)
consulting, getting/ giving advice, briefing, asking, information-seeking, questions (Bq)

3.1.2.5   Maintaining or Changing Social Order and Services (MC)

public order
making/ changing/ posting laws, rules, regulations
choosing formal role occupants (by discussion, voting, etc.)
deciding on/stating goals, determining means, discussing policies or decisions
making judgments, settling conflicts, issuing reward/ punishment

orating/ speech making
making restitution (jail, fine, apology, banishment)
issuing currency
policing
bribing/being bribed
feuding or rioting
providing/receiving military protection (incl. drilling, warring, making weapons)
public services
building, maintaining communication and transport
maintaining public safety (building dikes, shelters)
responding to disasters (fire fighting, rescue)
providing public assistance services to people in crisis situations
paying/ gathering tithes, taxes, tributes
private order
marrying, paying bride wealth/ dowry, divorcing
practicing population control (birth control, infanticide, abortion, euthanasia)
creating/ becoming ritual kin (adoption, god parents, blood sisters/ brothers)
3.1.2.6   Religious & Ritual types of activities (R)
addressing, sacrificing, manipulating gods, spirits, etc.
ritually secluding/being ritually secluded
making religious objects, symbols
meditating
ritual questing/pilgrimages
ritual cleansing
burying/ formal mourning
wearing ceremonial garb, etc.
making oaths, vows
cannibalistic and other ritual eating
contacting spirits, divining, interpreting omens
being in a trance/ non-ordinary state
fasting
alms giving/ philanthropy
3.1.2.7   Converting energy & materials to human use
3.1.2.7.1 Primary conversion (PC)
providing for food
hunting
gathering
fishing
irrigating
hoeing
plowing
planting
weeding
fertilizing
harvesting (raised crops)
herding and feeding animals
milking
marking/ branding
butchering

veterinary
looking for water supplies /digging wells
water getting
salt getting/ processing
preserving food
cooking/ preparing food
providing shelter, heat, light
gathering/ processing fuel
making/ tending fire/ heat source/ light source
gathering building material (lumbering)
building shelter (animal or human)
providing clothing
obtaining fiber (shearing, cutting flax) or hide
spinning/ tanning (preparing for use)
weaving/ knitting/ sewing (making into clothes)
providing mineral resources
    mining, drilling
    processing minerals (smithing, smelting, refining)
3.1.2.7.2   Secondary conversion or support (SC)
  individual work activity
    making tools, vehicles, machines, containers
    keeping useful (repairing, mending, cleaning)
    making objects for household comfort (soap, furniture)
    transporting/storing
    obtaining things made by others (buying, selling, trading, bargaining)
    doing, receiving personal service (maids, servants, hair dressers)
  group or industrial work activity
    working in a factory
    supervising work (i.e., on the spot, giving orders, instructions)
    managing industry or trade (usually from an office)
    designing (as architects, engineers)
  owning and possessing
    inheriting
    dividing goods/ property
    lending/ borrowing/ renting/ collecting interest
    accumulating surpluses or wealth/ displaying it
    giving/ collecting salary/ wage/ welfare
3.1.2.8   Doing/ suffering something defined as wrong/ committing a crime (W)
stealing, wrecking - property crime
raping/ seducing/ adultery/ incest - sex crime
assaulting
murdering/ suiciding
violations of the social order such as lying/ committing fraud
not paying debts
violating religious laws or taboos
doing sorcery - psychological crimes
harming self or others through neglect or carelessness
3.1.3   Group Size and Composition
  3.1.3.1   Group Size
    3.1.3.1.1   Individual (I)
    3.1.3.1.2   Small 2-10 (S)
    3.1.3.1.3   Medium 11-40 (M)

3.1.3.1.4 Large 40+ (L)
3.1.3.2   Group composition (all codes indicate mixed groups unless a code for a
           sex/authority indicates otherwise)
3.1.3.2.1 Parent-Sibling Group (P)
    Single sex
        primarily same sex (s)
        primarily opposite sex (o)
    Equality/ Authority
        just siblings (=)
        just parents (a)
3.1.3.2.2 Kin group (K)
    Single sex
        primarily same sex (s)
        primarily opposite sex (o)
    Equality/ Authority
        primarily junior or equals (=)
        primarily seniors/ authorities (a)
3.1.3.2.3 Friends and acquaintances (F)
    Single sex
        primarily same sex (s)
        primarily opposite sex (o)
    Equality/ Authority
        primarily junior or equals (=)
        primarily seniors/ authorities (a)
3.1.3.2.4 Mixed group of parents, siblings, kin, friends, or acquaintances (MC)
    Single sex
        primarily same sex (s)
        primarily opposite sex (o)
    Equality/ Authority
        primarily junior or equals (=)
        primarily seniors/ authorities (a)
3.1.3.2.5 Mixed group of familiars and strangers (MF)
    Single sex
        primarily same sex (s)
        primarily opposite sex (o)
    Equality/ Authority
        primarily junior or equals (=)
        primarily seniors/ authorities (a)
3.1.3.2.6 Group of strangers (S)
    Single sex
        primarily same sex (s)
        primarily opposite sex (o)
    Equality/ Authority
        primarily junior or equals (=)
        primarily seniors/ authorities (a)
3.1.4 Relational Expressive Atmosphere
    3.1.4.1   Sleep: relaxed -- eyes closed, snoring, etc. (M)
    3.1.4.2   Boredom/Lethargy: all biol. & indiv./ stim. measures near bottom --
               blankness, heaviness of limb, energy lacking (B)
    3.1.4.3   Relaxation: loose muscles, loose focus -- yawns, comfortable (R)
    3.1.4.4   Sadness: activity, focus, biological measures very low, intensity absent --
               heavy eyes, drooping face (S)

3.1.4.5   Love: physical closeness, touching, endearing terms, baby talk, hugging, kissing (L)

3.1.4.6   Depression/ Dejection: although quiet, there is some activity -- sobbing, moody silence, abrupt or suppressed movement, side focus (D)

3.1.4.7   Happiness: definite movement, moderate arousal, laughing, joking, nicknames, informal (H)

3.1.4.8   Resentment/Unhappiness: low but definite bodily movement, generalized focus -- crying, complaining, mourning (U)

3.1.4.9   Task oriented: moderate arousal -- most attention and activity directed toward a task or activity like music production, may be formalized, may be a sports activity (T)

3.1.4.10   Judgmental/Competitive: moderate arousal, attention less single, activity lower and less intense than .12/.13 -- bragging, boasting, daring, sharp remarks, ridiculing, blaming (J)

3.1.4.11   Wonder/surprise: high focus, moderate arousal, less intense and active, moderate biological disturbance (W)

3.1.4.12   Elation: high arousal -- yelling, marching, dancing, loud laughing (E)

3.1.4.13   Anger/Disgust: high arousal, focus, activity, loud yelling, arguing, expressions of pain (A)

3.1.4.14   Fear: highest arousal, very focused, intensive activity -- screaming, fighting,hiding, running, panic (F)

3.2 Patterns of Control/Response

3.2.1   Accepting non-instructional responses (A)
            includes learner in conversation/ task, makes room, gives materials
        looks on or observes learner performance
        no response -- just continues task/activity

3.2.2   Implicitly instructional reactions (I)
        strong positive response, such as praise, give reward, touch, pat, kiss, thank, etc. (++)
        strong negative response, such as spank, slap, push away, withhold privileges, vilify, curse, beat (--)
        moderately positive response, such as smile, nod, praise indirectly (+)
        moderately negative responses, such as gestures of anger or disapproval, adverse indirect comment (-)

3.2.3   Responds to learner initiatives (L)
        acts on learner's request, suggestion, direction (++)
        gives in to learner reluctantly, ungraciously, annoyed (--)
        denies request, withholds permission (--)

3.2.4   Purposeful but indirectly instructional responses (P)
        encourages learner to continue (+)
        tries to get learner to think (+)
        asks learner question (+)
        offers reward, bribe, conditional promise (-)

3.2.5   Mixed, reversed or contradictory responses (M)

3.2.6   Directly instructional or directive responses (D)
        gives directions, instructions that accept learners actions (++)
        correct actions, instruct by centering on mistakes, criticize (--)

References

Abrahamson, D. 1985. Tamarins in the Amazon. *Science* 227:59–63.

Ainsworth, M. 1973. The Development of Infant-Mother Attachment. In *Review of Child Development Research*, Vol. 3, ed. B. Caldwell and H. Ricciuti, 1094. Chicago: University of Chicago Press.

Albert, E. M. 1956. The Classification of Values: A Method and Illustration. *American Anthropologist* 58:221–48.

Aldis, O. 1975. *Play Fighting*. New York: Academic.

Amoss, P. T., and S. Harrell. 1981. Introduction: An Anthropological Perspective on Aging. In *Other Ways of Growing Old*, ed. P. T. Amoss and S. Harrell, 1–24. Stanford: Stanford University Press.

Ashby, R. 1968. Variety, Constraining, and the Law of Requisite Variety. In *Modern Systems Research for the Behavioral Scientist*, ed. W. Buckley, 129–36. Chicago: Aldine.

Bagley, N. 1963. The Life-Span as a Framework of Reference in Psychological Research. *Vita Humanitas* 6:125–39.

Baldwin, J. D., and J. I. Baldwin. 1978. Reinforcement Theories of Play, Creativity and Psychosocial Growth. In *Social Play in Primates*, ed. E. O. Smith, 231–57. New York: Academic.

————. 1979. The Phylogenetic and Ontogenetic Variables That Shape Behavior and Social Organization. In *Primate Ecology and Human Origins*, ed. I. W. Bernstein and E. O. Smith, 90–116. New York: Garland.

Baltes, P. B., H. W. Reese, and L. P. Lipsitt. 1980. Life-Span Developmental Psychology. *Annual Review of Psychology* 31:65–110.

Baltes, P. B., and S. L. Willis. 1976. Toward Psychological Theories of Aging and Development. In *Handbook of Psychology of Aging*, ed. J. E. Birren and K. W. Schaie. New York: Van Nostrand Reinhold.

————. 1979. Life-Span Development Psychology, Cognitive Functions, and Social Policy. In *Aging from Birth to Death: Interdisciplinary Perspectives*, ed. M. W. Riley, 15–46. Boulder: Westview Press.

Barry, H., J. L. Child, and M. K. Bacon. 1959. The Relation of Child Training to Subsistence Economy. *American Anthropologist* 61:51–63.

Beall, C. 1984. Theoretical Dimensions of a Focus on Age in Physical Anthropology. In *Age and Anthropological Theory*. ed. D. Kertzer and J. Keith. Ithaca, NY: Cornell University Press.

Beals, A., G. Spindler, and L. Spindler. 1967. *Culture in Process*. New York: Holt, Rinehart & Winston.

Becker, H. S., B. Geer, E. C. Hughes, and A. L. Strauss. 1961. *Boys in White: Student Culture in Medical School*. New Brunswick, NJ: Transaction.

Benedict, R. 1934. *Patterns of Culture*. New York: Mentor.

Berlyne, D. S. 1971. *Aesthetics and Psychobiology*. New York: Appleton Century Crofts.

Bernardi, B. 1985. *Age Class Systems: Social Institutions and Polities Based on Age*, trans. D. I. Kertzer. Cambridge: Cambridge University Press.

Bertalanffy, L. von. *See* von Bertalanffy.

Bierele, J. M. 1974. Analysis Reliability Reports. *Behavioral Science Research* 9:327–29.

Bierele, J. M., and S. Witkowski. 1974. HRAF Coding Reliability. *Behavioral Science Research* 9:57–65.

Binstock, R. H., and E. Shanas. 1976. *Handbook of Aging and the Social Sciences*. New York: Van Nostrand Reinhold.

Birren, J. E., and W. P. Cunningham. 1985. Research on the Psychology of Aging: Principles, Concepts and Theory. In Birren and Schaie 1985.

Birren, J. E., W. P. Cunningham, and K. Yamamoto. 1983. Psychology of Adult Development and Aging. *Annual Review of Phychology* 34:543–75.

Birren, J. E., and K. W. Schaie. 1977. *Handbook of the Psychology of Aging*. New York: Van Nostrand Reinhold.

————. 1985. *Handbook of the Psychology of Aging*. New York: Van Nostrand Reinhold.

Black, J. E., and W. T. Greenough. 1986. Developmental Approaches to the Memory Process. In Martinez and Kesner 1986:55–77.

Bloom, B. 1964. *Stability and Change in Human Characteristics*. New York: Wiley.

Bloom, F. E., A. Lazerson, and L. Hofstadter. 1985. *Brain, Mind and Behavior*. New York: Freeman.

Bornstein, M., and M. Lamb. 1984. *Developmental Psychology: An Advanced Textbook*. Hillsdale, NJ: Erlbaum.

Bowden, E. 1969. A Dimensional Model of Multilinear Sociocultural Evolution. *American Anthropologist* 71:864–70.

Bowlby, J. 1969. *Attachment and Loss*, Vol. 1, *Attachment*. New York: Basic Books.

————. 1972. *Attachment and Loss*, Vol. 2, *Separation*. New York: Basic Books.

Breuggeman, J. A. 1978. The Function of Adult Play in Free Ranging Macaca Mulatta. In *Social Play in Primates*, ed. E. O. Smith, 169–91. New York: Academic.

Brim, D. G., Jr. 1966. Socialization Throughout the Life Cycle. In *Socialization After Childhood*, ed. O. G. Brim, Jr., and S. Wheeler, 1–49. New York: Wiley.

Brown, J. K. and V. Kerns, eds. 1985. *In Her Prime: A New View of Middle-Aged Women*. South Hadley, MA: Bergin and Garvey.

Bucher, R., and A. Stelling. 1977. *Becoming Professional*. Beverly Hills, CA: Sage.

Buchler, I., M. Fischer, and J. R. McGoodwin. 1968. Ecological Structure, Economics and Social Organization: The Kapauku. In *New Trends in Mathematical Anthropology*, ed. G. De Meur. London: Routledge and Kegan Paul.

Buckley, W. 1967. *Sociology and Modern Systems Theory*. Englewood Cliffs, NJ: Prentice-Hall.

Burton, A. 1978. Anthropology of the Young. *Anthropology and Education Quarterly* 9(1):54–71.

Burton-Jones, N. 1972. *Ethological Studies of Child Behavior*. Cambridge: Cambridge University Press.

Cairns, R., and J. Valsiner. 1984. Child Psychology. *Annual Review of Psychology* 35:553–77.

Calvin, W. H. 1983. The Computer Methaphor in Neurobiology. In *The Throwing Madonna*. New York: McGraw-Hill.

Campbell, J. W. 1973. Women Drop Back In: Educational Innovations in the Sixties. In *Academic Women on the Move*, ed. A. S. Rossi and A. Calderwood, 93–124. New York: Russell Sage.

Cancian, F. 1975. *What Are Norms? A Study of Beliefs and Action*. Cambridge: Cambridge University Press.

Cancian, F. 1965. *Economics and Prestige in a Maya Community*. Stanford, CA: Stanford University Press.

———. 1972. *Change and Uncertainty in a Peasant Economy*. Stanford, CA: Stanford University Press.

Chagnon, N. 1968. *Yanomomo: The Fierce People*. New York: Holt, Rinehart & Winston.

Chalmers, N. 1980. *Social Behavior in Primates*. Baltimore, MD: University Park Press.

Chance, M. R. A. 1978. Attention Structure and Social Organization (Roundtable Discussion). In *Recent Advances in Primatology*, ed. D. J. Chivers and J. Herbert, 93–97. New York: Academic.

Chance, M. R. A., and C. J. Jolly. 1970. *Social Groups of Monkeys, Apes and Men*. London: Jonathan Cape.

Changeux, P. 1985. *Neuronal Man: The Biology of Mind*, trans. Lawrence Garey. Paris: Pantheon.

Chapple, E. 1970. *Culture and Biological Man: Explorations in Behavioral Anthropology*. New York: Holt, Rinehart & Winston.

Cherniak, C. 1986. *Minimal Rationality*. Cambridge, MA: MIT Press.

———. 1987. Logic and Anatomy. Paper presented at the Minnesota Center for the Philosophy of Science, February 9, at the University of Minnesota, Minneapolis.

Chevalier-Skolnikoff, S., and F. E. Poirier, eds. 1977. *Primate Bio-Social Development: Biological, Social and Ecological Determinants*. New York: Garland.

Chodorow, N. 1974. Family Structure and Feminine Personality. In *Women, Culture and Society*, ed. M. Z. Rosaldo and L. Lamphere. Stanford: Stanford University Press.

———. 1978. *The Reproduction of Mothering*. Berkeley: University of California Press.

Chun, K. 1984. Status Mobility and the Role of Individuals in a Korean Lineage Group. In *The Study of Transitional Ways of Life*, Volume 3, 157–209. Seongnam, Korea: Korean Academy.

Cohen, J. J., and L. R. Squire. 1980. Preserved Learning and Retention of Pattern Analyzing Skill in Amnesia: Dissociation of Knowing How from Knowing That. *Science* 10:207–10.

Collier, J. 1973. *Law and Social Change in Zinacantan*. Stanford, CA: Stanford University Press.

Collier, J. F. and M. Z. Rosaldo. 1981. Politics and Gender in Simple Societies. In *Sexual Meanings*, ed. S. Ortner and H. Whitehead, 275–329. New York: Cambridge University Press.

Condon, W., and L. Sander. 1974. Neonate Movement Is Synchronized with Adult Speech: Interactional Participation. *Science* 183:99–101.

Crain, W. 1985. *Theories of Development: Concepts and Applications*, 2nd ed. Englewood Cliffs, NJ: Prentice-Hall.

Csikszentmihalyi, M. 1981. The Socialization Effects of Culture Role Models in Ontogenetic Development and Upward Mobility. *Child Psychiatry and Human Development* 12(1): 3–18.

Curtiss, S. 1977. *Genie: A Psycholinguistic Study of a Modern-Day "Wild Child."* New York: Academic Press.

DaBassis, M. S., and W. R. Rosengren. 1975. Socialization for Occupational Disengagement. *Sociology of Work and Occupation* 2:133–49.

Dager, E. Z., D. Hines, and J. B. Williams. 1976. Social Identification, Social Influence and Value Transmission. Paper presented at the seventy-first annual meeting of the American Sociological Association, New York.

DeCasper, A. and W. Fifer. 1980. Of Human Bonding: Newborns Prefer Their Mothers' Voices. *Science* 208:1174–76.

Devore, I. n.d. *Baboon Development: The Young Infant—Birth to Four Months and Baboon Development: The Older Infant—Four Months to One Year*. Newton, MA: Education Development Center. Films.

Dobbert, M. L. 1975. Another Route to a General Theory of Cultural Transmission: A Systems Model. *Anthropology and Education Quarterly* 6:22–26.

———. 1982. *Ethnographic Research: Theory and Application for Modern Schools and Societies*. New York: Praeger.

———. 1984. An Application of a General Systems Model of Constraints in Cultural Transmission. Paper presented at the Central States Anthropological Society, Lincoln, NE.

Dobbert, M. L., and R. Eisikovits. 1984. Observing Learning in Everyday Settings: A Guide to the Holistic Study of Cultural Transmission/Acquisition in Daily Life. Minneapolis: University of Minnesota. Photocopy.

Dobbert, M. L., R. Eisikovits, M. A. Pitman, J. K. Gamradt, and K. Chun. 1984a. Cultural Transmission in Three Societies: Testing a Systems-Based Field Guide. *Anthropology and Education Quarterly* 6:22–26.

Dobbert, M. L., D. P. McGuire, J. J. Pearson, and K. C. Taylor. 1984b. An Application of Dimensional Analysis in Cultural Anthropology. *American Anthropologist* 86:854–84.

Dobbert, M. L. and H. J. Nelson. 1975. *The Friends at Clear Creek: 1830–1930*. DeKalb, IL: Westland Press.

Dobbert, M. L., and Pitman, M. A. 1982. Cultural Transmission in Three Societies: Testing a Systems-based Field Guide. Paper presented at the Annual Meeting of the American Anthropological Association, Washington DC, December.

———. 1983a. Testing a Theory of Cultural Transmission II: Holistic Pattern Analysis of Data on the Relationship Between Older Children and Cultural Activity Patterns. Paper presented at the American Anthropological Association/Council on Anthropology and Education, Chicago, IL.

———. 1983b. Cultural Transmission in Three Societies: Testing a Systems-Based Model and Field Guide—Research in Progress. Paper presented at meeting of the American Educational Studies Association, Milwaukee, WI.

————. 1986. The Preparation of Childcare Workers: An Anthropological Study of the Hidden Problems of Professionalization. In R. A. Eisikovits and Y. Kashti, eds., *Qualitative Research and Education in Group Care*. New York: Haworth.

Dolhinow, P., ed. 1972. *Primate Patterns*. New York: Holt, Rinehart & Winston.

Dombeck, M. 1983. The Theme Centered Interactional Group Model in Professional Education. *Small Group Behavior* 16(3):275–300.

Dreyfus, H. 1979. *What Computers Can't Do: A Critique of Artificial Intelligence*, rev. ed. New York: The Free Press.

Dreyfus, H., and S. Dreyfus. 1986. *Mind Over Machine: The Power of Human Intuition in the Era of the Computer*. New York: The Free Press.

Dunbar, R. I. M. 1979. Population Demography, Social Organization, and Mating Strategies. In *Primate Ecology and Human Origins*, ed. I. S. Bernstein and E. O. Smith 66–88. New York: Garland.

Dunn, A. J. 1980. The Neurochemistry of Learning and Memory. *Annual Review of Psychology* 31:343–90.

Eddy, E. M. 1969. *Becoming a Teacher*. New York: Teacher's College Press.

Edel, M., and A. Edel. 1968. *Anthropology and Ethics*. Cleveland: Case Western Reserve University Press.

Eggan, D. 1956. Instruction and Affect in Hopi Cultural Continuity. *Southwestern Journal of Anthropology* 12:347–70. Reprinted in *Education and Culture*, ed. G. Spindler. New York: Holt, Rinehart & Winston, 1963.

Eich, J. E. 1980. The Cue-Dependent Nature of State-Dependent Retrieval. *Memory and Cognition* 8:157–73.

Eisenberg, R. 1975. *Auditory Competence in Early Life: The Roots of Communicative Behavior*. Baltimore, MD: University Park Press. (Cited in Murray and Trevarthen 1985:195.)

Elder, G. H. Jr. 1974. *Children of the Great Depression*. Chicago: University of Chicago Press.

Erickson, F. 1975. Gatekeeping and the Melting Pot: Interaction in Counseling Encounters. *Harvard Educational Review* 45:44–70.

————. 1986. Qualitative Methods in Research on Teaching. In *Handbook of Research on Teaching*, 3rd ed, ed. M. C. Wittrock, 119–61. New York; Macmillan.

Erickson, F., and Mohatt, G. 1982. The Cultural Organization of Participant Structures in Classrooms of Indian Students. In *Doing the Ethnography of Schooling*, ed. G. D. Spindler, 132–74. New York: Holt, Rinehart & Winston.

Erickson, F., and J. Schultz. 1981 When Is a Context? Some Issues and Methods in the Analysis of Social Competence. In *Ethnography and Language in Educational Settings*, ed. J. Green and C. Wallat, 147–60. Norwood, NJ: Ablex.

Erikson, E. H. 1959. Identity and the Life Cycle: Selected Papers. *Psychological Issues* 1:50–100.

Fagen, R. 1981. *Animal Play Behavior*. New York: Oxford University Press.

Faherty. V. E. 1983. Simulations and Gaming in Social Work Education: A Projection. *Journal of Education for Social Work* 19(2):111–18.

Falk, D. 1980. Language, Handedness, and Primate Brains: Did the Australopithecines Sign? *American Anthropologist* 82:72–78.

Fantino, A. 1973. Emotion. In *The Study of Behavior: Learning, Motivation, Emotion and Instinct*, ed. J. A. Nevin. Glenview, IL: Scott, Foresman.

Fendrich, J. M. 1976. Black and White Activists Ten Years Later: Political Socialization and Left Wing Politics. *Youth and Society* 8:81–104.

Field, T., and N. Fox, eds. 1985. *Social Perception in Infants*. Norwood, NJ: Ablex.

Forbes, J. L., and J. E. King. 1982. Vision: The Dominant Primate Modality. In *Primate Behavior*, ed. J. L. Forbes and J. E. King, 220–43. New York: Academic.

Fox, R. C. 1957. Training for Uncertainty. In *The Student Physician: Introductory Studies in the Sociology of Medical Education*, ed. R. K. Merton, G. C. Reader, and P. L. Kendall, 207–41. Cambridge: Harvard University Press.

Freedman, D., and M. DeBoer. 1979. Review of Studies on Biological and Cultural Differences in Children. *Annual Review of Anthropology* 8.

Freedman, D., and D. Omark. 1973. Ethology, Genetics and Education. In *Cultural Relevance and Educational Issues*, ed. F. Ianni and J. Storey. Boston: Little, Brown.

Freud, S. 1967. *Introductory Lectures on Psychoanalysis*, trans. James Trachley. New York: Liveright.

Friedan, B. 1963. *The Feminine Mystique*. New York: Norton.

Fry, C. L. 1979. Structural Conditions Affecting Community Formation Among the Aged: Two Examples from Arizona. In *The Ethnography of Old Age*, ed. J. Keith. *Anthropological Quarterly* (special issue) 52:7–18.

———. 1985. *Culture, Behavior, and Aging in the Comparative Perspective*, Birren and Schaie 1985: 216–44.

Fry, C. L., ed. 1981. *Dimensions: Aging, Culture, and Health*. New York: Praeger.

Fry, C. L. and J. Keith. 1982. The Life Course as a Cultural Unit. In *Aging from Birth to Death: Sociotemporal Perspectives*, ed. M. W. Riley, R. Abeles, and M. Teitelbaum. Boulder: Westview.

Funnel, R., and R. Smith. 1981. Search for a Theory of Cultural Transmission in the Anthropology of Education: Notes on Spindler and Gearing. *Anthropology and Education Quarterly* 12:275–300.

Gard, G. C., and G. W. Meier. 1977. Social and Contextual Factors of Play Behavior in Sub-Adult Rhesus Monkeys. *Primates* 18:367–77.

Gardner, H. 1986. Notes on Cognitive Development: Recent Trends, New Developments. In *The Brain, Cognition and Education*, ed. S. Friedman et al., P 259–86. Orlando, FL: Academic.

Gartner, A. 1976. *The Preparation of Human Service Professionals*. New York: Human Science Press.

Gautier, J., and A. Gautier-Hion., 1982. Vocal Communication Within a Group of Monkeys: An Analysis by Biotelemetry. In *Primate Communication*, ed. G. Snowdon, C. Bown, and M. Peterson, 5–29. New York: Cambridge University Press.

Gazzaniga, M. 1985. *The Social Brain: Discovering the Networks of the Mind*. New York: Basic Books.

Gearing, F. 1973. Where We Are and Where We Might Go From Here: Steps Toward a General Theory of Cultural Transmission. *Council on Anthropology and Education Newsletter* 4(1):1–10.

———. 1979. A Reference Model for a Cultural Theory of Education and Schooling. In F. Gearing and L. Sangree (eds.), *Toward a Cultural Theory of Education and Schooling*, 169–230. The Hague: Mouton.

Gearing, F., Carroll, T. Richter, L., Grogan-Hurlick, P., Smith A., Hughes, W., Tindall, B. A., Precourt, W., and Topfer, S. 1979. Working Paper 6. In F. Gearing and L. Sangree (eds.), *Toward a Cultural Theory of Education and Schooling*, 9–38. The Hague: Mouton.

Gearing, F., and L. Sangee, eds. 1979. *Toward a Cultural Theory of Education and Schooling*. The Hague: Mouton,

Gearing, F., and A. Tindall. 1973. Anthropological Studies of the Educational Process. *Annual Review of Anthropology* 2:95–105.

Gearing, F., A. Tindall, A. Smith, and T. Carrol. 1975. Structures of Censorship, Usually Inadvertent: Studies in a Cultural Theory of Education. *Council on Anthropology and Education Newsletter* 6:109.

Geertz, C. 1973. *The Interpretation of Cultures*. New York: Basic Books.

Gibson, M. 1976. Approaches to Multi-Cultural Education in the United States: Some Concepts and Assumptions. *Anthropology and Education Quarterly* 7:7–18.

Gilligan, C. 1977. In a Different Voice: Women's Conceptions of the Self and Morality. *Harvard Educational Review* 47:481–517.

———. 1979. Women's Place in a Man's Life Cycle. *Harvard Educational Review* 49(4):431–46.

Goodman, M. E. 1970. *The Culture of Childhood*. New York: Teachers College Press.

Gould, S. 1985. *The Flamingo's Smile: Reflections in Natural History*. New York: W. W. Norton.

———. 1986. Of Wasps and WASPS: Farewell to Pigeonholes. *The Family Therapy Networker* (January–February).

Greenwood, A. 1957. Attributes of a Profession. *Social Work* (July):47–55.

Gumperz, J. J. 1982. *Discourse Strategies*. Cambridge: Cambridge University Press.

Gutmann, D. 1977. The Cross-cultural Perspective: Notes Toward a Comparative Psychology of Aging. In Birren and Schaie 1977:302–26. New York: Van Nostrand Reinhold.

Hagestad, G. O., and B. L. Neugarten. 1979. Age and the Life Course. In *Handbook of Aging and the Social Sciences*, 2nd ed., R. H. Binstock and E. Shanas, 35–61. New York: Van Nostrand Reinhold.

Hall, K. R. L. 1968. Social Learning in Monkeys. In *Primate Studies in Adaptation and Variability*, ed. P. C. Jay, 383–97. New York: Holt, Rinehart & Winston.

Hansen, J. F. 1979. *Sociocultural Perspectives on Human Learning*. Englewood Cliffs, NJ: Prentice-Hall.

———. 1982. From Background to Foreground: Toward an Anthropology of Learning. *Anthropology and Education Quarterly* 13(2):189–202.

Harlow, H. F., and M. K. Harlow. 1962. Social Deprivation in Monkeys. *Scientific American* 207:136–46.

———. 1965. The Affectional Systems. In *Behavior of Nonhuman Primates: Modern Research Trends*, Vol. 2, ed. A. Schrier, H. Harlow, and F. Stollnitz, 287–334. New York: Academic.

———. 1966. Learning to Love. *American Scientist* 54:244–72.

Harrington, C. 1979. *Psychological Anthropology and Education: A Delineation of a Field of Inquiry*. New York: AMS.

Harris, M. 1968. *The Rise of Anthropological Theory*. New York: Crowell.

Harrison, A. A. 1977. Mere Exposure. In *Advances in Experimental Social Psychology*, Vol. 10, ed. L. Berkowitz. NY: Academic.

Hasher, L., and R. T. Zachs. 1979. Automatic and Effortful Processes in Memory. *Journal of Experimental Psychology: General* 108:356–88.

———. 1984. Automatic Encoding of Fundamental Information: The Case for Frequency of Occurrence. *American Psychologist* 39(12):1372–88.

Haviland, J. B. 1977. *Gossip, Reputation and Knowledge in Zinacantan*. Chicago: University of Chicago Press.

Henry, J. 1960. A Cross-Cultural Outline of Education. *Current Anthropology* 1:267–305.

———. 1963. *Culture Against Man*. New York: Random House.

———. 1971. *Pathways to Madness*. New York: Random House.

Herzog, J. D. 1974. The Socialization of Juveniles in Primate and Foraging Societies: Implications for Contemporary Education. *Council on Anthropology and Education Quarterly* 5:12–17.

Hilger, M. I., Sr. 1960. *Field Guide to the Ethnological Study of Child Life*. New Haven, CT: Human Relations Area Files Press.

Hill-Burnett, J. 1973. Event Description and Analysis in the Micro-ethnography of Urban Classrooms. In *Cultural Relevance and Educational Issues*, ed. F. Ianni and E. Storey. Boston: Little, Brown.

———. 1979. Anthropology in Relation to Education. *American Behavioral Scientist* 23(2):237–74.

Hoebel, E. A. 1972. *Anthropology: The Study of Man*. New York: McGraw-Hill.

Hofstadter, D. R. and D. C. Dennett. 1981. *The Mind's I: Fantasies and Reflections on Self and Soul*. New York: Basic Books.

Holloman, R. E. 1974. Ritual Opening and Individual Transformation: Rites and Passages at Esalen. *American Anthropologist*, 76:265–79.

Horton, D. L., and C. B. Mills. 1984. Human Learning and Memory. *Annual Review of Psychology* 35:361–94.

Hsu, F. L. K. (ed.) 1972. *Psychological Anthropology*. Cambridge: Schenkman.

Hubel, D. 1979. The Brain. *Scientific American* 241(3):44–53.

Huizinga, J. 1950. *Homo Ludens*. Boston: Beacon.

Hwang, H. 1984. Characters of Contemporary Tenancy Systems. In *New Approaches to Agricultural Problems in Korea*. Seoul: Dolbaegae Press.

Hymes, D. 1980. Ethnographic Monitoring. In *Language in Education: Ethnolinguistic Essays*, ed. D. Hymes, 104–18. Washington, DC: Center for Applied Linguistics.

Inkeles, A. 1969. Social Structure and Socialization. In *Handbook of Socialization: Theory and Research*, ed. D. Gosslin, 615–32. Chicago: Rand McNally.

Jacob, E. 1987. Qualitative Research Traditions: A Review. *Review of Educational Research* 57:1–50.

Jacobson, E. 1982. *The Human Mind: A Physiological Clarification*. Springfield, IL: Thomas.

Jakobsen, R., C. Fant, and M. Halle. 1965. *Preliminaries to Speech Analysis: The Distinctive Features and Their Correlates*. Cambridge: MIT Press.

Jenkins, J. J. 1974. Remember That Old Theory of Memory? Well, Forget It! *American Psychologist* 29(11):785–95.

John, E. R., and E. L. Schwartz. 1978. The Neurophysiology of Information Processing and Cognition. *Annual Review of Psychology* 29:1–29.

Johnston, T. D. 1981. Contrasting Approaches to a Theory of Learning. *The Behavioral and Brain Sciences* 4.

Judson, H. F. 1979. *The Eighth Day of Creation*. New York: Simon & Schuster.

Kaas, J. 1978. The Organization of the Visual Cortex in Primates. In *Sensory Systems in Primates*, ed. C. Norback, 151–79. New York: Plenum.

Kagan, J. 1977. The Child in the Family. *Vita Humanitas* 6:125–39.

Kagan, J. and H. Moss. 1962. *Birth to Maturity*. New York: Wiley.

Kanter, R. M. 1977. *Work and Family in the United States: A Critical Agenda for Research and Policy*. New York: Russell Sage.

Kay, P., ed. 1971. *Explorations in Mathematical Anthropology*. Cambridge: MIT Press.

Keesing, R. 1970. Kwaio Fosterage. *American Anthropologist* 72:991–1019.

————. 1971. Formalization and the Construction of Ethnographies. Sonoma, CA: Kay.

Keith, J. 1980. The Best Is Yet to Be: Toward an Anthropology of Age. *Annual Review of Anthropology* 9:339–64.

————. 1985. Age in Anthropological Research. In *Handbook of Aging and the Social Sciences*; ed. R. H. Binstock and E. Shanas, 231–63. New York: Van Nostrand Reinhold.

Keith, J., and D. I. Kertzer. 1984. Introduction. In *Age and Anthropological Theory*, ed. D. I. Kertzer and J. Keith, 19–61. Ithaca, NY: Cornell University Press.

Kesner, R. P. 1986. Neurobiological Views of Memory. In Martinez and Kesner 1986: 399–438.

Kimball, S. T. 1974. *Culture and the Educative Process*. New York: Teachers College Press.

————. 1982. Community and Hominid Emergence. *Anthropology and Education Quarterly* 13:125–32.

Kimball, S. T., and J. Burnett, 1973. *Learning and Culture*. Seattle: University of Washington Press.

Kimball, S. T., and J. McClellan. 1962. *Education and the New America*. New York: Random House.

Kleinginna, P. R., and A. M. Kleinginna. 1981. A Categorized List of Emotion Definitions with Suggestions for a Consensual Definition. *Motivation and Emotion* 5:345–79.

Kluckhohn, F., and F. Strodtbeck. 1961. *Variations in Value Orientations*. Westport, CT: Greenwood.

Kneller, G. F. 1965. *Educational Anthropology: An Introduction*. New York: Wiley.

Kohlberg, L. 1958. The Development of Moral Thinking and Choice in the Years 10 to 16. Chicago: University of Chicago Photoduplication Library.

Kozak, N., and E. Tronick. 1985. Mothers' Turn-Giving Signals and Infant Turn Taking in Mother-Infant Interaction. In Field and Fox 1985.

Kroeber, A. L. 1909. Classificatory Systems of Relationship. *Journal of the Royal Anthropological Institute* 39:77–84.

Kupferman, I. 1985a. Learning. In *Principles of Neural Science*, 2nd ed., ed. E. R. Kandel and J. H. Schwartz. New York: Elsevier.

————. 1985b. Hemispheric Asymmetries and the Cortical Localization of Higher Cognitive and Affective Functions. In *Principles of Neural Science*, 2nd ed., ed. E. R. Kandel and J. H. Schwartz. New York: Elsevier.

Lancaster, J. B. 1975. *Primate Behavior and the Emergence of Human Culture*. New York: Holt, Rinehart & Winston.

Lancy, D. 1980. Play in Species Adaptation. *Annual Review of Anthropology* 9:471–95.

Lashley, K. S. 1950. In Search of the Engram. *Symposium of the Society for Experimental Biology* 4:454–82.

Laudan, L. 1977. *Progress and Its Problems: Toward a Theory of Scientific Growth*. Berkeley: University of California Press.

Lazarus, R. S. 1982. Thoughts on the Relations Between Emotion and Cognition. *American Psychologist* 37 (9):1019–24.

Leeman, T. A. 1972. *The Rites of Passage in a Student Culture*. New York: Teacher's College Press.

Leonard, J. W. 1978. Discussion Note. In *Recent Advances in Primatology*, ed. D. J. Chivers and J. Herbert, 15. New York: Academic.

LeVine, R. 1973. *Culture, Behavior and Personality*. Chicago: Aldine.

———. 1982. *Culture, Behavior and Personality: An Introduction to the Comparative Study of Psychosocial Adaptation*. New York: Aldine.

LeVine, R., and B. LeVine. 1971. Age Groups and Role Change in Africa. In *Conformity and Conflict*, ed. J. Spradley and D. McCurdy. Boston: Little, Brown.

Levinson, D., ed. 1977. *A Guide to Social Theory: World Wide Cross-Cultural Texts*. New Haven: Human Relations Area Files Press.

Levinson, D. J. 1986. *The Seasons of a Woman's Life*. New York: Knopf.

Levinson, D. J., C. M. Darrow, E. B. Klein, M. H. Levinson, and B. McKee. 1978. *The Seasons of a Man's Life*. New York: Knopf.

Lewicki, P. 1986. *Nonconscious Social Information Processing*. Orlando, FL: Academic.

Lewis, M., and L. Rosenblum, eds. 1974. *The Effect of the Infant on Its Caregiver*. New York: Wiley.

Lewontin, R. C. 1984. *Human Diversity*. San Francisco: Freeman.

Lewontin, R. C., S. Rose, and L. J. Kamin. 1984. *Not in Our Genes: Biology, Ideology, and Human Nature*. New York: Pantheon.

Loftus, E. F., 1980. *Memory: Surprising New Insights into How we Remember and Why We Forget*. Reading, MA: Addison-Wesley.

Loftus, E. F., and G. R. Loftus. 1980. On the Permanence of Stored Information in the Human Brain. *American Psychologist* 35(5):409–20.

Luce, D. R. 1971. Similar Systems and Dimensionally Invariant Laws. *Philosophy of Science* 38:157–69.

Maddox, G. L., and R. T. Campbell. 1985. Scope, Concepts, and Methods in the Study of Aging. In *Handbook of Aging and the Social Sciences*, 2nd ed., ed. R. H. Binstock and E. Shanas, 3–34. New York: Van Nostrand Reinhold.

Mahew, B., T. James, and G. W. Childers. 1972. System Size and Structural Differentiation in Military Organizations. *American Journal of Sociology* 77:750–65.

Martinez, J., and R. Kesner, eds. 1986. *Learning and Memory: A Biological View*. Orlando, FL: Academic.

Maslow, A. H. 1954. *Motivation and Personality*. New York: Harper & Row.

Mason, W. A. 1965. Determinants of Social Behavior in Young Chimpanzees. In *Behavior of Nonhuman Primates: Modern Research Trends*, Vol. 2., ed. A. Schrier, H. Harlow, and F. Stollnitz, 335–64. New York: Academic.

———. 1978. Ontogeny of Social Systems. In *Recent Advances in Primatology*, ed. D. J. Chivers and J. Herbert, 5–14. New York: Academic.

Mass, H. S., and J. A. Kuypers. 1974. *From Thirty to Seventy: A Forty-Year Study of Adult Life Styles and Personality*. San Francisco: Jossey-Bass.

Masters, J. 1981. Developmental Psychology. *Annual Review of Psychology* 32:117–51.

Mauer, K. F. 1980. Factors Related to the Performance of Psychotherapists During Family Training. *South African Journal of Psychology* 10(1–2):110.

Maybury-Lewis, D. 1984. Age and Kinship: A Structural View. In *Age and Anthropological Theory*, ed. D. I. Kertzer and J. Keith. Ithaca, NY: Cornell University Press.

Mayes, A. (ed.) 1983. *Memory in Animals and Humans: Some Comparisons and their Theoretical Implications*. Workingham, Berkshire, England: Van Nostrand Reinhold (UK) Co., Ltd.

Mayr, E. 1982. *The Growth of Biological Thought*. Cambridge, MA: Harvard University Press.

McDermott, R. P., and D. R. Roth. 1978. The Social Organization of Behavior: Interactional Approaches. *Annual Review of Anthropology* 7:321–45.

McFarlane, A. 1975. Olfaction in the Development of Social Preferences in the Human Neonate. In *Parent-Infant Interaction Ciba Foundation Symposium* 33. Amsterdam: Elsevier. (Cited in Murray and Trevarthen 1985:180.)

McGaugh, J. L. 1983. Preserving the Presence of the Past: Hormonal Influences on Memory. *American Psychologist* 38(2):161–74.

McKenna, J. J. 1982. The Evolution of Primate Societies, Reproduction, and Parenting. In Forbes and King 1982:87–133.

Mead, M. 1928. *Coming of Age in Samoa*. New York: Morrow.

———. 1930. *Growing Up in New Guinea*. New York: Mentor.

———. 1956. *New Lives for Old*. New York: Morrow.

———. 1959. *Writings of Ruth Benedict: An Anthropologist at Work*. New York: Avon.

———. 1963a. Our Educational Emphases in Primitive Perspective. In *Case Studies in Education and Culture*, ed. G. Spindler, 309–20. New York: Holt, Rinehart, & Winston.

———. 1963b. Socialization and Enculturation. *Current Anthropology* 4:186–88.

———. 1970. *Culture and Commitment*. Garden City, NY: Natural History/Doubleday.

Mead, M., and G. Bateson. 1942. *Balinese Character: A Photographic Analysis*. New York: New York Academy of Sciences.

Mead, M., and F. C. McGregor. 1951. *Growth and Culture: A Photographic Study of Balinese Childhood*. New York: Putnam.

Mehan, H. 1978. Structuring School Structure. *Harvard Educational Review* 48:32–65.

Meltzoff, A. 1985. The Roots of Social and Cognitive Development: Models of Man's Original Nature. In Field and Fox 1985:1–30.

Meltzoff, A., and M. Moore. 1977. Imitation of Facial and Manual Gestures by Human Neonates. *Science* 198:75–78.

———. 1983. Newborn Infants Imitate Adult Facial Gestures. *Child Development* 54:702–9.

Miller, J. G. 1978. *Living Systems*. New York: McGraw-Hill.

Milner, B. 1972. Disorders of Learning and Memory After Temporal Lobe Lesions in Man. *Clinical Neurology* 19:421–46.

Modiano, N. 1973. *Indian Education in the Chipas Highlands*. New York: Holt, Rinehart & Winston.

Montague, A. 1970. *The Direction of Human Development*. New York: Hawthorn.

———. 1978. *Learning Non-Aggression: The Experience of Non-Literate Societies*. New York: Oxford University Press.

Mortimer, J. T., and R. G. Simmons. 1978. Adult Socialization. *Annual Review of Sociology* 4:421–54.

Moss, M. A., and J. Kagan. 1972. Report on Personality Consistency and Change from the Fels Longitudinal Study. In *Personality and Socialization*, ed. D. R. Meise, 21–28. Chicago: Rand McNally.

Murdock, G. P. 1982. *Outline of Cultural Materials*. New Haven, CT: Human Relations Area Files.

Murray, L., and C. Trevarthen. 1985. Emotional Regulation of Interactions Between Two-Month-Olds and Their Mothers. In Field and Fox 1985:177–98.

Mussen, R., ed. 1983. *Handbook of Child Psychology*, 4th ed. New York: Wiley.

Myerhoff, B. G. 1982. Rites of Passage: Process and Paradox. In Turner, V. (ed.), *Celebration: Studies in Festivity and Ritual*, 109–35. Washington, DC: Smithsonian Institution Press.

———. 1984. Rites and Signs of Ripening. In *Age and Anthropological Theory*, ed. D. Kertzer and J. Keith. Ithaca, NY: Cornell University Press.

Naroll, R. S., and L. von Bertalanffy. 1956. The Principle of Allometry in Biology and Social Sciences. *General Systems* 1:76–89.

Neugarten, B. L., ed. 1968. *Middle Age and Aging: A Reader in Social Psychology*. Chicago: University of Chicago Press.

Neville, G. K. 1984. Learning Culture Through Ritual: The Family Reunion. *Anthropology and Education Quarterly*, 15:151–66.

Newcomb, T. M. 1967. *Persistence and Change*. New York: Wiley.

Nihlen, A. S., and B. A. Bailey. 1988. Children's Display of Gender Schemas Through Interaction with Nontraditional Workers. *Anthropology and Education Quarterly* 2:155–62.

Norbeck, E. 1974. Anthropological Views of Play. *American Zoologist* 14: 267–73.

Norman, D. A. 1982. *Learning and Memory*. New York: Freeman.

Oakley, D. A. 1983. The Varieties of Memory: A Phylogenetic Approach. In *Memory in Animals and Humans: Some Comparisons and Their Theoretical Implications*, ed. A. Mayes. Workingham, Berkshire, England: Van Nostrand Reinhold.

Ogbu, J. 1974. *The Next Generation: An Ethnography of Education in an Urban Neighborhood*. New York: Academic.

———. 1978. *Minority Education and Caste: The American System in Cross-Culture Perspective*. New York: Academic.

O'Keefe, J., and L. Nadel. 1978. *The Hippocampus as a Cognitive Map*. London: Oxford University Press.

Ortner, S. B., and H. Whitehead. 1981. *Sexual Meanings: The Cultural Construction of Gender and Sexuality*. Cambridge: Cambridge University Press.

Overton, D. A. 1985. Contextual Stimulus Effects of Drugs and Internal States. In *Context and Learning*, ed. P. D. Balsam and A. Tomie, 357–84. Hillsdale, NJ: Lawrence Erlbaum Associates.

Pelto, P. 1970. *Anthropological Research: The Structure of Inquiry*. New York: Harper & Row.

Penfield, W., and P. Perot. 1963. The Brain's Record of Auditory and Visual Experience. *Brain* 86:595–696.

Penfield, W., and T. Rasmussen. 1957. *The Cerebral Cortex of Man: A Clinical Study of Localization of Function*. New York: Macmillan.

Perun, P. 1981. Comment on Rossi's "Life-Span Theories and Women's Lives." *Signs* 7(1):243–50.

Petersen, M. R. 1982. The Perception of Species Specific Vocalization by Primates: A Conceptual Framework. In *Primate Communication*, ed. C. Snowdon, C. Brown, and M. Petersen, 171–211. New York: Cambridge University Press.

Phillips, S. V. 1982. The Language Socialization of Lawyers: Acquiring the "Cant." In *Doing the Ethnography of Schooling*, ed. G. Spindler. New York: Holt, Rinehart & Winston.

Phillips, D. C. 1976. *Holistic Thought in Social Science*. Stanford: Stanford University Press.

Piaget, J. 1952. *The Origins of Intelligence in Children*. New York: Norton.

Pietsch, P. 1981. *Shufflebrain*. Boston: Houghton Mifflin.

Pitman, M. A. 1985. Continuing Education for Women—Checkmate? *Educational Horizons* 64(3):123–27.

Pitman, M. A., and M. A. Eisenhart. 1988. Experiences of Gender. *Anthropology and Education Quarterly* 19(2):67–69.

Pitman, M. A., J. Gamradt, M. L. Dobbert, K. Chun, and R. A. Eisikovits. 1984. Authors' Response to Commentaries. *Anthropology and Education Quarterly* 15:4:352–54.

Plutchick, R. 1980. Emotion: A Psychoevolutionary Synthesis. New York: Harper & Row.

Poirier, F. 1973. Socialization and Learning Among Nonhuman Primates. In *Learning and Culture*, ed. S. Kimball and J. Burnett. Seattle: University of Washington Press.

———. 1977. Introduction. In Chevalier-Skolnikoff and Poirier 1977:1–39.

Poirier, F. E., ed. 1972. *Primate Socialization*. New York: Random House.

Poirier, F. W., A. Bellisari, and L. K. Haines. 1978. Functions of Primate Play. In *Social Play in Primates*, ed. E. O. Smith, 143–68. New York: Academic.

Poirier, F. W., and L. K. Hussey. 1982. Nonhuman Primate Learning: The Importance of Learning from an Evolutionary Perspective. *Anthropology and Education Quarterly* 13:133–48.

Proctor, E. K., and L. E. Davis. 1983. Minority Content in Social Work Education: A Question of Objectives. *Journal of Education for Social Work* 18(2):85–93.

Raum, O. 1949. *Chaga Childhood: A Description of Indigenous Education in an East African Tribe*. London: Oxford University Press.

Read, M. 1960. *Children of Their Fathers: Growing Up Among the Ngoni of Malawi*. New Haven, CT: Yale University Press. Republished 1968 by Holt, Rinehart & Winston. Reissued 1987 by Waveland Press, Inc.

Reynolds, V. 1976. *The Biology of Human Action*. San Francisco: Freeman.

Rheingold, H. L. 1985. Development as the Acquisition of Familiarity. *Annual Review of Psychology* 26:1–17.

Riley, M. W. 1979. *Aging from Birth to Death*, Vol. 1. Boulder, CO: Westview.

Riley, M. W., and A. Foner. 1968. *Aging and Society*, Vol. 1, *An Inventory of Research Findings*. New York: Russell Sage.

Riley, M. W., M. Johnson, and A. Foner. 1972. The Succession of Cohorts. In *Aging and Society: A Sociology of Age Stratification*, ed. M. W. Riley, M. Johnson, and A. Foner, 515–82. New York: Russell Sage.

Ritzer, G. 1972. *Man and His Work: Conflict and Change*. New York: Meredith.

Roberts, J. I. and Akinsanya, S. K. (eds.) 1976. *Educational Patterns and Cultural Configurations: The Anthropology of Education*. New York: David McKay.

Rosaldo, M. Z., and L. Lamphere. 1974. *Women, Culture and Society*. Stanford: Stanford University Press.

Rose, S. 1973. *The Conscious Brain*. New York: Knopf.

Rossi, A. S. 1980. Life-Span Theories and Women's Lives. *Signs* 6(2):4–32.

Rubin, L. B. 1979. *Women of a Certain Age: The Midlife Search for Self*. New York: Harper & Row.

Rumbaugh, D. M. 1975. The Learning and Symbolizing Capacities of Apes and Monkeys. In *Socioecology and Psychology of Primates*, ed. R. H. Tuttle, 353–368. The Hague: Mouton.

Ryder, N. 1965. The Cohort as a Concept in the Study of Social Change. *American Sociological Review* 30:843–61.

Sacks, K. 1979. *Sisters and Wives: The Past and Future of Sexual Equality*. Westport, CT: Greenwood.

Sady, R. R. 1969. *Perspectives from Anthropology*. New York: Teachers College Press.

Sahal, D. 1977. Toward a Theory of Systems. *General Systems* 12:41–55.

Sanday, P. R. 1981. *Female Power and Male Dominance: On the Origins of Sexual Inequality*. Cambridge: Cambridge University Press.

San Giovanni, L. F. 1978. *Ex-Nuns: A Study of Emergent Role Passage*. Norwood, NJ: Ablex.

Sarles, H. 1977. *After Metaphysics: Toward a Grammar of Interaction and Discourse*. Great Britain: Peter deRidder Press. Reprinted as *Language and Human Nature*. Minneapolis: University of Minnesota Press, 1985.

Schon, D. 1983. *The Reflective Practitioner*. New York: Basic Books.

Schrier, A. M. 1984. Learning How to Learn: The Significance and Current Status of Learning Set Formation. *Primates* 25:95–102.

Schwartzman, H. B. 1978. *Transformations: The Anthropology of Children's Play*. New York: Plenum.

Scott, J. P., and M. Marston. 1950. Critical Periods Affecting Development of Normal and Maladjustive Social Behavior of Puppies. *Journal of Genetic Psychology* 13:25–60.

Searle, J. 1984. *Can Computers Think? Minds, Brains, and Science*. Cambridge: Harvard University Press.

Seyfarth, R. M., D. L. Chaney, and R. A. Hinde. 1978. How Monkeys See the World: A Review of Recent Research. In *Primate Communication*, ed. C. Snowden, C. Brown, and M. Petersen, 239–52. New York: Cambridge University Press.

Silvern, L. 1972. *Systems Engineering Applied to Training*. Houston: Gulf.

Snowdon, C. J., and S. J. Suomi. 1982. Paternal Behavior in Primates. In *Child Nurturance*, Vol. 3, *Studies of Development in Nonhuman Primates*, ed. H. E. Fitzgerald, J. A. Mullins, and P. Gage, 63–108. New York: Plenum.

Spence, M., and DeCasper, A. 1982. Human Fetuses Perceive Maternal Speech. Paper presented at the International Conference on Infant Studies, Austin, TX.

Spindler, G. 1974a. Schooling in Schonhausen: A Study of Cultural Transmission and Instrumental Adaptation in an Urbanizing German Village. In Spindler 1974b, 230–71.

Spindler, G., ed. 1974b. *Education and the Cultural Process*. New York: Holt, Rinehart & Winston.

Spindler, G., and L. Spindler. 1965. The Instrumental Activities Inventory: A Technique for the Study of Psychological Acculturation. *Southwestern Journal of Anthropology* 21:1–23.

———. 1971. *Dreamers Without Power*. New York: Holt, Rinehart & Winston.

———. 1981. Comment on Funnel and Smith. *Anthropology and Education Quarterly* 12:300–303.

Spindler, G. D. 1976. From Omnibus to Linkages: Cultural Transmission Models. *Council on Anthropology and Education Newsletter* 5.

———. 1987. Roots Revisited: Three Decades of Perspective. In *Education and Cultural Process*, 2nd ed., ed. G. Spindler, 70–77. Prospect Heights, IL: Waveland.

Spiro, M. 1965. A Typology of Social Structure and the Patterning of Social Institutions: A Cross-Cultural Study. *American Anthropologist* 67:1097–119.

Spitz, R. 1945. Hospitalism: An Inquiry into the Genesis of Psychiatric Conditions in Early Childhood. *Psychoanalytic Study of the Child* 1:53–74.

Squire, L. 1986. Memory and the Brain. In *The Brain, Cognition, and Education*, ed. S. Friedman et al., 171–202. Orlando, FL: Academic.

Stevens, C. 1979. The Neuron. *Scientific American* 241(3):54–65.

Suzuki, A. 1979. The Variation and Adaptation of Social Groups of Chimpanzees and Black and White Colobus Monkeys. In *Primate Ecology and Origins*, ed. I. S. Bernstein and E. O. Smith, 153–74. New York: Garland.

Symons, D. 1978. The Question Function: Dominance and Play. In *Social Play in Primates*, ed. E. O. Smith, 193–230. New York: Academic.

Tallman, I., and M. Ihinger-Tallman. 1977. A Theory of Socialization Process. Paper presented at the Theory Development Methods Workshop, twenty-ninth annual meeting of the National Council on Family Relations, San Diego.

Talmon, Y. 1972. *Family and Community in the Kibbutz*. Cambridge: Harvard University Press.

Taub, D. M., and W. K. Redican. 1984. Adult Male-Infant Interactions in Old World Monkeys and Apes. In *Primate Paternalism*, ed. D. M. Taub, 377–406. New York: Van Nostrand Reinhold.

Thomas, D. C. 1982. Stages of Professional Development in Child Care Work: A Proposed Model. *Child Care Quarterly* 11(2):147–48.

Triandis, H., and W. Lonner, eds. 1980. *Handbook of Cross-Cultural Research*, Vol. 3, *Basic Processes;* Vol. 4, *Developmental Psychology*. Boston: Allyn and Bacon.

Troll, L., and V. Bengston (with the assistance of D. McFarland). 1979. Generations in the Family. In *Contemporary Theories About the Family*, Vol. 1, ed. W. R. Burr, R. Hill, F. I. Nye, and I. L. Reiss. 127–61. New York: Free Press.

Tulving, E. 1985. How Many Memory Systems Are There? *American Psychologist* 40(4): 385–98.

Turnbull, C. 1978. The Politics of Nonaggression (Zaire). In *Learning Nonaggression*, ed. A. Montague, 161–221. New York: Oxford University Press.

Turner, V. 1969. *The Ritual Process: Structure and Anti-Structure*. Chicago: Aldine.

———. 1974. *Dramas, Fields and Metaphors: Symbolic Action in Human Society*. Ithaca: Cornell University Press.

Turner, ed. 1982. *Celebration: Studies in Festivity and Ritual*. Washington DC: Smithsonian Institution Press.

Vaillant, G. E. 1977. *Adaptation to Life*. Boston: Little, Brown.

Vaitl, E. 1978. Nature and Implications of the Complexly Organized Social Systems in

Nonhuman Primates. In *Recent Advances in Primatology*, ed. D. J. Chivers and J. Herbert, 18–30. New York: Academic.

Van Lawick-Goodall, J. 1971. *In the Shadow of Man*. New York: Dell.

Vessey, G. N. A. 1965. *The Embodied Mind*. London: Geo. Allen and Unwin. (Cited in Sarles 1977: 226.)

Vogt, E. 1969. *Zinacantan: A Maya Community in the Highlands of Chipas*. Cambridge: Harvard University Press.

———. 1970. *The Zinacantecos of Mexico: A Modern Maya Way of Life*. New York: Holt, Rinehart & Winston.

Vogt, J. L. 1984. Interaction Between Adult Males and Infants in Prosimians and New World Monkeys. In *Primate Pateralism*, ed. D. M. Taub, 346–76. New York: Van Nostrand Reinhold.

Voland, E. 1977. Social Play Behavior of the Common Marmoset (Callithrix Jaeinus Erxl, 1777) in Captivity. *Primates* 18:883–901.

von Bertalanffy, L. 1968. *General Systems Theory*. New York: Braziller.

Wagner, D., and H. Stevenson. 1982. *Cultural Perspectives on Child Development*. San Francisco: Freeman.

Walker, S. 1983. *Animal Thought*. London: Routledge and Kegan Paul.

Wallace, A. F. C. 1970. *Culture and Personality*. New York: Random House.

Walters, J. R. 1987. Transition to Adulthood. In B. B. Smuts, D. L. Cheney, R. M. Seyforth, W. W. Wrangham, and T. T. Struhsaker (eds.), *Primate Societies*, 358–69. Chicago: University of Chicago Press.

Washburn, S. L. 1973. Primate Field Studies and Social Science. In *Cultural Illness and Health*, ed. L. Nader and T. Maretzki, 128–34. Washington, DC: American Anthropological Association.

Watson, J. 1979. Perception of Contingency as a Determinant of Social Responsiveness. In *The Origins of Social Responsiveness*, ed. E. Thoman. Hillsdale, NJ: Erlbaum.

———. 1985. Contingency Perception in Early Social Development. In Field and Fox 1985: 157–76.

Wax, M., S. Diamond, and F. O. Gearing. 1971. *Anthropological Perspectives on Education*. New York: Basic.

Weinberg, G. M. 1975. *An Introduction to Systems Thinking*. New York: Wiley.

Whiting, B. 1963. *Six Cultures*. New York: Wiley.

Whiting, B., and J. W. M. Whiting. 1975. *Children of Six Cultures*. Cambridge: Harvard University Press.

Whiting, J. 1941. *Becoming Kwoma*. New Haven, CT: Yale Institute of Human Relations.

Whiting, J., and I. Child. 1953. *Child Training and Personality*. New Haven, CT: Yale University Press.

Whiting, J. W. M., et al. 1966. *Field Guide for a Study of Socialization*. New York: Wiley.

Whitten, P. L. 1987. Infants and Adult Males. In B. B. Smuts, D. L. Cheney, R. M. Seyforth, W. W. Wrangham, and T. T. Struhsaker (eds.), *Primate Societies*, 343–57. Chicago: University of Chicago Press.

Whorf, B. L. 1956. *Language, Thought, and Reality: Selected Writings*. Cambridge: Technology Press of MIT.

Williams, T. R. 1972. *Introduction to Socialization*. St. Louis: Mosby.

———. 1983. *Socialization*. Englewood Cliffs, NJ: Prentice-Hall.

Wittrock, M. C. 1980. Learning and the Brain. In *The Brain and Psychology*, ed. M. C. Wittrock. New York: Academic.

Wittrock, M. C., et al., eds. 1977. *The Human Brain*. Englewood Cliffs, NJ: Prentice-Hall.

Wolcott, H. F. 1982. The Anthropology of Learning. *Anthropology and Education Quarterly* 13(2):83–108.

Woody, C. D. 1986. Understanding the Cellular Basis of Memory and Learning. *Annual Review of Psychology* 37:433–93.

Wright, C. R. 1967. Changes in the Occupational Commitment of Graduate Sociology Students: A Research Note. *Sociological Inquiry* 37:55–62.

Zadeh, L. A. 1965. Fuzzy Sets. *Information and Control* 8:338–53.

———. 1971a. Qualitative Fuzzy Semantics. *Information Sciences* 3:159–76.

———. 1971b. Similarity Relations and Fuzzy Ordering. *Information Sciences* 3:159–76.

Zajonc, R. B. 1968. Attitudinal Effects of Mere Exposure. *Journal of Personality and Social Psychology Monograph Supplement* 9(2), Part 2:1–28.

———. 1980. Feeling and Thinking: Preferences Need No Inferences. *American Psychologist* 35:151–75.

———. 1984. On the Primacy of Affect. *American Psychologist* 39:117–23.

Zborowski, M. 1955. The Place of Book-Learning in Traditional Jewish Culture. In *Childhood in Contemporary Cultures*, ed. M. Mead and M. Wolfenstein. Chicago: University of Chicago Press.

Zipf, G. K. 1949. *Human Behavior and the Principal of Least Effort*. Reading, MA: Addison Wesley.

Index

About the Authors and Contributors

MARY ANNE PITMAN, Ph.D., is an Associate Professor of Educational Anthropology and Qualitative Research Methodology in the Department of Educational Foundations at the University of Cincinnati. Her reports of research in U.S. settings on the educative nature of the rituals of social relations have appeared in a number of journals and edited collections. She is currently at work on a community analysis of culture acquisition patterns in an intentional community in the rural northeastern United States.

RIVKA A. EISIKOVITS, Ph.D., is a Senior Lecturer in Anthropology and Education at the University of Haifa in Israel. Her publications on professional learning and the philosophy of research methodology have appeared in U.S., European, and Israeli journals. She is currently serving as the Director of the Laboratory for the Study of Cultural and Cross-Cultural Learning at the University of Haifa.

MARION LUNDY DOBBERT, Ph.D., is a Professor of Educational Anthropology and Ethnographic Research in the Department of Educational Policy and Administration at the University of Minnesota. Her publications include *Ethnographic Research: Theory and Application for Modern Schools and Society* (1982), which presents the rudimentary procedural bases for the holistic approach to educational research explicated in the present volume. She is currently at work on a structural analysis of classroom interaction that applies the holistic model of culture acquisition in a setting designed for deliberate instruction.

KYUNG-SOO CHUN, Ph.D., is an Associate Professor in the Department of Anthropology at Seoul National University in Korea. He has conducted field work in East Asia and Latin America and has written articles on that field work that address issues in ethnicity and ecological anthropology. His interest in culture theory is evident in his translation into Korean of Roger Keesing's *Modern Cultural Anthropology*.

BETTY COOKE, Ph.D., is a Faculty Research Associate in the Department of Home Economics Education at the University of Minnesota and a long-time parent educator. The focus of her current research in parent education explores the mental processes and knowledge structures that underlie expertise in parenting.

JAN ARMSTRONG GAMRADT, Ph.D., is a Lecturer in the Social and Philosophical Foundations of Education at the University of Minnesota and a Corporate Agency Consultant. She has a long-standing interest in holistic, cross-disciplinary approaches to educational research and has co-authored articles in *Anthropology and Education Quarterly* and in the *Journal of Ethology and Behavior*. She is currently at work on a comparative analysis of culture acquisition in developing nations and communities.

KYUNG-HAK KIM is a Research Associate in the Department of Anthropology at Seoul National University in Korea, where he is completing work on a doctorate. Kim is a former teacher whose major research interest is the application of anthropological theory to the study of education.